The Human Tide

The Human Tide

How Population Shaped the Modern World

PAUL MORLAND

JOHN MURRAY

First published in Great Britain in 2019 by John Murray (Publishers)
An Hachette UK Company

I

© Paul Morland 2019

A CIP catalogue record for this title is available from the British Library

Hardback ISBN 978-1-47367-513-1
Trade paperback ISBN 978-1-47367-514-8
Ebook ISBN 978-1-47367-515-5

Typeset in Bembo MT by Hewer Text UK Ltd, Edinburgh
Printed and bound by CPI Group (UK) Ltd, Croydon, CR0 4YY

John Murray policy is to use papers that are natural, renewable and
recyclable products and made from wood grown in sustainable forests.
The logging and manufacturing processes are expected to conform
to the environmental regulations of the country of origin.

John Murray (Publishers)
Carmelite House
50 Victoria Embankment
London EC4Y 0DZ

www.johnmurray.co.uk

To my children, Sonia, Juliet and Adam

Contents

CONTENTS

PART ONE

Population and History

I

Introduction

Joan Rumbold was nineteen years old in 1754 and living in the London district of Chelsea when she met John Phillips. Three years later, pregnant by Phillips and having contracted gonorrhoea, she was abandoned by him and with nowhere else to turn was admitted to a workhouse. When an opportunity to work in service came up, she was sent to nearby Brompton, leaving her son, John junior, in the workhouse, where he died two years later.[1] This unexceptional story of desperation, abandonment and infant death would today scandalise most societies in the developed world, triggering heart-searching and finger-pointing from both the social services and the press. In eighteenth-century England, and just about anywhere else at the time, it was completely normal. It had been so since the dawn of human history. Similar stories might be told of hundreds of thousands of girls across Europe and millions across the world at the same time or earlier. Life was lived against a background of material deprivation where, for most people, every day was a struggle against hunger, disease or some other form of disaster.

Historically, it was only yesterday that life was nasty, brutish and short. Almost any account of an aspect of the ordinary person's existence in pre- and early industrial society, whether of diet or of housing, of patterns of birth and death or of ignorance, of lack of hygiene or of lack of health, can easily shock today's reader. For Spanish peasants in wine-producing regions, for example, all hands were required in critical seasons of the annual cycle, including mothers of small children who left their offspring 'alone, crying and hungry in putrid diapers'; neglected, the children might end up with their eyes pecked out by domestic fowl allowed to wander in and out of their dwellings or have their hands chewed by pigs, or they might 'fall into the fire,

3

or . . . drown in pails and wash buckets left carelessly on doorsteps'.[2] Small wonder that between a quarter and a third of babies born in eighteenth-century Spain were dead before their first birthdays.

Life the other side of the Pyrenees for the ordinary French peasant – the vast bulk of the population – was little better. Today the department of Lozère is a charming region known for its kayaking and trout fishing, but in the eighteenth century most of its inhabitants were clothed in rags and lived in miserable cottages, 'surrounded by manure' which emitted a dreadful stink; the hovels rarely had windows and their floors were covered by scraps of canvas and wool serving as beds 'on which the old, decrepit man and the new-born child . . . the healthy, the ill, the dying' and often the newly dead lay side by side.[3] Similar descriptions of squalor and misery could apply to most places on the globe at almost any time since humankind adopted agriculture around ten thousand years or so ago.

So much for the idyll of rural life in earlier times, a myth only possible in a society so long urbanised as to have lost its memory of what pre-industrial country life was really like. This was the life which every penniless Jane Austen heroine on the hunt for a wealthy heir was trying to avoid, if not immediately for herself, then quite possibly for her children or grandchildren in a world of merciless, steady downward economic and social mobility and no welfare state.

Rural life across most of the world today is very different from that of the eighteenth-century country dweller of Spain or France. Urban life, too, has improved immeasurably from the miserable norms common as late as the nineteenth century even in what was then the most developed part of the world. This is well captured in the memoirs of Leonard Woolf, husband of the more famous Virginia. Woolf was born in 1880 and died in 1969 and witnessed a transformation of living conditions in south-east England where, but for a decade as a colonial administrator in Ceylon (now Sri Lanka), he spent all his life. He wrote towards the end of his life that he was struck by the 'immense change from social barbarism to social civilization' in London and indeed in most of Britain during his lifetime, considering it 'one of the miracles of economics and education'; slums, with their 'terrifying products', no longer existed and by the middle of the twentieth century, thought Woolf, it would be hard for those who had not experienced the London of the 1880s to imagine the condition of the poor in those days, living 'in their lairs, with poverty, dirt, drunkenness and brutality'.[4]

These changes were not restricted to Britain. Stefan Zweig, like Leonard Woolf a memoirist and born just a year after him in Vienna, noticed a marked improvement taking place in the years before the First World War with the arrival of electric light brightly illuminating once dim streets, brighter and better-stocked shops displaying a 'seductive new brilliance', the convenience of the telephone and the spread of comforts and luxuries once reserved for the upper classes but now reaching into the middle class. Water no longer had to be drawn from wells and fires no longer 'laboriously kindled in the hearth'. Hygiene was advancing and dirt retreating, and basic living standards were improving year on year so that 'even that ultimate problem, the poverty of the masses, no longer seemed insuperable'.[5]

Scenes of misery and material deprivation can still be seen in the worst slums of the developing world or in the last holds of rural poverty. But for most people across the world, such scenes would be recalled, if at all, as something of the past, a more distant past for those in some places, a less distant one for those in others.

The great improvements in material conditions, in nutrition, in housing, in health, in education, which have swept across most of the globe since the start of the nineteenth century, have clearly been *economic* but they have also been *demographic*, which is to say they have concerned not just the way people produce and consume but also the numbers of people born, their rate of survival into adulthood, the number of children they in turn have, the age at which they die and the likelihood of their moving region, country or continent. The improvements are reflected in the data on population and specifically births and deaths.

In a nutshell, the sorts of societies in which most people now live, as against the one into which Joan Rumbold lived and her unfortunate son was born in 1757, are marked by dramatically lower infant mortality, with far fewer babies or infants dying and almost everyone born making it at least into adulthood. They are marked too by generally longer life expectancy, in part the result of lower infant and child mortality but also of far fewer people dying in middle age and more living to ripe old ages and even to ages scarcely heard of a couple of hundred years ago. Women, given education and the tools of choice, have far fewer children in our societies. Many have no children at all and very few have the six or more common in Britain even until the middle of the nineteenth century. Having moved from the demography of Joan Rumbold's era to that of our own, the population has grown enormously. Back in the eighteenth century there were not a billion people on the face of the earth. Today there are more than 7 billion. Just as the politics, the economics and the sociology of societies today are radically different from those of the past, so is the demography.

This process, which started in the British Isles and among sister peoples in the United States and the British Empire around the year 1800, spread first across Europe and then to the whole world. Much of Africa has not yet completed the transition, but most of it is well on its way. Outside sub-Saharan Africa there are barely half a dozen countries today where women have on average more than four children, the global norm as recently as the 1970s. There is now no territory outside Africa with a life expectancy below sixty, again around the global norm in the 1970s and close to the European norm as recently as the 1950s. The achievement of the best in the middle of the twentieth century became the global average a few decades later. The global average of a few decades ago has become the bare minimum for most of the world today. This has been achieved through a combination of the most basic and the most complex means: the increased washing of hands, better water supply, often rudimentary but critical interventions in pregnancy and childbirth, improved general health care and diet. None of these would have been possible on a global scale without education, again often rudimentary but radically better than nothing, particularly of women, allowing life-preserving practices to be disseminated and practised. It has also required achievements of science and technology from agronomy to transportation.

Philosophers of history have long debated the fundamental factors which shape historical events. Some suggest that vast material forces are most important, determining the broad outlines if not the fine detail of the human story. Others see history as essentially the story of

6

the playing out of ideas. Still others claim that accident and chance are in the driving seat and that it is vain to look for large-scale causes behind the unfolding of events. Once historians talked of history as if it were the creation of 'great men'. None of these approaches is fully satisfactory and none can fully explain history. The interaction of human beings over time and space is just too vast and too complex for any one theory to encapsulate it. Material forces, ideas and chance, and even great individuals and their interplay must all be comprehended if the past is to be understood.

There has been a revolution of population over the last two hundred years or so, and that revolution has changed the world. This is the story of the rise and fall of states and great shifts in power and economics but also a story about how individual lives have been transformed; of British women who within a generation stopped expecting most of their children to die before adulthood; of childless Japanese elderly dying alone in their apartments; of African children crossing the Mediterranean in search of opportunities.

Some of these phenomena, such as the fall in infant mortality from high levels in the UK, are historical. Others, such as the sheer number of Japanese dying childless and alone and the African children heading to Europe, are still very much with us and likely to intensify. The demographic whirlwind – the ever-accelerating pace of change in population – has rattled through the globe from one region to another, tearing up old ways of life and replacing them with new. It is the story of the human tide, the great flow of humanity, swelling here, ebbing there, and how this has made a vast and too often overlooked or underplayed contribution to the course of history.

The fact that life has got immeasurably better for billions – and that the world should be managing to support 7 billion people and rising – should not obscure the dark side of this story. The West, which invented the conditions that allowed so many people to survive their early years and materially to flourish, has much to be proud of. Many of its critics would not be alive today, and certainly not enjoying rich, educated lives, were it not for scientific and technical advances from pharmaceuticals and fertilisers to soap and sewage systems. Yet this awesome achievement should not lead us to overlook the marginalisation and genocide perpetrated against non-European peoples, the decimation of indigenous populations from the Americas to Tasmania, the industrial-scale Atlantic slave trade which treated black people as disposable commodities.

The rise in nineteenth-century life expectancy in Britain was a great achievement but the Irish famine should not be forgotten. The fall of child mortality across Europe in the early decades of the twentieth century is to be celebrated but does not compensate for the barbarity of two world wars and the Holocaust. Infant mortality has fallen across the Middle East but this has contributed to the youth and instability of many societies where a mass of young people, unable to integrate into the workplace, resort to fundamentalism and violence. Rejoicing in the lengthening of life expectancy in large swathes of sub-Saharan Africa in recent years, we should not forget the Rwandan genocide in 1994 nor the appalling loss of life in the wars in Zaire/ Congo in the years shortly thereafter. Account should also be taken of actual or potential environmental damage posed by rising populations. The story of the human tide should not be a 'whiggish' one, that is, one painting a cheery picture of endless progress towards the light with History moving ever onwards to higher and brighter prospects. It is not surprising that such a view was common among much of the British elite in the nineteenth century, when the British found themselves the wealthiest and most powerful people in the world; it is not a view which can be supported today.

But for all the caveats, proper acknowledgement should be made of the great achievement that is the vast multiplying of human numbers and the provision of billions of people with a standard of living and health care and education which the wealthiest of earlier ages would have envied. The story of the human tide should be told warts and all, but it should also be told for what it is: nothing short of a triumph of humanity. The slave ships and the gas chambers should not be forgotten, but their horrors should not blind us to the fact that today countless parents like Joan Rumbold can confidently fear little for their children's health and that billions from Patagonia to Mongolia can expect to enjoy lives which, from a relatively recent historical perspective, are breathtaking in their richness and longevity. And this multiplicity of lives has increased the stock of human creativity and ingenuity, contributing in turn to achievements from vaccines to

8

placing a man on the moon and to – however incomplete – the spread of democracy and human rights.

What This Book Is About – and Why It Matters

The Human Tide is about the role of population in history. It does not argue that the great trends in population – the rise and fall of birth and death rates, the swelling and shrinking of population size, the surges of migration – determine all of history. Demography, it argues, is part but not all of destiny. The case is not made here for a simplistic, monocausal or deterministic view of history. Nor is the claim made that demography is in some sense a primary cause, a first mover, an independent or external phenomenon with ramifications and effects in history but not causes preceding it. Rather, demography is a factor which itself is driven by other factors, numerous and complex, some material, some ideological and some accidental. Its effects are varied, long-lasting and profound, but so are its causes.

Demography is deeply embedded in life. In a sense, it is life – its beginning and its ending. Population must be understood alongside other causal factors such as technological innovation, economic progress and changing beliefs and ideologies, but population does explain a great deal. Take for example the ideology and perspective of feminism. It is impossible to say whether the feminist movement prefigured demographic change and drove it or rather resulted from it, but we can chart how the two have worked together. Today, feminist ideas have permeated almost every aspect of (a still imbalanced) society and the economy, from the acceptability of premarital sex to female participation in the workforce. However, the revolution in social attitudes to sex and gender may not have taken place along these lines had it not been for the invention of the Pill and the fertility choices this allowed. But then again the Pill, in turn, was the product not just of the genius and grit of a number of women and men but a change in attitudes to sex, sexuality and gender which meant that research into it became acceptable within academia and fundable by both corporate and philanthropic interests. The ideology of feminism, the technology of the Pill and changes in social attitude towards sex and childbearing have all played a role in reducing fertility rates (that is, the number of children a woman can expect to have in her lifetime) and these in turn have had their own profound impact on society, the economy, politics and the course of history. Asking what came first – the social will or the Pill – is something of a chicken-and-egg problem; the story of the interplay between these forces can be told but it is futile to try to promote one as the supposed 'prime' or 'ultimate' cause and demote the others to mere effects.

Likewise, it would be a mistake to substitute a demographic for a pseudo-Marxian view of history, replacing 'class' with 'population' as the hidden factor that explains all world history. To leave demography out, however, is to miss what may be the most important explanatory factor in world history of the last two hundred years. For millennia, the same bleak story could be told of steady population progress reversed by plague, famine and war. Since around 1800, however, humankind has increasingly managed to take control of its own numbers, and to stunning effect. Demography has gone from the slowest- to the fastest-changing discipline. Population trends no longer move at a snail's pace, with occasional shocking interruptions like the Black Death. Fertility and mortality fall with growing speed and transitions which once took generations now take place in decades.

2

The Weight of Numbers

Imagine a car trundling slowly forward at more or less the same speed for mile after mile after mile. Imagine it then increasing its speed, gradually for the first few miles, then rapidly, until it achieves tremendous, even frightening, velocity. Then, after a relatively short distance hurtling along, the brakes are suddenly applied, resulting in rapid deceleration. This is what the world's population growth pattern has been like since 1800.

The question then arises: why the last two hundred years? Why the year 1800 as a starting point? The answer is that the end of the eighteenth century and the start of the nineteenth mark a discontinuity in demographic history, a great transformation. Before this time humanity had experienced without doubt dramatic demographic events, mostly on the mortality side of the equation, such as plagues and massacres, but these had been sporadic rather than part of long-term trends. What long-term trends there had been, such as population growth in Europe and in the world more generally, had been gentle and punctuated with unhappy setbacks.

By around 1800 the 'Anglo-Saxons' (essentially Britons and Americans) were escaping the constraints on population growth identified and defined by Thomas Malthus, an English clergyman, writer and thinker whose life spanned the late eighteenth and early nineteenth centuries and of whom much will be said later. Ironically, however, they were escaping these constraints precisely as they were being identified. This era marks a meaningful break in demographic history, a demographic corollary of the industrial revolution, a landmark pointing both geographically and historically to global and permanent change. Along with an industrially grounded population explosion went a boost to military and economic power and a great outpouring of settlers. These demographically driven events came to form a pattern which challenged, disrupted and in some cases over-turned established orders.

The Great Transformation

To get a sense of how completely revolutionary have been the changes of the last two hundred years or so, it helps to have a long view of demography. When in 47 BC Julius Caesar was appointed perpetual dictator of the Roman Republic his domain stretched from what is now called Spain to modern Greece, as far north as Normandy in France and much of the rest of the Mediterranean, a region that today contains over thirty countries. The population of these vast lands comprised around 50 million people, which was about 20% of a world population of approximately 250 million.[1] More than eight-een centuries later, when Queen Victoria ascended the British throne in 1837, the number of people living on earth had grown to some-thing like 1,000 million, a fourfold increase. Yet less than two hundred years after Victoria's coronation, world population has increased a further seven times – nearly twice the growth in a tenth of the time. This latter multiplication is astonishingly rapid, and has had a trans-formative global impact.

Between 1840 and 1857 Queen Victoria gave birth to nine chil-dren, all of whom survived into adulthood. Britain's previous female monarch, Queen Anne, had died in 1714, aged forty-nine. She had eighteen pregnancies but her tragedy was that not a single child survived her. By 1930, just twenty-nine years after the death of Queen Victoria, another great British matriarch, the Queen Mother, had produced only two children, Elizabeth (the present queen) and Margaret. These facts about three queens – Anne, Victoria and Elizabeth the Queen Mother – neatly represent the two trends that began in Britain between the eighteenth and twentieth centuries and which have subsequently spread across the world.

The first was a precipitous drop in infant mortality, with the death of a child becoming mercifully irregular rather than a common agony for parents. The second, which followed, was a dramatic reduction in the average number of children born per woman. In Queen Anne's time, losing child after child was common. In mid-Victorian Britain, having a large brood was still the norm. Its complete survival into adulthood was unusual (in this, Victoria had luck as well as wealth in her favour) but would shortly become usual. By the interwar years of the twentieth century, the Queen Mother's expectation that both her daughters would survive into adulthood was quite normal, in Britain at least.

When Queen Victoria was born in 1819, only a small number of Europeans – around 30,000 – were living in Australia. The number of indigenous Australians at that time is uncertain, but estimates range from between 300,000 to 1 million. When Victoria died at the start of the twentieth century, there were fewer than 100,000, while Australians of European origin numbered nearly 4 million, more than a hundred times as many as eighty years earlier. This transformation in the size and composition of a continental population occurred in the space of a single lifetime. It changed Australia completely and forever, and would have a significant impact beyond Australia's shores, as the country came to play a major role in provisioning and manning British efforts in both world wars. A similar story can be told of Canada and New Zealand.

These startling facts – the rapid but selective acceleration of population growth; plummeting infant mortality rates; falls in fertility; the nineteenth-century outpouring of European populations to lands beyond Europe – are all connected. They are born of the same profound social changes that accompanied the industrial revolution and have proved to be a formidable influence on the course of history, empowering some countries and communities at the expense of others, determining the fate of economies and empires, and laying the foundations of today's world. Yet when, after 1945, these trends became truly global, they caused an even greater tidal surge, one that contained similar eddies and currents to the nineteenth-century transformation but which occurred faster and more furiously than before.

The Great Population Trends, Past and Present

The acceleration that began in nineteenth-century Britain contains within it a complex story. It took hundreds of thousands of years from the dawn of humanity to the early nineteenth century for the world's population to reach a billion but only a couple of hundred years more for it to reach today's 7 billion. Now, however, there is a slowdown. In the late 1960s the number of people on the planet was doubling roughly every thirty years. Today it is doubling every sixty years. By the end of the current century there is a good chance global population will have stopped growing altogether. Some countries are already experiencing population decline.

Rapid population acceleration and deceleration send shockwaves around the world wherever they occur and have shaped history in ways that are rarely appreciated. For example, many people in the West would be surprised to learn that women in Thailand are having four children fewer than they were in the late 1960s, or that life expectancy for men in Glasgow is lower than for men in Gaza, or that the world's population is growing at barely half the rate it was in the early 1970s. Once this immense speeding up and then quite sudden slowing down are apprehended, it is possible to get a sense of the great fairground ride of world population change and our own position, today, of living at a turning point. This, in essence, is the human tide.

Within this big global picture there are striking contrasts between countries and continents. In 1950, for example, there were two to three Europeans for every person in sub-Saharan Africa. By 2100 there are very likely to be six or seven times as many Africans as Europeans. Over the same 150-year period, the ratio of Japanese to Nigerians will have gone from two to one in favour of Japan to nine to one in favour of Nigeria. Population change on this scale transforms everything, from geostrategy to macro-economics, from the demand for cradles to the need for graves. Neither the past nor the future can be considered properly without understanding this.

The great demographic transformation of humanity began in the British Isles and among those who originated there and who spilled out into North America and Australasia. Soon it spread to other European nations, and from them to the peoples of Asia and Latin America. Today, its powerful effects are to be seen at different stages across the world, in particular in Africa, where it is shaking and remaking a continent humanity first ventured from more than 100,000 years ago. Thus the great demographic transformation is returning to humanity's homeland. *The Human Tide* tells this story, from its origins in north-western Europe, and will trace its ever more rapid and dramatic impact across the entire globe. It focuses initially on those areas where demographic change first occurred. Following the trajectory, it will then move beyond Europe to China and Japan, to the Middle East, Latin America and south Asia and ultimately to Africa, as the human tide broke out of its originally narrow confines and became a truly global phenomenon. In each region some background will be given, but the story will essentially start when the old demographic order passed away and was replaced by the new, a process that occurs earlier in some places than in others.

How the Demography Equation Works

There is no bigger driver of population growth than the fall in the number of children dying in their early years. Queen Victoria may have had the advantages of the best care the era could offer as well as good health and good fortune, but as her reign drew to a close around one British baby in six did not make it to his or her first birthday. Today, just over a century later, only one child in three hundred born in England does not reach the age of one. In some parts of the world, in countries such as Afghanistan and Angola, things are not much better for infant survival now than they were in England a hundred years ago, although even there they are improving. In other parts of the world, however, progress has been even more rapid than in Britain. As recently as the 1920s almost three in ten babies in South Korea died before the age of one, but today that figure is barely three in a thousand, a hundredfold improvement in less than a hundred years. When progress happens this quickly, most people cannot grasp the scale of the transformation that has taken place. Nevertheless, such vertiginous falls in infant mortality can cause a population to quadruple in a few decades, with profound consequences for a country's economy and environment, its ability to raise an army or send migrants overseas.

In the absence of war, plague or some other natural calamity, the second biggest factor shaping population, after child mortality rates, is the number of children being born. This, too, has seen staggering shifts over the previous two hundred years. In the mid-Victorian period English women, on average, had around five children (a large number, though less than their sovereign); by the 1930s they were barely having two, in line with the Queen Mother. After the Second World War, to general surprise, the number went up for twenty years, as it did across the Western world, peaking at 3.7 in the US in the late 1950s and at just over three in the UK in the early 1960s, only to fall back again. In the twenty-first century, fertility has fallen all over the world. Today, women in Iran have fewer children than women in France, while women in Bangladesh have about the same number as French women.

The impact on society can be enormous. As the average age in a society rapidly rises, schools empty out and care homes for the elderly fill up. There is clearly a link between the peacefulness of Switzerland and the fact that its average citizen is well over forty years of age. It is equally likely that the violence in Yemen is connected to its average citizen being under twenty years old. Although other factors also play a part – Switzerland is very rich and Yemen is very poor – it is true that the countries with older populations tend to be much richer than those with younger populations. Among poor countries, it is often the youngest that are the most violent. South Africans are not much worse off economically than, say, Macedonians, but South Africa has a median age of around twenty-six and Macedonia of around thirty-eight. It is therefore not surprising that South Africa has a murder rate twenty times higher than Macedonia's. On the other hand, El Salvador and Bangladesh have similar median ages to South Africa – around twenty-seven – but the former has a murder rate that is double South Africa's while Bangladesh has one that is less than a tenth. Socio-economic and cultural factors are highly important too, and here, as elsewhere, demography cannot explain everything. Yet there is a strong correlation between age and violence; almost all the countries with high murder rates have young populations, even if a few countries with young populations have low murder rates.

The third factor remaking the world is migration. Contemporary Britain illustrates this very well. Once the destination of great waves of inflow – Anglo-Saxons, Vikings and Normans – the British Isles closed to mass inward migration after 1066. Before 1945 millions of Britons went to live overseas, peopling new areas on a continental scale. But the movement was almost entirely one way: outward. Huguenot immigration to the British Isles at the end of the seventeenth century – at most 200,000 and probably many fewer – was the only sizeable inward migration from outside the British Isles for hundreds of years,[2] while the late nineteenth- and early twentieth-century immigration of east European Jews probably never exceeded 12,000 per annum in its peak years.

Now this has been radically reversed. Britons still go to live overseas, though their destination is much more likely to be a retirement villa on the Costa del Sol than a hard-scrabble life on the Canadian prairies. Meanwhile hundreds of thousands of migrants from across the globe arrive in Britain every year. Regardless of whether this is desirable or not, to fail to recognise its historically unprecedented nature makes it much harder to understand how far it is transforming society. Those who in the 2011 UK census characterised themselves as 'white British' or whose ancestors were native to the British Isles from at least 1066 are likely to become a minority within the UK sometime after the middle of the current century.

The Difference Demography Makes

Many historical events would not have been possible without the human tide. Without its population explosion in the nineteenth century, Britain could not have populated vast territories across the world, including Australia, thereby creating much of what is considered 'global' today, from the ubiquity of the English language to the norms of free trade. Had it not been for the sheer drop in child death rates in Russia in the early twentieth century, Hitler's armies might well have taken Moscow in 1941, rather than encountering wave upon wave of Russian soldiers. An America that was unable to attract millions of migrants every year and which had not doubled its population since the 1950s might already have been eclipsed economically by China. A Japan that had not experienced more than half a century of falling birth rates would probably not have seen a quarter-century of economic stagnation. If Syria had an average age closer to Switzerland's than to Yemen's, it might never have collapsed into civil war, while Lebanon might have plunged back into civil war had its population not aged rapidly in the past forty years.

There is no guarantee that humanity has escaped forever the great natural forces that set population back – above all war, plague and famine. Indeed, since the dawn of the nuclear age, the potential for a war that eviscerates the global population has never been greater. Nor has disease had a greater opportunity to spread rapidly than since the invention of the jet engine and the arrival of mass rapid intercontinental travel. Environmental calamity may yet doom us all. To argue as a matter of fact that humanity has, over the past two hundred or so years, progressively liberated itself from the forces of nature that have previously always inhibited its demographic expansion, is not the same as saying that this will necessarily be the case in the future.

Numbers and Military Power

The first and most obvious way in which numbers of people have mattered in human history is through military force. The triumphs of small nations or armies over large ones are remembered precisely because they are the exception to the rule that the advantage belongs to the larger and heavier combatant, whether at the individual or collective level. In contrast, the many contests that have proven the rule rather than the exception are no more interesting than the headline 'Dog Bites Man'. Many cases where large nations or armies crushed small ones are long forgotten or are merely historical footnotes.

In antiquity, command of numbers mattered more than anything else in military conflict. The ancient annals are notoriously unreliable when it comes to numbers, and 17,000 Macedonian troops may not really have met 600,000 Persians at the Battle of Granicus, yet undoubtedly when Alexander the Great scored his first victory in Asia, it was against dramatic numeric odds.[3] Although contemporary medieval accounts, like ancient ones, often involve exaggeration and need to be viewed with a degree of scepticism, it is nevertheless thought that at Agincourt the conquering English were outnumbered by the French by a ratio of six to one.[4]

Yet these battles are so memorable because they went against the rule that numbers count. Far more common in the history of human warfare have been cases where numbers were decisive, and in almost all cases numbers counted for something. Indeed, quite small margins were often judged to be critical, especially where the quality of the troops was not vastly different and there was no great strategic advantage to be grasped. Prior to Waterloo, Wellington could not even consider taking the initiative against Napoleon because he had only 67,000 men against 74,000 on the other side.[5] In the grindingly predictable trench warfare of the First World War, fought with little scope for strategic advantage and troops of broadly comparable equipment, education and motivation, numbers were critical. The prospect of the entry of a first wave of 2.8 million American draftees in 1917/1918, threatening decisively to tilt the balance between the exhausted armies on the Western Front, drove Germany to desperate and ultimately futile measures.[6]

Behind the numbers on the front line are the numbers that comprise a society as a whole. In 1800, France's population comprised a little under a fifth of the European total, and France could attempt to dominate the whole continent; by 1900, with a population that was less than a tenth of Europe's, France was on the way to becoming a second-rank power. Ever since competing bands and tribes locked horns in pre-history, birth rate and population size have in most cases determined who has won and who has lost wars. Numbers of men on the battlefield, meanwhile, depend on numbers of babies in the cradle two or three decades earlier, particularly in eras of mass mobilisation or the *levée en masse* and total war.

Some societies have been more successful at mobilising their forces than others, but even higher mobilisation rates cannot fully compensate for a lack of numbers. Men left behind are often required for activities necessary for the support of the war effort and larger numbers of women meant, in modern times, more potential recruits for the factories producing armaments for the front. A state or an alliance of states with a demographic advantage – put simply, with more people and particularly with more men of fighting age – normally has a distinct advantage in a conflict. Through the translation of demographic weight into military edge, demography has come to have a powerful effect on world history.

Although missing from many histories, demography's salience in world affairs has often been noted, and there has been a correspondingly long pedigree of pro-fertility thought and writing from those of a patriotic disposition. Tacitus, the Roman historian and statesman, compared the small families of the Romans unfavourably to the fertile Germans, while Ibn Khaldun, the medieval Arab historian, associated depopulation with the desolation and reversal of civilisation.[7] Vauban, Louis XIV's great military architect, was under no illusion about what ultimately drove power; however innovative the defensive buildings might be, he declared that 'the greatness of kings . . . is measured in the number of their subjects'. Clausewitz, a Prussian theorist of war living in the Napoleonic era, considered superiority of numbers to be 'the most general principle of victory', and it was Voltaire who insisted that God was on the side of the big battalions. Adam Smith declared that 'the most decisive mark of the prosperity of any country is the increase in the number of its habitants'.[8] Asked which woman he loved most, Napoleon is reported to have replied: 'she who has the largest number of children'.[9]

Of course, a big technological advantage can undoubtedly be decisive. But often such an advantage, whether it be the Maxim gun or the atom bomb, cannot be indefinitely sustained, since it is invariably adopted by the enemy, whereupon population again becomes key. Iraqi and Afghan militants in recent decades were able to deploy devastating weapons against their first world invaders. Russian efforts to dominate Afghanistan in the 1980s and American attempts to dominate both Iraq and Afghanistan in the first decade of the twenty-first century were in large part frustrated by the fact that Afghanistan and Iraq had populations with a median age of under twenty, while those of the USSR and the USA were well over thirty. It could be argued that in the end what was lacking on the part of the Russians and Americans was not sheer numbers but will; but even here, demography has a role to play. A country with a fertility rate of two or less is much more likely to have a culture in which civilian or military losses are unacceptable than a country with a fertility rate of over seven or nearly five, as was the case in Afghanistan and Iraq respectively around the time of the US invasions in 2002 and 2003. Each mother in the former case simply has fewer sons to lose. It seems callous to imagine that mothers of large families are any more willing to lose their children in a conflict, but there is compelling evidence to suggest that societies with smaller families are generally less bellicose.[10]

Numbers and Economic Clout

Besides military power, the most decisive factor in determining a country's power is the size of its economy. A large economy itself contributes to military power through the ability to sustain large forces and, in modern times, to equip them with weaponry on an industrial scale. As well as contributing indirectly to state power through the support it is able to give to the military effort, a large economy is an asset to state power in its own right, providing leverage on world markets both as a buyer of goods and services and as a market for the goods of others. Again, this has been long recognised; Frederick the Great declared that 'the number of people makes the wealth of states'.[11]

In a world in which the majority of the population lives more or less at subsistence level, the size of an economy is very closely related to the size of the population. If almost everyone has broadly the same income, and the national economy is no more and no less than the aggregate of individual incomes, then the economy will vary in size between countries based purely on their populations. This changes once average incomes cease to be similar between countries. When incomes per head vary, countries with relatively small populations can have exceptionally large economies and those with large populations can be so poor that their economies are small.

This occurred most remarkably during the industrial revolution when first Britain and then other parts of Western Europe and North America began to transform their economies and to experience sustained per capita income growth. Around 1800 the average incomes in Western Europe and the eastern seaboard of the USA were roughly equivalent to those on the Chinese coast. A hundred years later they were probably ten times greater.[12] Thus the British economy was many times the size of the Chinese despite the fact that Britain had a much smaller population. The approximate correspondence of size of population and size of economy slipped out of kilter when some economies developed rapidly and others were left behind.

However, industrialisation has a tendency to spread, and it has done so dramatically in recent decades, nowhere more so than in China. The technologies which fuel economic growth are diffused with ever greater speed, and so it is not surprising that the economies of developing countries have grown more rapidly in recent years than those of developed countries. That is not to say that this is occurring everywhere or at the same pace, but it does mean that, globally, there is a great catching up occurring in terms of income per head, with many in poorer countries getting rapidly richer and most in richer countries seeing their incomes stagnate. In the pre-industrial world individual incomes did not differ radically across countries, and therefore the size of an economy was largely determined by the size of the population; likewise in today's world, with its overwhelmingly modern economy, the size of populations comes to matter more in determining the size of an economy.

The relationship between modernisation and demography is not straightforward, however.[13] It is true that in countries where most women are educated, most people live in towns and cities, and where there is a relatively high standard of living – that is, in all countries which meet our definition of 'modern' – fertility rates in almost all cases are no higher than three and life expectancy is well over seventy. Modernisation is a *sufficient* condition of moving through or having moved through the demographic transition to low fertility and long life expectancy. It alone will ensure that the demographic transition occurs. Women with university degrees will not, in general, have seven children. Office workers living in homes with sewage systems and having access to cars will live longer than did their peasant ancestors who toiled in the fields and relied for transport on their feet and, if lucky, their shoes.

But full modernity is not a *necessary* condition for having made the demographic transition. As the twentieth century progressed it was possible for a still relatively rural country with low levels of income and education to achieve low fertility rates and to lengthen life expectancy. Government-funded family planning, often assisted by international aid, and the provision of basic public health and medical facilities, again often internationally supported, can move demography ahead of modernisation. This is how a country like Morocco – where as recently as 2009 more than half of all women were illiterate – could have a fertility rate as low as 2.5 children per woman. It is how a country like Vietnam – with a per capita income a fifth or a sixth of the USA's – can achieve a life expectancy at birth of just a few years shorter than America's.[14] Cheap technology and private and public philanthropy allow the demography, as it were, to get ahead of the economics.

Once the mass of humanity has reached or is rapidly moving towards modernity, along with which goes higher income per head, it becomes impossible for countries with huge populations such as China, India and Indonesia to have relatively small economies, and it becomes less sustainable for countries with relatively small populations, like the UK or even Germany, to maintain their position at the top of league tables of absolute economic size. For example, on the basis that the population of Indonesia is three times that of Germany, the German economy will remain larger than the Indonesian as long as the average German is three times richer, but once the average German is less than three times richer than the average Indonesian – a still relatively distant prospect, but far less so than was previously thought – the Indonesian economy will be larger than the German even though the average German will still be much better off than the average Indonesian. Also, because industrial and commercial technology is now widely spread and large advantages are harder to establish

23

and maintain, population size is once more beginning to influence what determines the relative size of economies.

This view may be criticised on the basis that it looks rather crudely at the overall size of an economy, ignoring the importance of per capita income. There are two responses to this. First, demographic growth can itself assist in per capita economic growth; young, growing populations can provide a labour force and a domestic market. A large population creates the possibility of a large domestic market, which is particularly important where national markets are closed, as they have often been throughout history. Second, when it comes to power and what drives history rather than to measures of personal welfare, it is the overall size of the economy which matters. The Dutch continued to be prosperous in the eighteenth and nineteenth centuries, but lacking a large population they simply ceased to matter as much on the world stage as they had in the seventeenth century. Britain started to lose its pre-eminence to the United States as its population was overtaken by America's towards the end of the nineteenth century. One of the most prosperous countries in Europe today, Luxembourg, is also one of the least important; wealthy though its citizens may be, there are so few of them that its economy continues to be a minnow. By contrast, China could soon become the world's largest economy (indeed by some measures it already is), even though its people are on average still relatively poor, simply by dint of their great number. This gives China meaningful power in the world economy as both a buyer and a seller; it also allows it to access the resources required to be a major military player.

The question of 'soft power' is more subtle and perhaps less susceptible to numbers. Nevertheless, sheer population weight makes it more likely that a country will be able to play a role on the world cultural stage. The size of the population of India makes Bollywood a global phenomenon whereas the cinema of, say, Albania is not. The difference may lie partly in the quality or at least the general appeal of the product, but it also lies in the respective population sizes. It is less likely that Japanese design would have had such an impact on the world if there had been fewer than 10 million Japanese rather than more than 100 million. For sure, the extent of soft power is not demographically determined any more than military or economic power, but in all cases the weight of numbers counts – always for something, often for much.

Demography Within States, Not Just Between Them

Population matters not just to what happens between states but also to what happens within them. Had the United States been as 'white' in 2008 as it had been fifty years earlier, Barack Obama would not have become president. Obama won only 43% of white votes to John McCain's 55%, but he won an overwhelming majority of non-white votes at a time when the US was simply no longer 'European' enough for this smaller white vote to prevent his election. Conversely, with the projected ethnic shape of the US in 2040, a candidate like Donald Trump, who purports to champion white, blue-collar America, will find it almost impossible to win, despite America's electoral college system giving disproportionate weight to smaller, rural and predominantly white states such as Wyoming and North Dakota, both of which are around 90% white.

In 2016 those defining themselves as non-Hispanic whites comprised more than three-fifths of the US population and 71% of voters. Donald Trump had a large lead among whites in the 2016 election: 58% of voters who identified as 'white' voted for him (whereas only 37% voted for Hillary Clinton). Given the still significant white majority, this delivered Trump the White House. But when, towards the middle of the current century, white Americans slip below 50% of the total population, their support is very unlikely to be sufficient for a candidate to offset the very poor showing among non-white Americans that Trump received. Americans whose number one issue was inequality were significantly less likely to vote for Trump than those whose number one issue was immigration, which is testimony to the fact that concern about rapid demographic change was at the heart of the 2016 US election.

In England and Wales, the share of the population that does not categorise itself as white British has risen from around 2% in the 1960s and perhaps 7% in the early 1990s to nearly 20% in 2011. In predicting how an individual voted in the British Remain–Leave EU referendum, the strongest correlate with a 'leave' vote – after concern about European integration and the loss of British sovereignty – was a person's attitude to immigration. Analysis of the voting data shows that it was areas such as Boston in Lincolnshire and Stoke-on-Trent in Staffordshire, which had experienced the greatest rise in their immigrant populations in 2005–2015 (but interestingly not those like London, with the highest level of foreign-born residents), that were most likely to vote for Brexit, supporting the view that issues of identity in the face of changing local ethnic demography were vitally important in determining the vote.[15]

In France, it is unlikely that the government would have been moved to legislate against the burkini if there were hundreds or thousands of Muslims in the country rather than around 5 million. Quebec would probably have voted to break away from Canada had its predominantly Catholic French-speaking population maintained beyond the 1960s its exceptionally high fertility rate, which for a time was among the highest of any industrialised society. A few more French speakers would have tipped the independence referendum that Quebec held in 1995, when the noes won by just over 54,000 votes – barely a percentage point.

Shifts in the ethnic composition of states do not just affect the developed world, nor do they just impact on electoral politics; they are also associated with civil strife.[16] Demography has become more important in more recent times, particularly as a factor in intra-state conflict.[17] The sheer scale of demographic change and its acceleration over time – the demographic whirlwind – is one of the reasons. As birth rates hit unprecedented highs for lengthy periods while death rates plummet, populations can grow fast, as did England's in the nineteenth century. Indeed, those experiencing these changes later experienced population growth which far outstripped the UK's nineteenth-century achievement. Often such growth affects one ethnic group but not another because of different social or religious practices or different levels of socio-economic development. It has become harshly apparent that demographic strength between different ethnic and social groups can change with historically unprecedented speed, and this can have a dislocating and disorienting impact.

Although sometimes an *inter-state* phenomenon, these shifts are often experienced at *intra-state* level since most states contain ethnic minorities and many of those minorities display markedly different demographic behaviour from the majority. Chechens in Russia, Albanians in Serbia (or what was Serbia) and Catholics in Northern Ireland spring to mind. These are all cases where minorities have a higher birth rate than majorities, with the result being a shift in or challenge to the prevailing power structure. Sometimes it is the minorities who have a lower birth rate, such as the whites in South Africa or the Chinese in Malaysia, again with domestic political consequences.

Demography also matters more now than in the past because politics has become increasingly ethnic in its nature in the modern era, particularly since the French Revolution. The era in which an ethnically distinct elite rules over a majority, whether Normans in England, whites in South Africa or Alawites in Syria, appears to be coming to an end. In an increasingly democratic environment, numbers count, and where politics has an ethnic nature, the numbers of different ethnic groups relative to each other become particularly important.

Over the course of this modern period, as conflict is decreasingly between states and increasingly between ethnic groups, often within states, demography becomes important precisely because contending ethnic groups often have starkly different demographic profiles.[18] Given the importance of numbers to ethnic and national groups in conflict, one might expect such groups to adopt strategies which aim to advance their own demographic strength, either through increasing their own or decreasing those of rivals or both. These strategies, known collectively as demographic engineering, can be of the 'hard' or 'soft' variety. Hard demographic engineering involves the creation, destruction and movement of people through policies such as selective incentives to fertility, genocide or the encouragement of inward or outward flows of people from a given territory. Examples are sadly numerous. In the 1920s the United States explicitly shaped its immigration policy to preserve its 'Anglo-Saxon' character against further incursions from southern and eastern Europe. In the middle years of the twentieth century, Protestant leaders in Northern Ireland tacitly encouraged Catholic emigration while Catholics adopted higher birth rates in part to boost their numbers. Sri Lanka's Sinhalese-dominated government expatriated Tamils of relatively recent South Indian origin to boost the Sinhalese nature of the state. In Communist Romania, ethnic Hungarians were given readier access to contraceptives and abortions than ethnic Romanians while ethnic Germans and Jews were encouraged to leave the country altogether, all in the name of boosting the ethnic Romanian character of the country.[19]

Soft demographic engineering, by contrast, while still concerned with demographic policies aimed at enhancing the numbers of one group over another, uses means such as redrawing frontiers, manipulating identities or manipulating censuses and census categorisations. Examples include the consolidation of the Sinhalese identity in Sri Lanka out of Kandyan highlanders and people of the Low Country, or the suggestion that Turkey redefine Kurds as 'mountain Turks'.[20] This is one way in which demography is shaping destinies.

It is reckoned that whereas in the 1950s around half the world's conflicts were *between* states and half *within* them, in the 1990s the latter outnumbered the former by a ratio of six to one. Whereas 57% of conflict during 1945–2008 was 'ethnic', *all* conflict between 2000 and 2010 can be given that label.[21] Christians, once dominant in Lebanon, have been eclipsed by Muslims, who sustained a higher birth rate over a longer time and were less likely to leave the country. Today the main struggle for power in Lebanon is between Sunni and Shi'a Muslims rather than between Muslims and Christians. Whether in civil wars, referendums or elections, numbers make the difference between dominance and marginalisation, victory and defeat, at home as well as abroad. When some groups have sky-high birth rates or arrive in serried ranks while others have tiny families or up-sticks, it is usually demography that determines who controls communities, regions and countries.

It is worth spelling out at this point that nations and ethnic groups *are* real and that they matter in history. Humans are not a naturally solitary species, but live in groups. Loyalties are initially to the band or tribe. A shared sense of common ancestry, language and custom is universal in hunter-gatherer societies. How these sentiments are transformed in complex and modern societies is subject to much scholarly debate, but the fact that they exist is undeniable. These affiliations explain much of how the world works, and has worked in the recent past, including the outcome of conflicts and elections.

It is certainly true that many people would like to overlook the highly ethnic nature of politics around the world and assume that our cosmopolitan preferences will become more universal if we ignore the nationalism and ethnocentrism of others. However, in much of the world, ethnicity matters politically. And pretty much everywhere, it has mattered at least until recently. It may be that some genuinely post-ethnic, multicultural societies are beginning to emerge in some of the more urban and cosmopolitan parts of the West (coastal USA and London, for example), but even within those places there are populist backlashes. Both Brexit and Trump can be understood as part of that backlash.

A Brief Guide to Demography

To understand how demography has driven history it is necessary first to outline its three timeless fundamentals. The good news is that this is fairly simple. Only three things can change the number of people in a region or country: the first is births, which provide additions to the population; the second is deaths, which cause subtractions from it; and the third is migration, or the net movement of people in or out.

The birth rate (sometimes called the 'crude birth rate') is simply the number of births relative to the population. The death rate (known as the 'crude death rate', or 'crude mortality rate') is the number of deaths relative to the population. For example, in England and Wales in 2014 there were around 700,000 births in a population of 58 million, giving a crude birth rate of about twelve per thousand.[22] (Note that demographic data is often presented as 'per thousand' rather than per hundred or per cent.) In the same year, England and Wales had around half a million deaths, or a crude death rate of about eight and a half per thousand. Without any immigration or emigration, this would have given England and Wales a population growth rate of 3.5 (i.e. 12 − 8.5) per thousand, or 0.35%. This is equivalent to about 200,000 people, the gap between births and deaths. In the United States, the figures for the crude birth rate are about twelve and a half per thousand and the mortality rate is just over eight per thousand, which results in annual population growth, excluding immigration, of almost 1.5 million a year. In Germany, which has experienced years of declining population, the crude birth rate is around eight per thousand, whereas the crude mortality rate is just under eleven per thousand. Without immigration, the German population would be falling by nearly a quarter of a million a year.

In many developing countries, particularly (but not exclusively) in Africa, birth rates are very high while death rates have fallen considerably. Even very basic health care and nutrition improve infant mortality, extend life expectancy and so decrease death rates quite substantially. Sub-Saharan Africa as a whole has a crude birth rate of around thirty-eight per thousand, compared to Europe's modest eleven. In the middle of the twentieth century, Africa's crude death rate was not much short of thirty; today, it is not much more than ten. Both Iraq and Afghanistan have high birth rates (around thirty-five per thousand) and both, despite all the violence they have suffered, have managed to bring down their death rates; between the late 1990s and 2010–15 the death rate in Afghanistan fell from above thirteen per thousand to below eight, in Iraq from an already low 5.7 to 5.3. Most people would be surprised to learn that Iraq's death rate is lower than the UK's. It is testimony to the youthfulness of Iraq's population and to the fact that, as in Afghanistan, while the violence on our television screens concerns the deaths of tens or even hundreds of thousands, improvements in nutrition and health care affect tens of millions. This is why, even in the second decade of the twentieth century when Europe was plunged into the First World War, followed by a deadly influenza epidemic, the continent's population continued to grow.

The advantage of crude birth and death rates is that they are simple and they tell us how quickly a population is growing or declining. Their shortcoming – the reason why birth and death rates are often called 'crude' – is that they do not take account of the age structure of a country. You would expect to see more deaths relative to the population in a country like Japan, which is full of old people, than in Ireland, which is still relatively young. Likewise, you would expect there to be more births per person in Ireland where there are, relative to the population, more women of childbearing age, than in Japan. To adjust for this, demographers also measure total fertility rate and life expectancy. These indicators describe how many children the average woman can expect to have – regardless of how many young women there happen to be in a given population – and how long the average person can expect to live – regardless of how old the general population is. ('Fertility', therefore, means actual childbearing rather than the biological potential of bearing children. A woman who is perfectly fertile, that is, capable of having a child or many children, may for a variety of reasons never have any. When demographers speak of fertility they refer to children actually born.) These expectations are based on the actual births to women and the actual deaths of people at different ages. For more on this, see the Appendices at the end of this book.

Fertility rates are always quoted 'per woman' for a number of reasons. First, there is near certainty about who is the mother in each case of a birth; the father's identity is more uncertain. Counting births per father might mean double counting or leaving some births out. Second, the number of children a woman can have ranges from zero to very rarely more than fifteen. For a man it ranges from zero to (at least in theory) thousands, so the fertility rate as a number is more easily manageable for women. Third, there is greater certainty about the cohort of women likely to have children than there is about the cohort of men. Statistically, the fertility for women beyond the age of around forty-five can more or less be ignored. Older women do have children, but rarely enough for it to impact the statistics meaningfully. Men, by contrast, can in theory at least continue having children to the end of their lives. So demography invariably focuses on women, at least when it comes to births, although in doing so it sometimes has a tendency to view them as statistics or units, interesting to the extent to which they produce children or not. Whilst childbearing can and indeed must be viewed statistically, comparing it between places and between times and seeing how it changes, far more insight may be gained by viewing these changes through the lives and choices of individual women, giving voice to their aspirations, anxieties and decisions. This is not just about illustrating the data but also about showing how one of the most inspiring elements to the story of population in the last two hundred years is how women have progressively been able to take control over their own decisions and bodies.

The difference between crude birth rate and fertility rate may be illustrated by comparing South Africa and Israel. South Africa has witnessed a rise in women's education, urbanisation and concerted government efforts to provide birth control services, and as a result has experienced a sharp fall in fertility – in this it is well ahead of the rest of sub-Saharan Africa. But because, until fairly recently, fertility rates were high, there are many young people as a share of the total population, a reflection of the fertility choices of an earlier generation. Israel, in contrast, is an unusual case: a developed country that has actually seen the number of children born per woman rise in recent decades. South Africa has a slightly higher birth rate than Israel: twenty-two per thousand compared to twenty-one. But this is not caused by the average South African woman having more babies. Rather, there are simply more young women who are having babies. In Israel, a woman on average has more than three children now, versus less than 2.5 in South Africa. South Africa's marginally higher birth rate is a product of its recently (but no longer) high fertility rate; as recently as the late 1970s it was five children per woman. This has generated a young population, full of women of childbearing age, but they are now not choosing to have many children. In Israel, by contrast, the total fertility rate in the late 1970s was a child and a half lower than the South African level. There are fewer women of childbearing age as a proportion of the overall population in Israel, but they are each having more children, and so Israel has a high fertility rate (the average number of children born to an individual woman) but not a particularly high crude birth rate (the number of births relative to the population as a whole).

Total fertility rate is a good measure of the moment, a snapshot of what is happening to fertility at a particular point in time. A definitive measure is *completed* fertility for a cohort or generation, but this is only available, as it were, after the event, that is, when all of the women of that cohort have passed their fertile years. It is possible to compare the number of children German women born in the 1870s had to those born in the 1890s; none of them will be having any more. But it is more difficult to compare definitively the childbearing of German women born in the 1970s and the 1990s; both groups may still not have completed their fertility and may still have childbearing ahead of them. *Total* fertility is the best measure available for determining what is happening to fertility now.

Like mortality rates, birth rates give us a crude measure for the population as a whole; like life expectancy, fertility rates give us a measure tailored to the specific structure of the population. Take Japan and Guinea, in west Africa. Both countries have a crude mortality rate of ten per thousand. But the reasons for this similar level of mortality could not be more different. Japan is an old country; Guinea is a very young one. If they had the same life expectancy, Guinea would have a much lower mortality rate than Japan because there would be far fewer deaths among its population, which is young, than among Japan's, which is old. As the crude mortality rates of these countries are the same, and Guineans are on average much younger than the Japanese, then Guineans must be dying much younger than people in Japan. People in Japan can expect to live into their mid eighties. For most Guineans, life ends nearly thirty years earlier. Think of a boarding school and an old people's home, each with a thousand inhabitants. If twenty people died in both institutions in a given year, they would both have a crude death rate of twenty per thousand, but people in the elderly residential care home on average would be living much longer lives than people in the school.

The age structure of a population can also be analysed by showing what percentage are small children or are over sixty-five. The simplest way is to figure the median age: if all the population was lined up in age order, how old would the person in the middle be? In Guinea, the median age is below nineteen; in Japan it is over forty-six.

The Data

Understanding and tracking all of this depends on data. The data is certainly not uniform, nor is it uniformly accurate over time and space. Generally, the later the data and the more developed the country, the greater its reliability.[23] British censuses, which started in the early nineteenth century, are generally reliable in terms of overall population size. The birth of the life insurance industry – whereby insurers needed to calculate the probability of someone at a given age dying – means that we have a good idea of the mortality rates and life expectancies in some places dating back to the eighteenth century. In some places, local records, usually those of the parish, have been expertly extrapolated by demographers to build a picture of wider society. In other countries, censuses go back a long way. Indeed, the census is almost as old as the state, and testifies to an inherent desire of states to know about their inhabitants, sometimes predominantly for military reasons, at other times for tax purposes. There were censuses in ancient Egypt and China thousands of years ago, while the Bible speaks of censuses in ancient Israel – like the Chinese, the Romans had censuses mostly to determine military capacity. The Ottomans had censuses for the same reason, but therein lies the flaw, at least for the purposes of historians. Only Muslim men of a certain age were qualified to fight in Ottoman armies, so only these were of interest to the census officers. To figure out the size of the entire population at various times, extrapolations and assumptions are required. Censuses continue in most developed countries today, and recent proposals to end them – suggesting alternative sources of data were now available, that sampling would suffice given sophisticated statistical techniques, and that costs could be saved – have been vigorously and successfully opposed.

Today, demographers are blessed with a standard set of measures from a variety of sources, not least the United Nations, which offers records of birth and death rates, fertility, longevity and median age by country and continent, going back to 1950 and with projections to the end of the twenty-first century. No data is perfect, but that of the United Nations is recognised as being of high quality, and so it is heavily relied on for the later chapters of this book. Where the reliability and quality of data is open to question, I have used the best available sources but have not opened up the topic to lengthy discussion.

To get a sense of what the data means, Table 1 provides a useful guide to what is high, what is low and what is experienced today in the UK.

Table 1: Demographic Data: What's High, What's Low

Birth rate (births per 1,000)

High	51.8	Afghanistan, 1965–70
UK 2010–15	12.4	
Low	9.0	Hong Kong, 2005–10

Fertility rate (no. of children per woman)

High	9	Israeli Arabs, 1960s
UK 2010–15	1.9	
Low	1.4	Japan, 2010–15

Death rate (no. of deaths per 1,000)

High	37.3	South Sudan, 1950–5
UK 2010–15	9.0	
Low	1.5	UAE, 2010–15

Life expectancy at birth (years)

Short	24	Russia, 1750s
UK 2010–15	81.0	
Long	83.3	Japan, 2010–15

Annual population growth (%)

High	3.9	Kenya, 1982
Europe	0.20	1000–1800
World	0.06	AD 1–1750

What makes demography exciting, what makes it a more powerful tool for understanding the world than is generally appreciated, is that each of these numbers can be seen in three ways. First, in and of itself, as an illustration of something meaningful about a society. For example, the fact that the UAE has such an extraordinarily low mortality rate is testimony both to the huge recent growth of its population (there are few elderly people relative to the population: 2% of people in the UAE are over sixty compared to 12% worldwide and 27% in Germany), the extraordinarily long life expectancy (only a couple of years short of the USA's) thanks to world–class health care and public health and the enormous size of the immigrant population (90% of the total), most of whom are likely to go home to south Asia or Europe and not die in the UAE. By unpacking one piece of data, a great deal of light is shone on today's UAE.

Second, taken as part of a chain, it can illustrate extraordinary change. Kenya's population may have been growing at nearly 4% annually in 1982 but by the year 2000 the growth rate had fallen to 2.5% thanks to a success in reducing the fertility rate from seven to five. (Since then the growth rate has plateaued, meaning that Kenya's population continues to grow fast although somewhat less quickly than in the 1980s.)

Third, the data is but an aggregation of millions of individual stories, of elderly parents living longer than anyone had expected, of a baby's life hanging in the balance, of a choice to make a new life in a new land. The individual stories illustrate the data, but the data also illustrates the stories, placing the fate of families in the context of wider societies and the whole of the human race.

A Point of View

The human tide will continue to take its course regardless of what is written about it. The account I offer is essentially a historical rather than an evaluative one, an account of what has happened rather than what should have happened, or whether what happened is good or bad. Nevertheless, it is worth at this stage setting out my own values with regard to demography. There are only two that need be stated.

First, human life is an inherently good thing, and the saving and extension of it is a worthy pursuit. If it is good to save the life of a single child then all the more is it good to save the lives of millions of children, which is what happens when infant mortality is brought down. Healthy, civilised and long lives are better than nasty, brutish and short ones. Violent and catastrophic mass deaths are an inherently bad thing; if we regret the loss of a single life then the regret at the loss of multiple lives should be proportionately greater. What we do not wish for our families and friends we should not wish for other human beings, whether this is in the name of equality or environ-mentalism or any other potentially worthy but abstract goal.

Second, when women have control over their own fertility, they collectively make wise decisions, with or without input from their male partners. When women are educated and have access to contra-ception, they will not choose to have more children than they can support and, just as the hidden hand of the market works in econom-ics, so the hidden hand of demography will work if allowed to do so. Enforced limitations on childbearing are not only wrong; they are unnecessary. In matters of demography as in so many others, the decisions of ordinary people, given the educational and technical tools to take them, will turn out to be best for their societies and for the planet as a whole.

Demography is embedded in life and in a sense *is* life. The births, uprootings, couplings and deaths are life's great milestones. Just because demography looks at these matters in the aggregate does not, should not and must not detract from the value and sanctity of the lives and experiences of the individuals over which it casts its eye. The demographer and the historian, however much he or she generalises, must never lose sight of this. Indeed, those who have the privilege of aggregating and generalising have a special responsibility to remember that the numbers they are handling are nothing more and nothing less than the sum of the hopes, loves and fears of every individual human being.

PART TWO

The Gathering Tide: Among the Europeans

3

The Triumph of the Anglo-Saxons

Frank McCoppin was born in County Longford, in the middle of Ireland, in 1846. The same year, halfway across the globe, the Mexican region of Upper California was claimed for the United States, and the town that was to become San Francisco had barely 500 inhabitants; by the time McCoppin died, in 1897, it had around 300,000 inhabitants. It would have seemed astonishing at the time of McCoppin's birth that he should have served as mayor of a town which barely existed in 1846, and that he should have represented a state in the US Senate which did not even come under US control until 1848. By the end of the nineteenth century the establishment on the western extremity of North America of a small but vibrant metropolis populated predominantly by people of British and Irish origins was thought of as quite normal, as it is today. Stories such as McCoppin's abound, of people from small towns in the British Isles making their way to distant lands and there becoming rich or powerful representatives of new societies. Such stories could be told from Adelaide to Oregon, from Cape Town to Chicago, and they are all the product of a population explosion which created today's world.

England Leads the Way

Experts debate what came first – the rapid growth of industrial production or the great surge in population – and which caused which. Whether it was the rise in population which stimulated the industrial take-off or the industrial take-off which enabled the growth of population, one thing is certain: these two events were contemporaneous. Whichever came first, the one could not have got very far without the other. Only mass factory hands could man the industrial take-off and world-scale manufacturing, but only with mass industrial production and exports could a growing population support itself. What started in Britain went on to storm the entire world and shake it to its foundations in country after country, on continent after continent. Population explosion first allowed the peoples of Britain and then more widely the people of Europe to dominate the globe, then played a major role in forcing their retreat. That is the story of the human tide. In this chapter, the first stirrings of what were to become global phenomena will be charted, stirrings which took place among the people of the British Isles and the sister peoples often referred to at the time as 'Anglo-Saxons'.

The British Isles is where the demographic revolution began. It is important to get a sense of why and how it was revolutionary and genuinely different from what had happened previously. It is not that populations had never expanded rapidly before. But the population expansion which began in England in the late eighteenth century and progressed throughout the nineteenth was the first to occur alongside industrialisation and urbanisation. What started at the beginning of the nineteenth century was therefore not just an incident in a long history of rising and falling numbers, but part of a sustained pattern of rapid transformation which was in time to go global. It was therefore revolutionary both in terms of time and space: time, because it was not only a rapid but a sustainable growth of population; space, because it set a pattern which was to be played out across the globe. (It should be noted that the data for England, or England and Wales, is distinct from the data for Great Britain, including Scotland as well, and from the United Kingdom, which included in this period all of Ireland too. The best available data is for England.)

To get England's population take-off into perspective it is necessary to go back a couple of hundred years, to the end of the sixteenth century and the closing years of the reign of Queen Elizabeth I and the age of Shakespeare. When the Spanish Armada sailed – and failed – and when the Bard was at the height of his powers, there were about 4 million people in England, well up on the population of 3 million or so not that much earlier, at the end of the reign of Henry VIII. This rise by a third in half a century (which amounts to a little

over a half of one per cent per annum) was rapid by historical standards. England under the Tudors was a largely peaceful and prosperous
place, with a relatively stable political situation – despite the religious
controversies of the age – and an expanding trade internally and with
Europe. In addition, England was still making up for the losses of the
Black Death, the bleak years of the Wars of the Roses and other
calamities of the late medieval period. These had knocked the population back, so when the plague waned and a degree of stability
returned, there was enough land to support more people. 'Merry
England', then, was not entirely a myth of Victorian nostalgia
merchants. A rising population normally suggests improving living
conditions, and the Tudor and Elizabethan periods of the sixteenth
century were indeed merry in England, at least compared to what
had gone immediately before and to some extent what came after.

The growth of the population slowed and then went into a modest
reverse in the seventeenth century as civil war and plague returned,
but growth resumed in the early eighteenth century.[1] Average annual
population growth was around a third of one per cent in the first half
of the eighteenth century and nearly a half of one per cent in the
second half. So far so good, but also historically fairly normal. But
this is the point at which things change forever and the human tide
begins to flow along a completely new course. Population growth in
England accelerated in the nineteenth century, exceeding an annual
1.33% on average despite large-scale emigration. Natural growth,
excluding the effects of emigration, peaked at over 1.7% in the years
1811–25.[2] This was much faster than in any other period, whether the
high Middle Ages before the Black Death or in the Merry England of
the Tudors, and it delivered a far larger population than England had
ever seen before. When a population – or anything else – is growing
at 1.33% per annum, it doubles in around fifty years, then doubles
again in the next fifty years, and that is what the population of England
did during the course of the nineteenth century.

Just as this revolution was getting under way, the 'old regime' from
which it was breaking was at last being identified, by the Reverend
Thomas Malthus. Malthus was a country parson from Surrey, a prosperous county in southern England, who identified what he believed
was an iron law of history. In his famous *Essay on the Principle of*

Population, written, published and progressively revised between 1798 and 1830, he argued that a growing population would always outstrip the ability of the land to support it, which would lead inexorably to misery and death. In such circumstances, Malthus maintained, war, famine and disease would reduce population back to levels that the land could sustain. At that point, with numbers down and fewer people to share the available resources, the surviving people, reduced in number, would each get a larger share of what was available, enabling them to live a little better, live longer and bear more surviving offspring. But the population would soon grow back towards its natural limit and, without the checks of 'vice' (birth control) or 'restraints' (late marriage and sexual abstinence), universal misery would return. As Malthus put it: 'The power in population is so superior to the power in the earth to produce subsistence for man, that premature death must in some shape or other visit the human race.'[3]

Although Malthus had provided a landmark account of human development up to that point, the world was changing around him even as he wrote. With the arrival in his native Britain of the agricultural revolution followed by the industrial revolution, food production and trade were transformed, enabling the population to grow way beyond any previous bounds.[4] Population size was no longer constrained by what could be produced locally. An industrialised country could sell its products on world markets and buy its food from around the globe. New agricultural techniques meant that more could be produced; for example, in the eighteenth century new sowing and crop rotation techniques boosted yields and in the nineteenth century agriculture was increasingly mechanised. Yields per acre rose around 50% in the early nineteenth century, and in the second half of the century huge new acreages in Canada, the United States and Australia fell under European farming techniques and their produce became available for purchase by people back in Europe.

The settling of the new territories was often accompanied by the displacement and sometimes genocide of their inhabitants. Yet placing the land under modern agricultural techniques coupled with the advent of transport to sell the produce to people in Britain and elsewhere in Europe meant that millions of additional extra acres became available to feed a burgeoning number of mouths. Effectively, Britain was fuelling its population growth by opening up vast new acreages and farming them with the latest techniques. Only in Malthus's day was this new, more efficient and productive world becoming imaginable. Had Malthus lived and preached in Manchester, at the heart of the industrial revolution, or emigrated to serve a community in the New World, he might have glimpsed humanity's new future. But based in rural Surrey, he did not.

The growth of the country's population was not greeted by all as a national boon. Among intellectuals – and not only those who could be dismissed as conservatives or reactionaries – there was an upsurge of horror as the population spread and a mass civilisation and landscape came into view. In 1904 *The Times* lamented that the suburbs of south London were producing 'a district of appalling monotony, ugliness and dullness'. H. G. Wells despaired that 'England now for half of its area is no better than a scattered suburb' and spoke of the 'tumorous growth' of endless streets and indistinguishable houses. D. H. Lawrence was positively genocidal in his response to the masses: 'If I had my way, I would build a lethal chamber as big as Crystal Palace . . . then I'd go out in the back streets and main streets and bring them in, all the sick, the halt and the maimed.'

A snobbish contempt for the lower orders was at least as old as ancient Greece, but the peculiarly nauseous (and nauseating) sentiments expressed here can be seen specifically as a response to population growth on a scale never seen before. No one expressed it more bluntly or alarmingly than the German philosopher Nietzsche: 'The great majority of men have no right to existence, but are a misfortune to higher men.'[5] This is a sentiment less likely to have been heard when the population was small and growing slowly at best, and when most of the poor were not far from the edge of starvation.

Explaining Demographic Take-off

Why was demographic growth happening and why in particular was it happening in England? To some extent, it had to do with good luck. The sceptred isle of which Shakespeare had written, with a civil

45

war then still ahead of it, became once more a relatively safe place in the eighteenth century. In sharp contrast with much of the Continent, it suffered no marauding armies, at least after the Jacobite rising of 1745–6. Incidents of plague and other contagious diseases on a pandemic scale became less frequent, perhaps as standards of hygiene and nutrition started to rise. Some have even claimed the rising consumption of tea as a factor in explaining better health.[6]

When population rises, one of two things – and perhaps both – must be happening. The first possibility is that births are outstripping deaths. The second is that there must be more immigration than emigration. In the case of England in the nineteenth century, the second of these explanations can be dismissed out of hand. It may often be said that England has always been a land of immigration, but this is simply untrue. The rise of England's population between 1800 and 1900 most certainly did *not* have anything to do with immigration. On the contrary, during this period, Britain and Ireland were exporting huge numbers of people who were colonising the vast spaces of Canada, Australia and New Zealand and were for much of the period providing the largest immigrant group into the United States. It is true that there was much migration to England from Scotland and especially Ireland (both at that time within the United Kingdom) and, at the very end of the nineteenth century, of east European Jews, but this was dwarfed by the outward movement to the colonies and the USA. Estimates vary – the record keeping was not very good – and of course many people came back, complicating the picture, but one estimate is that in the 1850s alone, more than 1 million people left the country.[7] By contrast, in the peak year for immigration in the century before the First World War, barely 12,000 from outside the UK came to stay.[8]

Given that there was a mass migration *out* of England, and yet its population nearly quadrupled in the course of the century, the cause of the population growth must have been a vastly greater number of births than deaths, sufficient not only to generate this large domestic population growth but also to fuel the emigration. The poor, narrow streets of London's East End, into which Jews were packed by the end of the century, representing the bulk of immigration into the country, counted as nothing when compared to the vast spaces into which emigrants poured out from Britain, in Canada, the United States, Australia, New Zealand and beyond. Any excess of births over deaths had to compensate for the huge net emigration before it could contribute anything towards population growth. This is precisely what happened.

One of the first things to change as Britain's population revolution got under way was the average age at which people married. It got earlier, falling from twenty-six to twenty-three for women between the early eighteenth and the mid-nineteenth centuries.[9] That meant three more years of highest fertility when women would be having babies rather than waiting (mostly chastely) for a match.[10] At the same time (still on the question of chastity), the number of births outside marriage fell (along with the rising tide of Victorian morality). Overall, this was more than compensated for by the rise in births within marriage. Total fertility, whether inside marriage or out of it, rose from what had seemed quite low levels in the early eighteenth century, from four or five children, to about six children per woman in the early nineteenth century. This is one factor which makes England's population take-off slightly different from many that followed: whereas in most cases a high birth rate *stays high* and the death rate falls, in England's case the birth rate actually *rose*.[11]

Meanwhile, on top of people marrying earlier and having larger families, people started to live longer, which meant fewer deaths each year. In the late seventeenth century, when plague was still fairly common and living conditions highly unsanitary, the average person could expect to live little beyond thirty. By the early nineteenth century, insalubrious though much of life continued to be, it was improving, and life expectancy was over forty.[12] It was this steady fall of mortality which was the most important, consistent and sustainable contributor to the rise in population, even if the process was kicked off by a rise in the birth rate. And falling death rates were in turn made possible by changes in living standards – modest by our standards today but dramatic when compared with what had gone before – which were made possible by great technological changes ranging from cheaper and more hygienic clothing to more affordable food.

To us, the Victorian city may seem like a squalid place, but compared with the poverty-stricken village life of an earlier age, not to mention the death trap which was London in the Georgian period and earlier, the great 'improvements' of the age were contributing to a population explosion. Plague died out in England sooner than elsewhere in Europe, and cholera, when it appeared, had less severe effects.[13] Sewers were built, most famously in London by Joseph Bazalgette. Rudimentary medical care became more generally available. This was the age in which the railway made its first appearance. Pioneers such as Isambard Kingdom Brunel laid out lines which connected all parts of Britain, and their successors ensured that within decades railways were spanning other nations and continents. Steamships came to plough the oceans and road surfaces improved. This meant quicker, cheaper transport, which, when coupled with innovations in agriculture, meant more, cheaper food. Local food shortages were less likely to result in famine when food could easily and cheaply be brought in from outside.

Opening its market to the world after the repeal of the Corn Laws, Britain allowed for its people to be fed from wherever food could be brought in economically, and as transport technology progressed, that meant a wider and wider area. Britain's purchases of American cotton alone would have required, to produce equivalent quantities of wool, the use of almost all of Britain's pastureland, leaving nothing for the wool that actually was produced or for the production of meat. For the equivalent of a year's coal production, Britain would have had to fell a forested area equivalent to more than seven times its total forested area – every year.[14] Changes to public and private health and to diet greatly reduced death rates and so boosted the overall size of the population.

Although England was setting a pattern to be followed globally, as we have already seen, its population explosion differed from others in that it included not just a fall in the death rate but also at first a modest rise in the birth rate.[15] Another characteristic of England's demographic transformation was that, while the population boom was certainly fuelled by falling general mortality, it was not particularly marked by falling *infant* mortality. In most population booms which followed and which will be described later, as living standards improved and fewer died each year, it was usually highly vulnerable babies and small children whose mortality improved the fastest. In

Yemen, for example, the death of children before the age of one has fallen from one in four to one in twenty since 1950, which is a major factor in explaining why, during this period, its population has grown from less than 5 million to more than 25 million (at least, this was the case until the recent outbreak of civil war).[16] In England, infant mortality did not fall much from around 150 per thousand for most of the nineteenth century, and only began falling sharply after 1900.[17] Once people had cleared the hazardous years of childhood they did live longer, reducing the mortality rate and boosting the population, but the early years remained, for now, just as dangerous.

In nineteenth-century England child survival was no higher in the town or city than it was in the countryside, a fact that would surprise someone presently working in the field of economic development. Today, a family in Jakarta, for example, is more likely to get better health care and have access to superior amenities than one in an outlying Indonesian island, and urban infant mortality rates are lower than rural ones. Back in the eighteenth century, at least in England, the reverse was true; London in particular was a much less healthy environment for a young child than was the countryside. In the nineteenth century, although towns and cities were improving, it was still the case that they were less healthy than the countryside. So as the population moved from country to town, it moved from areas of lower to higher infant mortality. This slowed the fall in England's infant mortality whereas for countries urbanising today, it speeds it up.[18]

Generally, however, the pattern observed in England starting from the late eighteenth century would become a classic feature of societies in transformation, and has come to be called the 'demographic transition'. As living conditions improve, people live longer. Yet for a time, people continue to have very large families of six or seven. Only later do family sizes decline.

Overseas Comparisons

What, meanwhile, was happening across the Channel in continental Europe?

France, traditionally seen as Britain's main rival, was not only geographically larger but supported a larger population. In the reign of Queen Elizabeth I, England's population had been a fifth of France's.[19] In 1800, with Napoleon Bonaparte in control and soon to be crowned Emperor, France had nearly four times as many people as England. British victories over France in the preceding centuries, victories which secured the global supremacy of Britain, had happened despite, not because of Britain's population size. However, over the course of the nineteenth century France started to fall behind not only industrially and militarily but also in terms of population. By 1900, far from having four times as many people as England a century earlier, it had barely a quarter more (and fewer than the UK as a whole).[20]

This is even more extraordinary in view of the fact that while England had had mass emigration, few people had left France in the intervening century. It is true that France had lost the provinces of Alsace and Lorraine in 1871, but this is a small part of the explanation. The strange fact is that French family sizes were simply much smaller than those in England. Its women had fewer children. Many explanations have been offered for this: French inheritance laws; the role of the Church in recruiting priests, nuns and monks who had no children; or, perhaps most intriguing of all, a knowledge among French peasants about how to practise birth control which simply did not travel across the Channel. Whatever the cause, France was, demographically speaking at least, stuck in a rut in the nineteenth century. Just as population expansion, urbanisation and industrialisation went hand in hand in Britain, so in France slow population growth was accompanied by limited industrialisation and a continuation of a predominantly rural lifestyle. By the middle of the nineteenth century England passed the point where half of its population lived in towns or cities; this did not happen in France until the middle of the twentieth century. With France's stagnant population size and limited industrialisation came a loss of power. Indeed this was the start of a French fixation with demography and a fear that its inferior numbers would doom it forever to inferior status, if not subservience.

Two countries whose populations did rise as quickly as England's, or almost so, were Denmark and Scotland. Denmark, however, hardly counted for much on the international stage by this point, while Scotland was bound to England in the United Kingdom, experiencing the same take-off of industry and urbanisation and also the same high levels of emigration.

For much of the nineteenth century it is not really possible to speak of 'Germany' as a single entity, since it did not unify until 1871, but taking it as the lands which were eventually to become Bismarck's Reich, England and its fellow members of the United Kingdom made relative progress here too. In the first half of the century the population of Great Britain (England, Wales and Scotland but excluding Ireland) rose from barely 40% of what was to become Germany to around 60%. Germany was still behind England in implementing those rudimentary reforms which cause the death rate to fall and the size of the population to rise. Other parts of Europe, such as Spain, Italy and the Austro-Hungarian Empire, were further behind still and so experienced even slower population growth.

The fact that England's population was growing so fast mattered. As the human tide always shows us, numbers count, whether because more people means the ability to field larger armies or because it leads to a bigger economy, sucking in and churning out more resources. The rise of England and more generally of Great Britain within Europe in population terms was a major part of Britain's rise as the leading power during the course of the nineteenth century. When taking into account the simultaneous rise of people of British origin beyond Europe during the period, it was fundamental to Britain's emergence as the leading global power. But before we examine the impact of England's population revolution on the world, it is necessary to look at Ireland, where a very different and much darker demographic story was unfolding.

Ireland: An Exception within an Exception

While the population growth of England in the early nineteenth century was exceptional, Ireland's loss of population was an exception within an exception.

Ireland was an agricultural country whose climate and soil were well suited for the potato. However, the potato did not arrive in Ireland until the reign of Elizabeth I, and when it did, it had major population implications. As Malthus pointed out, the soil can only support so many people. Once in a very occasional while, however, something extraordinary can happen which can dramatically enhance the land's ability to support people, and in the case of Ireland, it was the arrival of the potato from the New World. When Walter Raleigh brought back the potato from America, he carried in his cargo the fate of Ireland. It took a while for the crop to spread and for it to affect population, but whereas in 1600 Ireland's population was perhaps 2 million (the data, as so much data from earlier periods, is contestable), it spiked to well over 8 million by around 1840.[21] This was despite considerable emigration in the preceding decades to the United States of the mostly Protestant population from Ulster, which settled the Appalachian backwoods and became what the Americans call the 'Scotch-Irish'.

The life of the Irish peasants who relied on the potato may have been materially miserable, but they were burgeoning in number nonetheless, and that was precisely Malthus's point: unchecked, numbers would expand to the frontier of misery. In the absence of any kind of developed industry to provide exports to pay for the import of food, Ireland's population could never have reached such dramatic heights without the potato and its ability in the damp Irish climate to support far more people than wheat, barley or any other crop could possibly have done.

Then in 1845, potato blight struck. What is most shocking about the Irish famine – which was hardly the greatest or the latest famine in human history but was nonetheless one of the most remembered in Europe – was that it happened when much of the British Isles was moving beyond the cruel Malthusian trap whereby populations that had grown too large to be supported were ground back down by the vicissitudes of nature and war. While England was heading into the modern age, Ireland was heading into a medieval nightmare. The hard-hearted attitude of British officialdom in the face of the Irish famine was informed by a Malthusian mindset undoubtedly supplemented by a degree of racism quite unfathomable from today's perspective: a belief that, if the starving masses were fed, they would only breed in greater number and exhaust the land. It was the anti-philanthropy (or misanthropy) of the bottomless pit. Any attempts to alleviate the misery, to feed and tend to the poor and their sickly offspring, would just lead to more of them surviving and eating up the limited resources, pushing them again into misery. (This is the same approach that Victorians took to the poor in general and is familiar to us through the writings of Charles Dickens, parodying and condemning this outlook in, for example, *Oliver Twist* and *Bleak House*.) So as commercial exports of wheat and barley continued, the population remained unfed.

Charles Kingsley, author of *The Water-Babies* and the Queen's private chaplain, spoke of the Irish as 'white chimpanzees'. Some contemporary commentators were more sympathetic, as this report from County Cork in the *Illustrated London News* of February 1847 shows:

> I saw the dying, the living and the dead lying indiscriminately on the same floor, without anything between them and the cold earth, save a few miserable rags upon them . . . not a single house out of 500 could boast of being free of death and fever, though several could be pointed out with the dead lying close to the living for the space of three or four or even six days, without any effort being made to remove the bodies to a last rest place.[22]

The effects of famine were shattering for Ireland. In the seven years between 1845 and 1852 around a million people died of starvation and another million emigrated under dire and often fatal conditions. Hundreds of thousands more left in the ensuing decades, transforming the great cities of the American north-east as the earlier Protestant emigrants from Ulster had transformed the Appalachians. Today there are seven times as many people claiming Irish descent in the USA as there are in Ireland, north and south combined. Hundreds of thousands more came to England and Scotland, often to the great and growing conurbations of Liverpool, Glasgow and Birmingham.

Famine and mass emigration consolidated British rule during the course of Queen Victoria's reign. From 1837 to 1901 Ireland's population fell from 8 to 4 million, and its share of the UK's population fell from nearly a third to less than a tenth of the whole population of the British Isles, not only because of this calamitous drop but also because of the rise of population in the rest of the country.[23] This had significant long-term impact, not least on British politics. During the course of the nineteenth century Britain extended the franchise to Catholics and, in due course, to working-class men and agricultural labourers. By the end of the century the male Catholic peasantry of Ireland (aided by the general over-representation of Ireland given its newly diminished demographic condition) could return enough MPs to swing many parliaments. Had Ireland still represented a third of the population rather than a tenth in this newly democratic era, the issue of Home Rule, which so preoccupied late Victorian and Edwardian Britain, would have loomed even larger. The demands of Irish nationalism would have been harder to resist; Home Rule, if not complete independence, would probably have come sooner, and partition may not have been a viable option.

Yet if Ireland was an exception within the UK, then Ulster was an exception within Ireland. It was in the north that industrialisation and urbanisation stirred while the rest of the island remained an agrarian society. Shipbuilding in Belfast and shirt-making in Londonderry meant Ulster was booming, integrating itself not only into the British but also into the imperial economy. As the Protestants of Ulster became the majority, both within the six counties which were later to form the Northern Irish State and even – more tenuously – within the wider nine counties which traditionally constituted the region, some of the more outlying and predominantly Catholic areas of Ulster suffered a fate closer to that of the rest of Ireland. Booming Belfast, meanwhile, the symbol of industrial, Protestant Northern Ireland with close links to Britain and its empire, went from having 20,000 people to having 350,000.[24]

Workshop of the World: How Population Made Britain the World's Leading Economy

Britain's imperial expansion in the nineteenth century was intimately tied to its becoming the workshop of the world. It was the first and the pre-eminent industrial power, leading the way in the production of clothing, the manufacture of iron and steel and the laying out of railways. This was the age when scientists such as Humphry Davy led advances in chemistry, and applied them to making mining safer, and when inventors such as Henry Bessemer changed the way steel was made, turning it into a material that could be used far more widely than ever before. There is no denying the importance of these individuals, their inventions and the changes to production they enabled. Yet it was only against the background of a rapidly growing population that these innovations could transform Britain into the world's first great industrial power. Industrialisation supported Britain's expanding population by providing work and, through trade, sustenance for its burgeoning numbers, but population expansion also drove industrialisation, providing the navvies to build the transport infrastructure and the factory hands to work on the shop floors.

It is true that a country with a small population can be rich and a country with a big population can be poor. So to say that Britain became the workshop of the world and, for a time, its leading economy, because its population ballooned is simplistic. Plenty of countries have had rapidly rising populations but remained poor while others have become rich as their population growth slowed. On the other hand, the link between these two events – the rise of Britain's population and the rise of its industry – cannot be ignored. There are two basic ways in which a country's population size contributes to its economic clout. First, there is the simple weight of numbers. Luxembourg is rich, its people on some scores twice as well off as Americans, but it is not a major player on the economic stage, unlike, say, India or China. Luxembourgers have prospered individually, and they have built a rich and successful country, but it has hardly any economic clout because it is so small. It has been possible for India and China to be very populous and to be so very poor that they too had no weight on the international economic stage – that was true of both countries for much of the twentieth century. But as soon as a country of many hundreds of millions starts to get going, even moving from abject to moderate poverty for its average citizen, the weight of numbers starts to count. The United States, meanwhile, is not the largest economy in the world because its people are very much richer than people in the individual European countries or Japan, but because there are so many more of them.

Second, a country the size of Luxembourg can only thrive today because it lives within a zone of free trade – deeply embedded within the European Union and to a considerable extent, through the World Trade Organisation, with the wider world. Luxembourgers have been able to specialise in high-value services which enable them to buy necessities and luxuries from the rest of the world. Forced back entirely on their own resources, they would be living at subsistence level, as would any group of a few hundred thousand people cut off from global trade. Today, small countries can make their way in the world thanks to the rules and regulations of free trade. The world's economy was not so open when Britain began its demographic take-off at the beginning of the nineteenth century. Under less liberal trading circumstances, a larger population provides not only more hands for factories but more consumers and a larger market. It builds the economy both from the supply side and from the demand side. The ability to reach real scale in production and manufacturing requires either access to a wide global market or at least access to a sizeable one at home.

Comparing the populations and economies of Britain and France is informative. The data for the size of the economy is more contentious than that for the size of the population, but taking what is probably the best data available, the economy of the UK grew steadily from less than a third of that of France in 1700 to more than a third larger by the outbreak of the First World War.[25] Relative to France's economy, therefore, Britain's quadrupled. Over the same period, the UK's population went from less than half of that of France to around 15% more. So a good part of Britain's economic growth relative to that of France must be attributed to the relative growth of its population.

Without its great nineteenth-century population growth, Britain could not have developed either into the workshop of the world early in the century or into the world's greatest financier in the second half. Even ignoring the impact of a growing population on increasing the market and enriching the population and simply looking at how sheer growth increased the economy, about half of the economic growth was the result of population increases alone. Just as a rising population contributed to economic growth, so economic development led to rising population. With greater wealth, Britain was able to invest in better public health, and its people were able to eat better, thanks to trade with their brothers and sisters settling the Canadian prairie and the Australian outback. Britain had the population scale to become the world's factory and then, based on the wealth it accumulated, to become the world's financier. And just as its leading economic role would not have been possible without its population boom, neither would its leading imperial role.

For Queen and Mother Country: Populating the Empire

The great cultural historian Fernand Braudel said of the Spaniards that they could conquer but not *grasp* Central and South America.[26] The suggestion is that although the Spaniards had a vast empire on paper, in practice they had little impact or control over much of it, even before losing most of it early in the nineteenth century. In large part this was because there were simply not enough Spaniards to make a real population impact on the lands they conquered, even if they succeeded – intentionally or otherwise – in wiping out large swathes of the populations who had been there beforehand. When the US annexed the northern half of Mexico in 1848 (including what are today the states of California, Arizona and New Mexico) they were able to do so easily because there were hardly any Spaniards or Mexicans there. This is in sharp contrast to the British, who *peopled* their empire – for which, of course, *people* were required. And people is what Britain came to have in abundance. The difference between the Spanish and British in this respect depended critically on the fact that Britain was undergoing a population explosion at the time, producing enough people to grow the population dramatically at home while exporting millions to the colonies and beyond. Spain had never been able to do this.

Great waves of people from the British Isles settled in the imperial territories of Canada, Australia and New Zealand, bringing with them diseases that devastated the indigenous peoples – much as the Spaniards had done in Latin America two or three centuries earlier – while themselves rapidly growing in number. It might seem surprising that a few million migrants could dominate a continent the size of Australia within half a century, but it is less extraordinary when the relatively small size of the indigenous population is borne in mind as well as its decline in the face of European diseases and violence, and the robust health and reproductive powers of those Europeans who were able to double their numbers every generation even without migration. When a settler agriculturalist population replaces a largely hunter-gatherer one, that process is often aided demographically by the high birth rate and low death rate of the former (who are able to access new lands for cultivation and thus at least temporarily escape Malthusian constraints) and a high death rate of the latter (sometimes at least in part the result of genocide but often largely the result of diseases brought in by the newcomers).

The motives which drove the migrants – the pull and push factors – are complicated and vary in each case. Migration to the colonies itself pre-dated the population explosion by a couple of hundred years, it is true, but migration on the scale witnessed in the nineteenth century would not have been possible without depopulating Britain had a population explosion not been under way at home. To some extent, the surfeit of people generated its own outward pressures. The colonies were distant and travel to them was often difficult and dangerous, but they held out opportunity and possibility. Often migrants failed overseas and returned, and sometimes they might have regretted going, but there were many success stories. In colonies where men outnumbered women, women could be tempted to move out. Ellen Clancy, who emigrated to Australia in 1853, wrote back home years later:

If you can go under suitable protection, possess good health and are not too fastidious or 'fine ladylike', can milk cows, churn butter . . . the worst risk you run is that of getting married and finding yourself treated with twenty times the respect and consideration you may meet with in England.

She added that thanks to their fewer numbers relative to men, women 'may be pretty sure of having our way'.[27]

It would be hard to overstate the degree to which this gave Britain a head start over its rivals. British emigrants settled in areas whose indigenous peoples, still following the population patterns described by Malthus, were easily outnumbered and pushed aside, sometimes brutally, by armies of newcomers who cornered resources such as land and water. Britain's ability to escape Malthus's constraints was the secret that allowed its people to wrest continental-sized territories away from their original inhabitants. It was the weight of numbers – combined with new industrial technologies – that enabled the British and their offspring to make their language, culture and political institutions the global norm.

Although England had led the way in population growth, Scotland was in close step. Wales was often included in the English data, but Ireland was different. Whilst aware of these differences and similarities, it is possible to talk of a population explosion which was not just English but which encompassed Britain as a whole. This was important in terms of the British Empire, because both Scotland and Ireland played a disproportionate role in providing immigrants for the lands beyond Europe. Britain's rise to global pre-eminence was based not just on the population explosion at home but also on its people coming to dominate vast continental spaces abroad. If, as historian Timothy Snyder has argued, speaking of late 1940 and early 1941, the Soviet Union and Nazi Germany had remade Europe 'but Great Britain had made the world', they did so by exporting people.[28]

It is worth distinguishing between three different areas in which the British had an impact. First, there were colonies into which British people poured, where they overwhelmed the indigenous populations and forcibly shaped new societies in their place. In this category would be included Canada, Australia and New Zealand.

Second, there was the United States, where Britain was no longer in control but which had been formed by people of British origin and which continued for much of the nineteenth century to be populated by waves of immigrants coming predominantly from the British Isles. Finally there was India and eventually vast areas of Africa where large numbers of colonists did not settle but where domination by the British was facilitated by its rising population (more boots to put on the ground) and by its industrialisation (particularly of its military), which meant that huge colonised populations could be dominated and controlled in their own homeland.

Let us start with Canada, the world's second largest country by surface area. Much of it, it is true, is uninhabitable wasteland, but much is not, and is suitable for intensive agricultural settlement. The population of this vast area was less than 2.5 million in the middle of the nineteenth century, but it had nearly tripled by the outbreak of the First World War to well over 7 million. This was a growth rate fuelled by immigration, and that immigration came from England, Scotland and Ireland. By 1914 well over half the people of Canada hailed from the British Isles, either directly or by origin. The French-Canadian share, concentrated in Quebec, slid from nearly a third to not much more than a quarter of the total. French Canadians had a famously high birth rate – interpreted by some as a 'revenge of the cradle', a getting their own back on the British for defeating France in Canada – and this went some way to counteracting the impact of immigration from the British Isles and ensuring that they remained a majority in what would become the province of Quebec. Many, however, emigrated to the United States during the course of the nineteenth century, while very few arrived from France to supple-ment their number.[29]

Immigrants from Britain and Ireland had been pouring in both before and after the creation of the Dominion (a formal union of the Provinces into a country called Canada) in 1867, and in due course the indigenous population of Canada was reduced to less than one in thirty. Some Irish immigrants kept up a tradition of antagonism towards Britain, but nevertheless the British imprint was placed firmly on this vast territory – in terms of its language, place names, constitu-tion and politics. There was also a huge impact back home. Canada became one of the primary exporters of food to the United Kingdom, posing competitive challenges for British farmers in the high days of free trade but meaning more and cheaper food and a tangible improvement in the standards of living of the working classes in the two or three decades before the First World War. During that war, food from Canada became a lifeline for Britain, while men from Canada rushed to fill the trenches in the service of what was still very much thought of as the mother country.

The story of Australia is similar. In the hundred years to the outbreak of the First World War the European population of Australia went from fewer than 10,000 to more than 4 million, and again this number was made up overwhelmingly of emigrants from the British Isles. Nearly 200,000 came in the 1880s and nearly twice that number in the 1890s.[30] This was a predominantly young population (immigrants usually are), encouraged to 'open up' the territory and incentivised by cheap land. Unsurprisingly, this meant a high birth rate and low death rate (typical of young populations), which in turn swelled numbers even more. Again as in Canada, the indigenous population, never very large to start with, was reduced to the status of statistical insignificance. By the early 1920s there were barely 3,000 indigenous Australians in the areas of most intense British settlement, namely Victoria, South Australia and New South Wales. Throughout Australia as a whole, the people who little more than a hundred years earlier had had the continent to themselves represented barely 2% of the population. In contrast, over 80% of those born overseas had been born in Britain and the overwhelming majority of those born in Australia were born of British immigrant parents or grandparents.[31]

The population of New Zealand grew tenfold to a million in the half-century before the First World War, and although the Maoris were more successful at holding on than the indigenous populations of Canada or Australia had been (their population share rising significantly as the century progressed), they still represented barely 5% of the population early in the twentieth century.[32] Again like Canada, Australia and New Zealand provided not only huge territories on to which British culture and norms could be imprinted through vast population movement, but also large quantities of food in peacetime and – even more crucially – in wartime, as well as more willing volunteers to man the trenches when the call from the Motherland came.

What is noteworthy in all these cases is that although Britain had nominally held colonies in North America since the early seventeenth century and in Australasia since the eighteenth century, it was only once a population boom at home could fuel mass emigration that these territories came under meaningful control of Britain through a process of settlement. Without the population boom there would have been no mass settlement, and without mass settlement Britain's imperial claims to these territories might have remained as insubstantial as those of Spain to most of Latin America. Equally, without mass settlement these lands could not have become the great granaries and providers of meat and other essentials to a global trading system of which a newly industrialised Britain was the heart.

Just as Ireland was the exception within an exception in the British Isles, so South Africa was the exception that proved the rule within the British Empire. Whereas most of Africa was judged unsuitable for European settlement, its climate unhealthy, malaria rampant and transport to its interior untenable, South Africa was seen by the British as a land of emigration thanks to its more amenable climate. People were also drawn by the lure of diamonds and gold. As in Canada, people from the British Isles were not the first Europeans to come to this conclusion, and the history of Britain in South Africa is as much one of displacement of the Dutch settlers as it is of displacement of the Africans. The point, however, is not the ins and outs of British and Dutch relations and the Boer Wars, but rather this: that precisely where the Europeans were unable to dominate demographically, wherever their populations did not numerically overwhelm those of the indigenous people, their foothold was built on shaky and ultimately unsustainable grounds. It is true that today Canada, New Zealand and Australia have populations of decreasingly British, and indeed European, origins, as they have opened their doors to immigration from the wider world. However, when immigrants arrive they still conform to a society that is effectively British in its origins. English continues to be the predominant language (along with French in Canada). The political institutions continue to bear the mother country's stamp, as do important symbols like the flag (in Australia and New Zealand) and the head of state (in all three) – in other words, they continue to be predominantly 'white' countries.

In contrast, the European presence in South Africa never became dominant against the presence of Africans – whether strictly 'indigenous' or more recent arrivals from neighbouring territories north of the Limpopo – and so the imprint of Europe has proved less permanent. In the year that Nelson Mandela was born, more than one in five South Africans was white. In the year he died, the figure was less than one in ten. Had the trend gone the other way, it seems unlikely that he would ever have become president of the republic and a numerically bolstered white population would probably have continued to hold on to a monopoly of power for longer. Long before Mandela became president, however, population weakness had been gnawing away at white control.

The British arrived in the Cape in 1814 and for a long time their primary goal was ensuring dominance over the pre-existing Dutch Afrikaner population rather than over the Africans. Eventually the Dutch moved into the hinterland, setting up territories which the British came to regard as blocks to further African expansion, and the result was the Boer Wars. Dutch and British migrants arrived, but on a dramatically smaller scale than in, say, North America. By 1870 around a quarter of a million Europeans had migrated to South Africa, far less than a hundredth the number in the (albeit much larger) territories of North America.[33] The gold rush brought more at the turn of the century, but by 1904 whites, whether Dutch, British or other, represented barely one in five of the people in South Africa. This contrasts sharply with the situation in Australia, New Zealand and Canada at the same time.

The white share in South Africa was about the same in 1960: more had come and the population had undergone natural expansion, but by now the modernisation which causes population expansion was well under way among Africans. Africans had much larger families than Europeans and now they too were benefitting from falling infant mortality rates and experiencing rapid population growth while the white population had adopted the lower fertility patterns and lower population growth rates which by then had become common among peoples of European origin. Apartheid can be seen as whites trying to put off their inevitable demographic destiny, attempting to maintain dominance in the face of numerical weakness, but demography triumphed in the end. By the time Apartheid ended, whites comprised around 13% of the population of South Africa,[34] and there simply were not enough of them to control the blacks or indefinitely disenfranchise them. Twenty years later, whites were well below 10% of the population of the new South Africa.

Anglo-Saxons in America

The term 'Anglo-Saxon' sounds somewhat bizarre in the context of the USA. In the UK, at least, it has come to be thought of as the name for arrivals from Germany and Scandinavia, who came to England around a millennium or more before Christopher Columbus even thought of crossing the Atlantic and thirteen hundred years before the American Declaration of Independence. The US is thought of as a great melting pot whose people come from all over the world, including Native Americans, Europeans from across the continent, people of African origin and, increasingly, people from Latin America and Asia. It comes as something of a surprise therefore to learn that Americans took it for a commonplace in much of the nineteenth century that they were Anglo-Saxons. Thomas Jefferson had wanted the Saxon chiefs Hengist and Horsa to feature on the seal of the United States, seeing them as the true founding forefathers of liberty in distinction to the later imposition of the Norman yoke.

To an extent, the name 'Anglo-Saxon' provided a convenient label. On the one hand, following the War of Independence and the establishment of the Republic, Americans did not wish to describe themselves ethnically as 'English'. Perhaps fancifully, some thought themselves not only the ethnic but also the spiritual heirs of a 'free people' who had had Norman rule cruelly imposed upon them seven hundred years earlier. (For these purposes, King George III was portrayed doubling as his distant ancestor William the Conqueror, the alien oppressor.) Also, not all white Americans were of English origin: not an insignificant number were of German extraction, even as early as the time of independence (many more Germans would come later) and there were other peoples of European origin. There were, of course, also the African Americans, but they were overwhelmingly slaves and not considered part of the nation at the time. Increasingly, the United States attracted immigrants from parts of the British Isles which were not English (that is, Scotland and Ireland), and while referring to such people as Anglo-Saxons was inaccurate, nevertheless it seemed less glaringly inaccurate than calling them English. So the term stuck and was often worn with pride by Americans of that era, while today it remains in the acronym 'Wasp' – white Anglo-Saxon Protestant.

Despite the rather spurious use of 'Anglo-Saxon' in nineteenth-century America, it needs to be remembered that at the time of independence, the people of the United States, and particularly their governing elite, were overwhelmingly of English, or at least British, origin. During the decades that followed, the United States grew away from its east coast origins and spread deep into the North American continent, absorbing the Appalachians, purchasing vast areas of the mid-west from France (the Louisiana Purchase) and acquiring still larger areas as part of the Oregon Treaty with the UK and from the ex-Spanish colony of Mexico, thus reaching the Pacific coast. None of this would have been possible, or meaningful, without the people to back it up. When the United States made the Louisiana Purchase in 1804, it had a hundred times more people than there were French men and women in the area of the Purchase.[35] Napoleon wisely saw that without a strong French presence there was no way he could hold on to the territory in the face of the swarming Anglo-Saxons. The human tide was pressing west, and at that point it was speaking English. By 1820 the USA had 10 million people and the numbers kept growing thanks both to new arrivals – still largely from the British Isles – and a high birth rate. American women in those days were giving birth to seven children. The population was mostly of British origin and its demography was an essential part of its dynamism and ability to brush aside rival French and Spanish colonists as well as Native Americans. Malthus had been well aware of conditions in the United States and specifically the opportunities for population to double in a generation where a fresh supply of agricultural land was unlimited. American founding father Thomas Jefferson had been aware of Malthus and commended his work.

As the USA's geography kept growing, so did its population, reaching 23 million by 1850 and 76 million by 1900, far exceeding Britain's. The ease with which the US absorbed what had been the northern half of Mexico after 1848 provides a graphic example. These huge territories contained an indigenous and Hispanic/Mexican population of barely 100,000. Within a few years of the annexation there were three times that number of whites in California alone.[36]

Initially the surging population of the United States that poured into these areas was the product of continuing high immigration from the British Isles and to a lesser extent Germany, buoyed by its own high birth rate and relatively low death rate. It brushed aside the natives, who were always relatively few in number – according to a Congress report, which may well have undercounted, there were barely 6,000 in the original thirteen founding states by 1830, their numbers decimated by disease and the loss of ancestral lands.[37] African American numbers did continue to rise even after the slave trade was abolished and no new arrivals came from Africa, but by the start of the twentieth century they were barely 12% of the total US population, a smaller proportion than at independence. (They are a similar percentage today.) French settlers in the Louisiana area of the Spaniards or Mexicans were remarkably thin on the ground.

The African American experience, and the legacy of slavery in particular, is one part of the dark side of this story, the other part being the marginalisation and sometimes genocide committed against the indigenous populations. It is true that slavery had been part of almost every society, and true too that the British were pioneers in abolishing the slave trade and driving it out of the Atlantic. It is true that the Arab slave trade long pre-dated that of the Europeans and outlived it. Yet the sheer industrial scale of the Atlantic slave trade, not only to the US but also to the Caribbean and Brazil, continues to stagger. The value of the lives of those transported was callously disregarded, and in the US slavery lived on and was not abolished until 1865. Thirty years later, black labourers in Alabama still received barely 60% of the nutrition they required.[38] The legacy survives, manifest in racial tensions in the US, and until recently in the underpopulation of Africa, although this is now fast reversing.

As the nineteenth century progressed, Europeans continued pouring into the United States but from increasingly diverse parts of the continent. In the hundred years up to 1920, when serious immigration controls started to be put in place, it is estimated that more than 8 million came from Britain and Ireland, 5–6 million from Germany, 4 million each from Italy and Austro-Hungary, more than 3 million from Russia and 2 million from Scandinavia.[39] The scale of the challenge – settling an area as vast as the United States and turning it into the world's greatest economy and superpower in the twentieth century – was simply too great even for the fertile people of the British Isles. But more than any other people, they contributed to populating the Republic. As the early as well as the most numerous immigrants, British Islanders provided the language other immigrants had to learn, and, very largely, the culture into which they had to integrate. As with those territories which remained within the British Empire, the United States, as it developed from its foundations until today, bears an unmistakably 'Anglo-Saxon' mark, and that was only possible because its great spaces were settled by people from East Anglia, Perthshire, Antrim and County Kerry. These were the people who won the West, and they won it largely because their numbers were increasing the fastest at the time.

Hubris

The world in 1900 was very different from the world in 1800. That can be said of any century, but in the nineteenth century something truly extraordinary stirred, and it stirred first and foremost in England and in the wider British Isles. This was the century that saw manufacturing industry grow in scale from low-level domestic activity to the employment of millions; which saw great continents settled by newly arrived populations and an international trade boom. Cities of millions sprang up across Europe and North America as Anglo-Saxon societies and then other European countries became increasingly urban. The population explosion lay at the heart of this. Without such economic change and development, the population of England, its colonies and its daughter republic, the USA, could not have grown sustainably. Equally, without the great boom in population, economic, social and political change could not have happened.

When in 1848 America debated what to do with Mexico, which it had just captured, some people argued for annexing the whole country, not just its northern part. They thought that its population, which was most certainly not welcome within the young United States, would melt away just as the 'Red Indians' had. Many thought that people of Anglo-Saxon origin would come to dominate the world. J. R. Seeley, whose famous lectures were published as *The Expansion of England* in 1883, declared that while 10 million Englishmen beyond the seas was admirable, it was 'absolutely nothing compared with what will ultimately . . . be seen'.[40] Cecil Rhodes, the famous (and, for some, infamous) British imperialist in Africa, not only shared this vision of an ever-expanding Anglo domain but believed it to be the work of God: 'I shall devote the rest of my life to God's purpose,' he said, 'and help Him to make the world English.'[41]

This kind of hubris was the product of the Anglo-Saxon lead in the demographic race. It seemed to those who were first out of the Malthusian trap that their advantage would last forever. They did not fully appreciate to what extent global dominance, whether imperial or economic, was built on foundations of population expansion, and that those forces which had caused the population expansion among the peoples of the British Isles and their colonial and American offspring could not be bottled, patented or otherwise restricted so as to prevent others from enjoying them in the fullness of time. In fact, others were not far behind. Population-expanding habits and technologies were, it turned out, not to be the preserve of Anglo-Saxons, and while Anglo-Saxons were destined to shape the planet they were not destined to have exclusive dominion over it.

4

The German and Russian Challenges

When, during the carnage of the First World War, wave after wave of soldiers met in battle on the Western Front, what ultimately mattered was not superiority of courage, technology or strategy but sheer weight of numbers. In the end it was the side that could continue to send men over the top that won. When the two sides had more or less slaughtered each other to a standstill, what was decisive was the arrival – or at least the prospect – of seemingly endless numbers of fresh recruits from the United States.

The importance of numbers did not come as a surprise. In the decades preceding 1914, the rival powers had been sizing each other up, worrying about their birth rates and those of their potential enemies, as though already conscious of the attritional slaughter that lay ahead. The *Daily Mail* lamented as early as 1903 that the decline in Britain's birth rate 'is now beginning to menace the predominance of our race'. A French work entitled *The Expansion of Germany* (perhaps consciously echoing Seeley's earlier *The Expansion of England*), published on the eve of the war, worried that 'fecundity is a permanent feature of the German race' and that 'the growth of this population assures Germany . . . a parallel growth in its military power'.[1] Meanwhile the influential German historian Friedrich Meinecke fretted that 'almost the entire Slavic race points to an inexhaustible fertility'.[2] Bethmann-Hollweg, chancellor at the outbreak of war, expressed concern about a Russia that 'grows and grows and lies on us like an ever-heavier nightmare'. Hollweg's despondent analysis contributed decisively to Germany's now or never gamble that led to war.[3] The dynamic changes in Europe's population – and in the population in countries settled by Europeans such as the United States, Canada, Australia and New Zealand – in the years leading up to the onslaught, were part of the cause of the war and contributed to its outcome.

It turns out the bizarre vision of Cecil Rhodes – that the whole world would be 'made' English – was simply not to be; neither was the vision of Anglo-Saxon supremacists in the US – that other peoples would 'melt away'. It is true that today's world was greatly shaped by the first ethnic/national group to experience a modern-style, sustained, industrially based population explosion, namely the people of the British Isles: their language predominates in the media, international business, diplomacy and academia; the states they founded remain (for now) the most powerful; and, taken as a group, they remain the richest and most economically powerful people on earth. But not only are they now in retreat in many fields on the world stage (in the face of rising Chinese power, for example); they have significantly retreated as an ethnic group *within their own states*. The US, Canada, Australia and the UK are all countries that are decreasingly populated by people who, to jumble nineteenth- and twenty-first-century phrases, could be labelled 'of Anglo-Saxon heritage' or indeed any wider origin within the British Isles.

What appeared an unbeatable and unique demographic formula turned out to be only a bit of a head start. Others learned to adopt precisely those techniques which had given the Anglos-Saxons their lead and, at least from a population perspective, caught up and overtook them, with major consequences for the balance of power and the outcome of history. In the last seventy or more years, it has been the people beyond Europe and North America who have made the running demographically, but the first challengers to Anglo-Saxon hegemony came from closer to home. Unsurprisingly, the technologies that allowed the British and their American cousins to take the first steps were copied by peoples most closely related to them culturally and geographically, namely other Europeans. As one might expect, when something new catches on, it is likely to catch on first among those closest to the source of the original innovation.

In the first place, it was the Germans and Russians who were in hot pursuit of the Anglo-Saxons. They were the first, thrusting, dynamic challengers to the Anglo-Saxon population leaders. In what follows we will look at why and precisely when this came to be the case, and at some of the also-rans – other European powers, who were slower off the block. (Russians are here considered as European, and we will not enter the great debate which consumed late nineteenth-century Russian intellectuals – whether they were European or not.) We will also see why all of this mattered and maybe even determined the outbreak and outcome of the First World War.

England Slows Down

Demography is not a competitive national sport. Aiming to get to the largest population through the highest birth rate and lowest mortality rate is rarely a chief policy goal of governments, although most are conscious that a falling birth rate (unless accompanied by a rising survival rate) will mean fewer potential soldiers and fewer potential producers (and consumers) in time, with military and economic consequences to follow.

As has been shown, England, and more widely Britain and its related overseas populations, maintained high or even rising birth rates with steady falls in mortality rates in the early nineteenth century, boosting its population size, but in the second part of the century changes began to set in. The most important of them was that women started to have fewer children. In the early part of the nineteenth century women had between five and six children on average, a level common in our day only among the least developed African states. It is possible to get a sense of this from Victorian novels, and those who are older may even have memories of it within their own families. Queen Victoria famously did more than her national duty, having nine children, all born in the early part of her reign. There is a tendency to think of the Victorian period as something of a mono-lith, but in fact conditions changed dramatically between 1837, when Victoria ascended the throne, and 1901, when she died. In the middle of his mother's reign, Victoria's son, later Edward VII, had five chil-dren with his wife Alexandra (a sixth died when only a day old), born in the 1860s, a decline from the number his mother had had and more in line with the nation as a whole at that stage. Later generations were markedly smaller. Of course, the British royal family is not typical of the UK. For one thing, it was not constrained by the same financial limits that influence most people and family size. But in a rough sort of way, it does illustrate what was happening generally to the population of the country. From the middle of the nineteenth century, when the average woman in England was still having around five children, there was a clear downward trend. By the outbreak of the First World War, the average woman was having just three. The birth rate (births per thousand of the population) fell by a third – from 36 to 24 – between 1876 and 1914. Women who married in the 1860s had more than six births each; those who married in the 1890s had slightly more than four; and those who married in 1915 had less than two and a half.[4]

It is easier to determine why this was happening than how it was achieved. What was happening in late Victorian and Edwardian England (and more widely across the United Kingdom) was a modernisation process which involves populations increasingly living in cities, more people wanting to invest in their children (who now require education to progress) rather than seeing them as a source of labour in the fields and an insurance policy for old age. Also, when more children survive childhood, the message eventually gets through that parents can have fewer in the first place since nature is less likely to deprive them of them.

In country after country, continent after continent, fertility falls when infant mortality drops, or at least when infant mortality *has fallen*. This is an essential part of the pattern that is the human tide. It takes longer for the reality of lower infant mortality to translate into lower fertility rates in some places than in others, and there are exceptions to the rule. Change in population is not physics, it is not governed by iron laws, or at least by very few. But nevertheless the general pattern will become clear. And as the nineteenth century proceeded, so the conditions that are thought of as Dickensian – open sewers, child factory workers and chimney sweeps, the workhouse – started to change. By 1914 there had been great steps forward in public health, the provision of clean water and even the basics of a welfare state. The Great Stink of 1858, when Britain's parliament had to be evacuated because of the unbearable miasma wafting from the polluted Thames, and the cholera outbreaks which had preceded it, were unimaginable in the London of fifty years later with its sewers and orderly public hygiene.

After 1870 at least a basic education was available to all, and an educated population was almost inevitably longer-lived, being better able to understand how to take care of itself and its children. And it was not only conditions at home that improved: thanks to the opening of the prairies of North America, the spread of the railways and the introduction of iron-clad and steam-powered ships and of refrigeration, food was becoming cheaper and more plentiful. Ordinary people were beginning to live in more salubrious conditions and enjoy better diets. Between 1870 and the outbreak of the First World War, life expectancy increased from around forty to the mid fifties. Perhaps this seems modest by today's standards, when people expect to live to eighty or beyond, but it seemed revolutionary at the time.

Moreover, infant mortality was finally beginning to fall, from at or above 150 per thousand in the latter years of the nineteenth century to around 100 per thousand by 1914. The advances of Pasteur, Koch and Lister, an understanding of disease and the need for cleanliness in the preparation of food and drink and in medical procedures, generally helped reduce mortality but were particularly beneficial in saving the lives of the young. At this point, infant mortality started decisively on its sharp downward path from over 100 per thousand babies never making it to their first birthday to below 30 per thousand by the middle of the twentieth century and to around 4 per thousand today. This effect was compounded by the fact that there were more young women of childbearing age than in previous decades (the result of past population growth) and as more of the children born were surviving, so the population continued growing, albeit more slowly.

Preventing Births: A Brief Aside on Contraception

Lower infant mortality and the longer life expectancy with which it was associated was followed, as it almost always came to be, with a drop in the number of children being born per woman (lower fertility rate). But how was this being achieved? Effective contraception was not available at this time, certainly not cheaply and accessibly to the population as a whole. The convenience and simplicity of the Pill was decades ahead and what was available was expensive, cumbersome and difficult to get hold of.

Contraception has existed in some form since at least the days of ancient Egypt, and at least one method of controlling births – *coitus interruptus* – is recorded in the Bible. There is evidence that the ancient Egyptians understood that prolonged breastfeeding helped spread conceptions out, resulting in fewer in total, and this in part explains why in ancient Egypt, annual population growth was probably barely 0.1% on average.[5] The Spartans famously practised infanticide, and this was probably common in many societies, although largely obscure, until fairly recent times, along with abortion. The eleventh-century Persian thinker Avicenna recommended spermicides, potions to take away passion and what is now called the rhythm method. The Catholic Church opposed such potions (although not the careful timing of sex) in the thirteenth century, instituting a Catholic pro-natalism which has not yet been formally abandoned by the Church (although the data suggests that it is now ignored by most Catholics). Sheaths were openly on sale in major European cities by at least the eighteenth century, albeit often illegally, often as much to prevent the spread of venereal diseases as to check conception.[6] Delaying weaning was in many places understood to delay the next conception.

In many places, legal blocks hindered those seeking to plan their families in any but the most natural ways. The American doctor Charles Knowlton was prosecuted, fined and sentenced to hard labour in the 1830s for publicising his book *The Fruits of Philosophy, or the Private Companion of Young Married People*. In the 1870s it was published in Britain by Charles Bradlaugh and his extraordinary companion Annie Besant (a one-time vicar's wife, organiser of the matchgirls' strike and later a founder of the Indian National Congress). Bradlaugh and Besant were also prosecuted, with the perverse outcome that the trial probably did much to popularise the use of rudimentary contraception among those who could afford it.

Although opposition to publicising contraception was fierce, other opinions were coming increasingly to the fore. Malthus had urged restraint and late marriage, but Richard Carlile, a populariser of birth control among the working classes, thought this a bad idea, claiming that 'women who have never had sexual commerce when about twenty-five years of age . . . become pale and languid . . . nervous fidgetiness takes possession of them'.[7] The complete dominance of the medical profession by men at this time – and often unimaginative ones at that – gave rise to all sorts of strange ideas about sex. William Acton, the best-known writer of the nineteenth century on sexual complaints, suggested that 'a modest woman seldom desires any sexual gratification for herself. She submits to her husband's embraces, but principally to satisfy him and were it not for the desire of maternity, would far rather be relieved of his attentions.'[8] To some extent the fall in fertility was achieved by later marriage. More women put off marriage, perhaps assisted by the start of what could be deemed 'middle-class' jobs for women. (The typewriter was invented in 1868 and its use became widespread in the decades thereafter, creating a demand for typists and secretaries, often considered a suitable and 'respectable' female occupation.) In the 1870s barely one bride in ten was over thirty on her wedding day; by the Edwardian period (specifically 1906–11) the share was nearly twice as high.

So fewer women of childbearing age were married, and many were now spending all or at least part of their fertile years outside of marriage, at a time when notions of respectability were becoming more widespread and fewer births were occurring outside marriage. And not only were more women staying outside marriage for longer (and becoming less likely to have children outside marriage); even within marriage, birth rates were falling. In 1905 *The Lancet* calculated that 300,000 fewer children each year were being born to married couples than would have been the case if the birth rate had remained at the level of the 1870s.

It is impossible to know whether this was achieved through abstinence from sex or careful timing (either within the act itself or within the menstrual cycle) or a bit of both; exactly what was going on in the bedrooms of our great-great-grandparents remains something of a mystery. Nevertheless, there are some intriguing clues. At the top end of society, shortly after the First World War Margot Asquith, wife of former Prime Minister Herbert (Henry) Asquith, reportedly spoke to British politician Oswald Mosley's first wife Cynthia (the daughter of

Lord Curzon and an early Labour woman MP) after the birth of her first child, warning her not to rush another: 'Henry always withdrew in time, such a noble man.'[9] In this Asquith was obviously more adept or concerned than his monarch's father, the late Prince Albert, of whom Queen Victoria complained: 'Oh! If those selfish men – who are the causes of all one's misery, only knew what their poor slaves go through! What suffering – what humiliation to the delicate feelings of a poor woman . . . especially with those nasty doctors.'[10]

At the lower end of society, there is no reason to imagine that practices were all that different to that of the Asquiths, although the memoir of Aida Hayhoe, a woman living in the Fens in rural eastern England, suggests an alternative approach, recounting how she would 'sit up at night, after my husband had gone to bed. He say [sic] "Aren't you coming to bed?" I say, "I've got to mend these before I go to bed. They'll want them in the morning. You can go but these have got to be done tonight."' Mrs Hayhoe's motives were clear: 'See, I had three children. And I didn't want no more. My mother had fourteen children and I didn't want that. So if I stayed up mending, my husband would be asleep when I came to bed. That were simple, weren't it?'[11]

While the battle for the acceptance and popularisation of birth control continued, new allies were found for those who favoured it, namely eugenicists, who valued and wished to manage the *quality* of what they unapologetically referred to as the country's human 'stock'.

When the trends towards smaller families later hit other countries, there came to be a distinct gap between the modernising populations in towns and cities, who rapidly adopted the nuclear family, and the peasants and agricultural labourers who remained in the countryside and continued to have large families. Here England was an exception. Given the country's small size, rural dwellers of England were perhaps too close to cities not to be heavily influenced by them. A sizeable town was almost always only a short railway ride away from even the remotest rural dwelling. There was nothing equivalent to *la France profonde*, a lost imaginary arcadia removed from modern influences, or to the American backwoods, never mind deepest, darkest peasant Russia, a day's trek or more from the nearest road. So even in the countryside, the English adopted the modern ways of the town and moved quickly to smaller family size.

Mass Emigration Continues

Between 5 and 7 million people left the UK (including Ireland) in the second half of the nineteenth century. Once large flows of immigrants started to go to the US from more distant and poorer parts of Europe such as Italy and the Jewish Pale in Russia (the western parts of Russia to which Jews were restricted), migrants from the British Isles tended increasingly to be diverted to the colonies, mostly Canada and Australia, and away from the US. This overall high level of emigration reduced population growth at home. In one way, simply by dint of the numbers leaving, emigration reduced population growth at home. On the other hand, as we have seen, the productive farming many of these emigrants engaged in and the cheap food they produced and exported boosted living standards of the working class back at home and helped them live longer, thus tending to increase the UK's population size.

As the gathering of population data improved, three incontestable factors were revealed to be at work in determining the growth of population. First, women were having fewer children – partly by delaying marriage, partly by a greater awareness and availability of methods to control conception – but also because of past population growth, there were still more young women having children than there had been, and so still plenty of births. Second, fewer people were dying each year, particularly fewer young children at least from the start of the twentieth century. Third, large-scale emigration continued and immigration from outside the UK (which at this time included Ireland) was still very limited. (The exception was immigration of Jews from Russia, mostly between 1880 and 1905, which never exceeded much more than 10,000 in any one year and produced a population of British Jews which never amounted to more than 1% of the total population, so not big enough significantly to affect total size.)[12] The net impact of these three effects was a population which continued to grow, but whose growth was beginning to fall from about 1.35% per annum in the first half of the twentieth century to only a little over 1% in the second half. A slower annual population rise over such a long time meant that the population at the end of the period was a lot smaller than it would have been had it continued growing at the same pace. Meanwhile, on the other side of the North Sea, a similar story was unfolding, resembling that of the United Kingdom but a few decades behind. And as England was starting to slow down, so Germany was just getting into its stride.

Germany Awakens

The first half of the twentieth century is often identified by a global clash between Britain and Germany. At the start of the nineteenth century, that would have been surprising. The history that tends to be taught in schools focuses on the efficiency – and ultimately the geno-cidal cruelty – of the German war machine and the size and power of its industry and economy. It is widely known that Germany was able to take on the combined might of the British Empire, Russia and the US by 1914, even if it was not able to overcome them, but it is often forgotten that in the early nineteenth century, as Britain was well into its industrial revolution, Germany was not only still politically divided into dozens of mini-states but still economically fairly backward and widely seen as a land of poets and thinkers, of princelings and petty dukedoms, more medieval than modern, more fairy-tale castle than blast furnaces.

This was the Germany of Goethe and Schiller, of Beethoven and Schubert, of Kant and Hegel, a land rich in thought and art and crea-tivity but constitutionally and regionally fragmented, agricultural and, compared with bustling London and Paris or booming Manchester, not at the cutting edge of nineteenth-century urban progress. There are many aspects to Germany's rise to prominence as a challenger of the world's mightiest powers, political, industrial, economic and military included, and the demographic one is often overlooked. Germany, Bismarck said, was built on blood and iron. We too often think about the iron – the industrial might which provided the heavy weaponry – and too rarely about the blood – not only the quality but also the quan-tity of young German men willing and able to die for the fatherland.

In sheer numbers, Germany (by which is meant the territory which was finally to become a single empire in 1871 after Bismarck's wars of unification) always had a larger population than the UK, but the balance changed over the course of the nineteenth century. In 1800 the UK's population was less than half that of Germany. With the UK's developmental head start, this rose to two-thirds in 1900, but at that stage it was falling back quickly, given its lower birth rate and higher emigration, and this meant that by 1913 the British gains had fallen back to 62%.[13]

Germany's demographic rise can be seen in relation to France as well as to Britain. A century before the outbreak of the First World War, during the reign of Napoleon Bonaparte, there were around 10% more French men and women than Germans in the fragmented states that would become Bismarck's empire. By 1914, the French population had sunk to less than 60% of Germany's. Germany had successfully joined Britain in a post-Malthusian world of industrial-isation, urbanisation, high birth rates (which persisted for a time) and plunging mortality rates. France, by contrast, experienced a quite different demographic fate, one marked by low fertility and low population growth, despite low emigration. German population growth relative to that of its neighbours caused considerable concern in Britain and created a kind of paranoia in France, which was still highly conscious of its defeat by Prussia in 1870 in a conflict that saw Paris occupied and which led directly to the unification of Germany a year later.

Germany's rise had a double impact. If it had remained a country divided up into a patchwork of states, the growth of its population would not have mattered that much. On the other hand, had it united but remained fairly modest in population terms, it could not have posed such a challenge to its neighbours. It was the combination of political unity *and* population growth which allowed Germany to be the major player it became, even if this turned out not to be enough to achieve either the European or global domination it came to seek.

What was happening in Germany was no more than a later replay of what had already happened in the UK. Twenty-five million Germans in 1800 became 40 million by 1870 – an annual average rise of about two-thirds of one per cent – and 67 million by 1913, an annual average rise that was almost twice as fast.[14] By the middle of the nineteenth century, the land of poets and thinkers was turning into the land of blood and iron, not to mention steel and coal. The industrialisation which had come to Britain was coming to a Germany with many of the same advantages Britain had, namely a sober, relatively literate and hard-working population and access to the necessary raw materials. Between 1880 and 1913 German manufactures rose from a third of Britain's to overtake them.[15]

Conditions in early industrial Germany were harsh, just as they had been in Britain, but as in Britain they slowly improved, eventually providing the urban worker and his family with a higher living standard than his peasant forebears had been able to hope for. That meant more children could survive, people could live longer and so at first, while fertility remained high, the population grew fast. Like Britain, Germany was escaping the Malthusian trap. But whereas Britain had been at the cutting edge, where progress was hard won, Germany was following a now beaten path, and could therefore move faster. This is a trend which will show itself as the story of the human tide unfolds. The later a country comes to industrialisation, the quicker it is able to adopt it, and the faster the transformation of its society, so the faster the initial population growth.

It is true that German women were starting to have fewer children by the end of the nineteenth century, but infant mortality was tumbling too, helping to hold up population growth. Like Britain, Germany benefitted from the arrival of cheap food from beyond Europe (and also from Russia), as well as an increased output from home as the area of cultivated land grew and technology improved. Farm machinery grew more efficient and fertilisers were more widely used. And while the German government was more prepared to prop up and protect its farmers through tariffs, which meant its population did not enjoy the full benefits of cheap food from overseas, and although Germany had no vast empire to exploit but merely colonial scraps, the benefits of cheaper food and healthier cities were considerable nevertheless. The government of the newly unified country put a stress on education and a welfare state, both of which helped people at the lowest levels of society to escape the kinds of lives associated with high infant mortality and, even for many who survived infancy, an early death. When Bismarck unified the country, the average German could not expect to live to forty; by the outbreak of the First

World War, he or she could expect to live to almost fifty. In this, Germany still lagged behind Britain, but it was clearly catching up.[16]

Looking beneath the surface, it is possible to gain some insight into how the picture varied within and across the country. Unlike in Britain, there was a real gap between the number of children had by women in towns and those in the countryside. Country people in Germany continued to have large families while their urban cousins started to adopt smaller ones, a pattern different to Britain's but more typical of the subsequent pattern elsewhere. The larger the town, the fewer children in the family. (This came to be seen later in the Nazi concept of the healthy, fertile peasant, uncorrupted by city life, continuing to produce babies for the master race, as against weakened and decadent townsfolk, who were too diverted by material pursuits to do their childbearing duty for the fatherland.) At a national level it mattered, because as more and more people came to live in towns and cities, the country as a whole came increasingly to reflect urban rather than rural patterns. As the German population swelled, so it became increasingly urban; Berlin, for example, grew from less than 200,000 to over 2 million between 1800 and 1910.

As well as differences between town and country, there were class differences, and here the picture was much more like the one in Britain. Generally, the poorer the family, the larger the family; traditionally higher infant mortality among the poor had meant that the families of the richest were the largest, but with the adoption of contraception from the top of society, filtering only gradually downward, and generally improving survival rates, this pattern was reversed. Just as the urban–rural divide came to be a pattern which repeats itself again and again across the world, so too did the class divide. Large families came to be associated with the poor, the uneducated and the primitive. The nuclear family of one, two or at most three children came to be seen as the hallmark of richer and more urban people, wishing to limit their family size in order to give their children a head start in life and able and willing, by whatever means available, to practise some form of birth control. Later marriage in Germany, as in the UK, was part of the picture of falling fertility.

Finally, a further investigation of the national data for Germany reveals that there was something of a Catholic–Protestant divide, with the former having larger families and taking later and more slowly to artificial birth control.[17] This divide becomes fairly common within countries (Germany, the USA, French-speaking versus English-speaking Canada) and when comparing countries (Italy versus Sweden, Ireland versus Britain) until well into the second half of the twentieth century, although it declines thereafter as Catholic obedience to Church strictures on birth control wanes.

In short, although German families were shrinking by the time of the First World War, they were still bigger than those in Britain, and mortality was falling quickly. These two factors fuelled the population rise in the half-century or so before 1914. In addition, there was another major factor driving German population growth at this time, in sharp contrast to Britain's: that is, *falling* emigration.[18] British emigration had been higher to start with; in the 1880s, for example, it was twice the level of German emigration. But by the period immediately preceding 1914 it was nine times the level.

Germans had left their home country throughout the nineteenth century in search of a better life overseas, often going to the US where they formed a large share of the population. President Eisenhower's family came from Saarland, in western Germany, and Donald Trump's father's family came from Karlstadt in south-west Germany. However, once Germany started to industrialise and particularly after its unification, there were more opportunities at home. So while the wider English-speaking world and particularly the lands of the Empire offered an enticing prospect for many Britons, where they would find family links and a familiar language and political system, the appeal of emigrating to the alien Anglosphere diminished for Germans once their home country went from a patchwork quilt to a united and fast-developing state. In a sense, unguided though it may have been, the migration patterns of these two great countries, the UK and Germany, were reflected in their strategies in the twentieth century. Germany's burgeoning population at home allowed it eventually to field great armies on the battlefields of the Eastern and Western Fronts in both world wars. Britain's mass emigration meant it could raise a smaller army from its home population but could call on the assistance of a worldwide network in wartime, for food, equipment and men.

Russia Stirs

As the nineteenth century wore on, Britain became less and less confident that the future belonged to it and its colonial offspring. Hubristic voices like those of Rhodes became rarer, and more often voices came to be heard like those of Rudyard Kipling, who in his 1897 poem *Recessional* wrote:

> Far-called, our navies melt away;
> On dune and headland sinks the fire:
> Lo, all our pomp of yesterday
> Is one with Nineveh and Tyre!

More than the fall of the biblical Nineveh and Tyre, it was the decline of the Roman Empire that haunted the British. Population growth pointed to who would eclipse the British Empire. The United States was steaming ahead, its population far exceeding the UK's by the end of the nineteenth century and its capacity to maintain a large population much greater. Here the British could comfort themselves with the fact that the US was a long way off and, in any case, a sister nation. In those days there may have been no talk of 'a special relationship' but the seeds of that relationship were already sown, although there was undoubtedly much rivalry and suspicion. France, although still large in population terms, had failed to grow by anything like as much as Britain either demographically or industrially. Germany, as we know, was clearly rising, and this came to dominate British concerns. Japan was geographically distant and, in times when racism was deeply ingrained, and particularly before the Russo-Japanese War of 1905, was not taken seriously as a threat to the Empire. The only other country which was starting to show that combination of industrial dynamism and population growth which could pose a threat was Russia.

If it takes both industrial weight and population size to become a player on the world stage, Russia in the late nineteenth century was setting out from both a very low and a very high starting point. It was still an overwhelmingly agricultural country, a country of peasants not raised from the level of serfdom until the 1860s; a country with very limited industry and few large towns or cities. The government feared industrialisation and urbanisation, believing, correctly, that these would create revolutionary forces of instability that would threaten the Tsarist regime. On the other hand, to fail to develop, at the very least to build railways and armaments factories, was to consign Russia to defeat on the battlefield, as the Crimean War had demonstrated.

Even without the advantages of industry, however, its enormous numbers were to enable Russia to overwhelm its neighbours to the west, east and south, and to build the world's largest contiguous political unit, which it remains today. Still, as long as the country remained relatively backward, with the majority of its people illiterate serfs, its population advantage could take it only so far. Thus was posed the question of where Russia was to go. Would Russia stay eternally true to its Orthodox, peasant roots or change, and if so, would it follow the pattern of the West or find its own, special way forward? These are the questions which haunt late nineteenth-century Russian thought and literature, from Herzen to Tolstoy. Perhaps it is no coincidence that in the end, Tolstoy's heroine Anna Karenina throws herself in front of a train; having abandoned the traditional role of a Russian wife, she ultimately chooses to be destroyed by the mechanical monster which epitomised change. Ultimately, the forces of modernisation, including rapid population growth, proved irresistible. But if Russia's starting point industrially was very low, its starting point in terms of sheer population size was very high. By the start of the twentieth century, Russia had three times as many people as the UK and rising.[19]

To grasp the scale of Russia's population rise, it is really only necessary to understand three pieces of data. First, Russia's population more than quadrupled in the course of the nineteenth century, accelerating towards the end of it, which meant that as Britain was starting to slow down, Russia was gathering pace. Second, by the time of the outbreak of the First World War, Russia's population was growing at a full 1.5% per annum, faster than Britain and by then faster too than Germany. At that speed, population almost doubles in a couple of generations. Third, by 1914 Russia's population was a colossal

132 million, unprecedentedly large for a European country.[20] Conditions in Russia were extremely harsh, however, for both industrial workers and even more so for the peasantry. A follower of Tolstoy's, assisting him in the relief campaign for the famine of 1891, despaired that

> with every day the need and misery of the peasants grew. The scenes of starvation were deeply distressing, and it was all the more disturbing to see that amidst all this suffering and death there were sprawling huge estates, beautiful and well-furnished manors, and that the grand old life of the squires, with its jolly hunts and balls, its banquets and its concerts, carried on as usual.[21]

Yet from a longer-term perspective the misery of the peasants was not growing. Life for ordinary Russians may have been materially miserable and the contrast between rich and poor was certainly stoking the anger which would break out into revolutionary violence, but things were getting better, not worse. Even here the railways were penetrating, new techniques were being adopted to make food more available, and very rudimentary public health was being practised. Plagues were starting to take the lives of fewer people, and bad harvests to become less frequent. From the perspective of today, and even from the perspective of contemporaneous Britain or Germany, Russia seemed a poor and primitive place, yet as long as people prioritise their own lives and the lives of their children, so (as material conditions improve) resources will be focused on preserving life, and in these circumstances improvements in survival rates, death rates and thus population size can be dramatic. In Russia, moreover, family sizes were staying large. Russian women were bearing seven children during the nineteenth century, with early marriage and many children within marriage very common, and although this was beginning to fall slightly by the time of the First World War, significantly more of the children born were surviving, contributing to the growth of the population.

The Also-Rans of Europe and the Huddled Masses

In the population race, Britain was first off the block, with Germany and Russia close behind. France remained surprisingly still, lingering near the start, whilst the rest of Europe was beginning to stir but lagged far behind.

While some European countries were following Britain's demographic take-off, others, for much of the nineteenth century, were not. Italy, Spain and Austria-Hungary were still largely mired in the peasant-dominated misery of large family size but high infant mortality. In 1900 in Spain, for example, life expectancy was still under thirty-five while in England it was over forty-eight. Parts of Austria-Hungary did start to see improvement in the latter part of the nineteenth century and the early twentieth, and its loss of ground against Britain slowed. This was less so for Spain and Italy. Indeed, it is telling that, at the time of the Spanish Armada, Spain had a population twice the size of Britain's, while 300 years later it was half the size. Over those years, Britain went from seeing Spain as its most dangerous rival and existential threat to a country barely worthy of strategic attention. Of course, this had much to do with Spain's loss of empire and internal economic decline, and its failure to modernise and industrialise beyond a few very limited areas, but it also had a lot to do with the relative shifts in the population balance. The Britain of Queen Victoria had much less to fear from Spain than had the England of Queen Elizabeth I, to the point where Spain was seen not as the principal global threat but as no more than a hot, dusty backwater. Population explains much of the reason for this change.

Italy and the Austro-Hungarian Empire began by the late nineteenth century to send populations beyond Europe, as Britain had been doing for centuries. Had the great cities of America not filled with Sicilian peasants and Jews from the furthest-flung Hapsburg provinces (as well as the Russian Pale) as the twentieth century dawned, the populations left at home would have been larger; in Italy, for example, the death rate fell between 1850 and 1913 from nearly thirty per thousand per year to just over twenty, while the birth rate fell more steadily, so the natural increase between these dates rose from around eight to around thirteen per thousand per annum. Just as the arrival of the railways brought cheaper food and modern ways deeper into the European continent, allowing more children to survive, so they also took more of those children away to the New World, limiting population growth in the Old Country.

Four million Italians emigrated to the US in the thirty-five years before the start of the First World War, and many more left for other places such as Argentina. Emigration from these countries was a boon to the United States, where numbers were swollen by a huge pre-First World War wave of migrants. In the generation after the Statue of Liberty was dedicated in 1886, her torch would welcome fewer immigrants from traditional lands – the British Isles and Germany – and more from the further reaches of Europe. These were people suffering from poverty and (in the case of Jews) persecution at home but who were also experiencing their own population expansions. These huddled masses and their offspring would soon be turned into Americans, providing their new homeland with the population advantage that would propel it to world leadership. Although their fertility rates soon began to fall once they arrived in the New World, they were still high, and so their numbers continued to swell for the first few decades after their arrival. The 6 million Jews of the United States today are overwhelmingly the product of this late nineteenth- and early twentieth-century population movement, as are the 60% of Argentinians who today claim Italian descent.

Although conditions and survival rates for the passage improved over time, and the cost fell, it should not be imagined that even early in the twentieth century the experience for the masses coming from southern and eastern Europe to Ellis Island was pleasant. A US government inspector, sent incognito to report back on conditions for those migrating to the US, reported on her experiences and related that 'during the twelve days in steerage, I lived in disorder and in surroundings that offended every sense. Only the fresh breezes of the sea overcame the sickening odors.' Meat and fish reeked and vegetables were a 'queer, unanalysable mixture'. One boy who left eastern Europe at around this time recalls of the crossing that 'we were huddled together in steerage literally like cattle'.[22]

Although the new immigrants were largely expected to assimilate into the predominant culture, they changed America. After the First

World War, President Woodrow Wilson warned the British that they should not expect too much familial favour from himself or from his compatriots: 'You must not speak of us who come over here as cousins, still less as brothers; we are neither. Neither must you think of us as Anglo-Saxons, for that term can no longer rightly be applied to the people of the US.'[23]

Pride and Panic: Reactions to the Changing Population Balance

In the first years of the twentieth century Britain's population growth was living on borrowed time. The population had grown rapidly in recent years, so there were many young people having children and fewer old ones dying. That meant that, even if each mother had fewer children, there were still a lot of children born each year to replace the deaths. It was a case of a high birth rate but a falling fertility rate. In time, however, fewer and fewer births per mother would lead to the population size stabilising and then falling. Because the study of population at the time was fairly rudimentary, this was not fully understood and many were complacent. Still, in these years there was in Britain the first evidence of what has come to be called 'anti-Malthusianism', or a concern not that the population would be too big (as Malthus had feared) but that it would be too small. In a way, this was not new.

People have often worried about the size of their country's population particularly in relation to those of rival countries. The French became quite paranoid on the topic after their decisive defeat in the Franco-Prussian War. One commentator early in the life of the French Third Republic complained that 'the government of France is a committee of bachelors presiding over a country which is depopulating itself'. In Britain, however, this was the first time a country was consciously reacting to a slowdown in its population caused by the processes of modernisation. There was talk of 'race suicide', and in 1906 John Taylor, president of the British Gynaecological Society, lamented 'with supreme dissatisfaction and disgust' that selfish couples, in employing contraceptives, were countering the patriotic efforts of doctors to preserve life, adding: 'all this work is swept away as though it had never been by the vicious and unnatural habits of the present generation'.[24]

British concerns were not just about quantity but also about quality, as is seen in the rise of the eugenicists. During the Boer War, right at the start of the twentieth century, army recruiters had complained about the poor health of working-class boys from the inner cities, with rickets and asthma. There was a worry that in its inner cities, Britain was breeding a race unfit for the military, and the difficulty the Empire had had in defeating the Boers was a wake-up call. At the same time, an ideology some have called 'Social Darwinism' was spreading. Inspired by Darwin's writings a few decades earlier about how animals and species engaged in a constant battle for survival, many intellectuals came to see nations as engaged in such a struggle. They started to worry that not only would there be more Germans, but that they would be fitter and stronger than the boys from the East End of London or the slums of Glasgow. Such thinking was in part behind the setting up of the rudimentary welfare state which came into being in those years, driven by Lloyd George and the young Winston Churchill. Others, influenced by the eugenics movement, preferred to let the least fit go to the wall rather than patch them up. One eugenicist, Dr John Berry Haycraft, praised tuberculosis in his 1895 work *Darwinism and Race Progress*, commenting: 'If we stamp out Infectious Diseases we perpetuate these Poor Types.'[25]

The slowing growth of the population became a concern of the press. The *Daily Mail* in 1903 was worrying about the 'decline of the race' linked to the slowing birth rate. It believed that victory would belong 'to the large unit; the full nursery spells national and race predominance'. J. A. Spender, editor of the *Westminster Gazette*, suggested in 1907 that fertility decline was generally regarded as 'a sign of decay'. Worries that problems of quantity would be compounded by problems of quality were fuelled by the findings James Barclay published in 1906, suggesting that the better off were breeding less while the poor remained fecund. In the days of Malthus, when life was so much harsher, the better off could afford to keep more of their children alive while the poor lost more, leading to the natural expansion of the better off relative to the poor; given that a relatively static economy could only keep so many people in top places, this inevitably meant that many of those born into the upper echelon had to find for themselves a place lower down the pecking order.

Now this seemed to have reversed, with the better off opting for smaller families while the poor were able to keep more of their children alive.[26] In London in 1911 wealthy Hampstead had a birth rate of 17.5 per thousand while that of Shoreditch, in the impoverished East End, was nearly twice as high.[27] The importance of the issue of national population in the public consciousness can be seen in the establishment of the National Birth Rate Commission, set up not by any official body but by the National Council for Public Morals whose 1911 manifesto was endorsed by three MPs, the heads of two Cambridge colleges, seven bishops and luminaries such as General William Booth, founder of the Salvation Army, Beatrice Webb, pioneering Fabian, and Ramsay MacDonald, a future Labour prime minister. The commission itself was chaired by Bishop Boyd Carpenter and Dean Inge and its vice chairman was Sir John Gorst, previously the Solicitor General. It began its work in 1913 and its results were published in 1916. The Commission concluded that it was not a lack of food and housing but the use of contraception which lay behind declining birth rates. It did not argue explicitly that a declining birth rate meant a decline in national power and prestige and it took some comfort from the evidence that the decline was general across north-western Europe, but the interest it aroused at least suggests the prominence of the topic in the national mind as the nation entered the First World War. While the commission was not official, it was eagerly reported in the press and Prime Minister Asquith stated in the House of Commons that there would be no royal commission into the subject until the National Commission had reported.[28]

In an age when snobbery was as unapologetic as racism, this led some to claim that the quality of the nation would inevitably decline, with the higher echelons of society dying out and the masses breeding so that the best and brightest 'blood' (today the term used would be 'genes') was pushed out by that of inferior quality. At that time it was not only a question of class but also of race, it seemed. In 1906 *The Lancet* reported the work of Sydney Webb, later Lord Passfield and a founding member of the Fabian movement and Labour Party, deploring the loss of 'one fifth part of every year's "normal" crop of babies' and decrying it as 'a national calamity seriously threatening the future welfare of our race'. The problem was not only an overall drop in numbers but also ethnic composition; Webb lamented that half the people were limiting their families while children were being 'freely born' to Irish Catholics and immigrant Jews.[29]

Not all voices expressed concern at the decline of the birth rate and consequent slowdown in growth of the population. Some, such as the Malthusian liberal economist and MP John Mackinnon Robertson, deplored the 'rhetoric about decay of national energy, the approaching extinction of the Anglo-Saxon, the fall in the vitality of the higher races, and the rest of it'. Dissenting voices welcomed the fact that smaller family sizes would allow for improved welfare and were themselves a sign of social advance. Smaller families would allow parents to take greater care of their children and allow them to be better nourished.[30]

Concern in Britain at falling population growth was not just about what was going on in the country itself but was also fuelled by a growing sense of rivalry with Germany. Germany was seen not just as a rival or potential rival in its economic dynamism and growing international trade, nor just in its quest for colonies and a navy, but also in its population growth. Population was fundamental to the challenge Germany posed to Britain. A one-time citizen of the Austro-Hungarian Empire, Emil Reich, published a book in 1907 with the title *Germany's Swelled Head*, a book that was republished in 1914. It suggested that the Germans were looking forward to having 104 million people by 1964, 150 million by 1980 and 200 million by the year 2000. Apparently, Reich's book was read keenly by Edward VII, a British monarch generally known for his antipathy towards Germany and in particular towards his nephew Kaiser Wilhelm II. The king recommended it to leaders of the army and, among others, the Bishop of Durham.[31]

It was not only the British who worried about German population growth (along with more general British worries about German economic and naval rivalry). The French, with their own demography much weaker than Britain's and well behind Germany's, had been fretting about birth and conscription rates since at least 1871, following the Franco-Prussian War, the loss of Alsace-Lorraine and the subsequent unification of Germany. Indeed, worries about French demographic decline can be dated back to the start of the nineteenth century if not earlier still. And although it was clear by the time the First World War broke out that German population growth was slowing and that in 1910 only 800,000 had been added to the population rather than the 850,000 of five years earlier,[32] nevertheless it was feared that this might be a merely temporary pause, that Germans would always have larger families and that by 1950 the German population would reach 95 million. Most alarmingly of all, it was feared that the population growth of Germany would provide it with a leading edge on the battlefield for at least half a century to come.[33]

With their own burgeoning population, Americans could hardly feel that they compared poorly to Germany from a demographic perspective. In addition, from the American point of view, there was no direct threat of German population and military power being translated into an invading army such as France or even Britain feared. American concerns, rather, hinged on the large population of Germans living in the United States. These fears were worked on by those militating for a pro-Allied stance during the war and who were concerned to put America on its guard against what in later years would be called 'fifth columnists'. One such doomsayer, Howard Pitcher Okie, in his luridly entitled *America and the German Peril*, pointed out in 1915 that there were precisely 1,337,775 German-born males in the US according to the 1910 census, that 40% of them were aged between twenty and forty (and therefore, he supposed, had probably done German military service) and as many as 10 million people in America were either German-born or had two German-born parents. Okie went on to note that there were twice as many German males in New York alone as in the entire standing US Army.[34]

German perceptions of their population growth were less clear-cut. They may have been boasting about it, at least according to Emil Reich (although perhaps never to the same extent as the hubristic Anglo-Saxon visions of world domination discussed in the previous chapter). Paul Rohrbach, a writer and publicist of Baltic extraction and an advocate of German world power, suggested that Germany's population growth should be interpreted as a sign of its 'natural and moral strength'.[35] On the other hand, as in the UK, there was awareness that the lower orders were outbreeding their betters in the years before the First World War and, again as in the UK, this was understood against a background of social Darwinism and a eugenicist outlook. Ferdinand Goldstein, a social commentator warning against the over-population of Germany, feared that 'the proles will capture the world' leading to 'the triumph of mediocrity as in France today'. In addition, while Germany's population was growing faster than Britain's, it was growing more slowly than Russia's, and this in turn was giving rise to German fears.[36]

Just as the British and even more so the French looked eastward and worried about Germany's population, so the Germans looked eastward and worried about the population of Russia. This can be seen in the writings of German academics and journalists of the time, people now long forgotten but influential in their day, who helped to create an atmosphere of rivalry and xenophobia which accompanied the approach of the First World War and in part caused it. While Ferdinand Goldstein was fretting that the wrong sort of Germans were too fertile and the right sort insufficiently so, he was also worried that 'the only real danger is the mindless breeding of the Slavs'. Friedrich Lönne, writing in 1917, argued that the slowdown of Germany's demographic growth would lead to military and economic eclipse, that 'nations whose population continues to grow will usurp our place in the world economy', and that Germany 'will lose her place in the sun'.[37] There were various efforts to legislate before the war against the spreading of methods of contraception, most such efforts being unsuccessful and in any case motivated as much by concern for public morals, and spearheaded by the Catholic Centre Party, as at that stage by any real concern for German military or economic power. Later, after the war was over, Hans Albrecht feared that 'in the final analysis, all the disarmament clauses of the Versailles Diktat will not be as fateful as the fact that Germany will simply not have enough men to bear arms'.

The seeming inexhaustibility of Russia's population growth was a real worry to German commentators, just as French commentators seemed to think that fecundity and Germanness were somehow inextricably linked. Influential voices such as those of the historian Friedrich Meinecke fretted publicly about Russia's inexorable rise, with burgeoning population, industry and military capacity contributing decisively towards Chancellor Bethmann-Hollweg's 'now or never' decision for war in 1914. Bethmann's secretary Kurt Riezler records his boss as talking a few years before the outbreak of war of 'Russia's increasing claims and immense explosive force' which would 'No longer to be resisted in a few years'.[38]

Not only was there a widening gap between the population growth of the early adopters of demographic transition and those who experienced it later, in favour of the latter; this fact was now being noticed, commented on and worried about. And this worry contributed to and was part of the general atmosphere of inter-state rivalry and tension which marked the international environment and marred international relations in the years leading to the First World War.

Two qualifying points must be made, however. First, demography was only part of the concern; there was more worry in Britain about being out-manufactured and out-traded by Germany than there was about being out-bred and out-manned. While the Germans were extremely concerned about Russia's military build-up, the population growth which accompanied it, although recognised, was in itself not the main concern; it was something which might cause problems in the future, whereas commercial rivalry was causing problems at the time and so was a more immediate worry. The second qualification is that population worries were not only focused on the question of international competition; there were still Malthusians, by now perhaps neo-Malthusians, who thought that a growing population was a problem and others, both in Britain and in Germany, who were more concerned about the domestic implications of how the growth was made up (too much breeding among the lower orders) than they were about the overall size or international implications.

Combining concerns about national population that were both quantitative and qualitative (the latter driven by racism and eugenics), the Fascists, who emerged after the First World War, would lay the foundations of the Second. Nevertheless, the factor of population amid pre-war international tensions was real and inextricable from other aspects of rivalry, and significant differences in rates of population growth were noted and reacted to in important ways.

How the Cradles Rocked the World

Without doubt, population in the main countries of Europe in the decades leading to the First World War and the way they were perceived contributed to the first catastrophe of the twentieth century. But what about the impact of population on the outcome of the war itself? There are two aspects to the answer. The first has to do with economics, industry and productive capacity; the second to do with the ability to place armies in the battlefield.

If the sheer growth in numbers was clearly one of the essential conditions to Britain becoming the workshop of the world, and thrust it to the forefront of the world's economy, then the population growth of its rivals had at least the potential to have the same effect for them. On the one hand China, with its hundreds of millions, remained an economic backwater in the absence of significant industrial development. On the other hand, the countries of Scandinavia and what would be termed 'Benelux' remained economic minnows because, although they developed industrially and economically, they were simply too small in population terms to have much impact. For an economy to matter, it must have a relatively large population *and* that overall population must be prosperous or becoming prosperous.

Looking at Britain in the years 1820–70, it is possible to attribute about half its annual economic growth (around 2.5% per annum on average) to the growth of the population and about half to the population's growing wealth. After 1870 Germany's economy and particularly its industry began growing much faster than Britain's so that, for example, by 1914 Germany was producing half as much pig iron again as Britain where, in 1870, it had produced barely a quarter of the British total. On the eve of the First World War, Germany was producing twice as much steel as Britain.[39] This came to matter when the young men of the two nations were hurling metal at each other. Without the great population explosion Germany had experienced it could never have become the industrial and economic giant capable of taking on Britain and its allies.

Just as population growth underpinned the economic and industrial rise of Germany, so likewise it was essential to the rise of Russia.

From 1885 to 1913 Russia's economy grew by a startling 3.4% per annum on average, faster than Germany's although from a much lower base. Again, this was partly because of the population growth and partly because each Russian employed was producing and consuming more. Russia was able to send 750,000 people to Siberia in a single year, underwriting its claims to the vast and sparsely populated territory.[40] Industrial production in Russia trebled in the last two decades of the nineteenth century and industrial employment in the first thirteen years of the twentieth century grew by nearly 50%.[41] This was replicated in armaments production in Russia, which doubled in the five years to 1913.

By the outbreak of war in 1914, Russia was still well behind Germany or even France in its output and prosperity, but it had rapidly closed the gap in the preceding years. The burgeoning population as well as mass urbanisation were essential components of this. When the Bolsheviks took power in 1917, claiming to represent the industrial working class in line with Marx's theory, it was frequently pointed out that the industrial working class in Russia represented a tiny share of what was still very largely a peasant society; not that much earlier, there was simply no industrial working class to talk of at all. When war came in 1914, Russian industry struggled to maintain the supply of armaments to its troops but still it kept them fighting for over three years. Without the breakneck industrialisation of the previous decades, intimately connected to the growing population, even this would not have been achievable. Meanwhile, the war boosted demand for industrial labour, bolstering the potentially revolutionary proletarian class. And it also disrupted the movement of food from countryside to town or city, making it hard to feed the urban population.[42] This young, uprooted and underfed population was ripe for revolution.

But if the link between population growth and economic and industrial growth came to matter in times of war, even more directly linked are population growth and the sheer weight of military force, particularly in arenas such as the First World War where, more than by any great stroke of strategic genius, battles were fought by a sheer grinding process of attrition, each side trying to wear the other down. Outside the confines of Europe, small numbers of men representing the European imperial powers were able to control large populations whose societies and economies were much less advanced. Even within Europe, the tightly organised and disciplined German troops had some advantage over their French and British enemies, at least initially, and a considerable advantage over the Russian soldiers. Yet for all of this, numbers were supremely important. The ability to recruit and keep recruiting men and pouring them into the battlefields, particularly in the static trench warfare on the Western Front, proved crucial, as did the ability to keep providing men at the front line with the products of an industrial economic base, a base which was in considerable degree linked to demography.

Britain was in a unique position as a naval power, although it was only as the First World War progressed that it managed to recruit and then conscript an army of scale. Britain's naval power, not highly dependent on large-scale manpower, kept the sea lanes open for the Allies, allowing resources and men to arrive from beyond Europe. Those extra-European men and resources were largely possible only because emigration had been fuelled by Britain's earlier population growth. As the French Army struggled under the weight of persistent German assault and Germany's greater ability to put men into the field, the contribution of British manpower, both in the factory and at the front, proved critical in allowing the Allies to hold out in the west.

Naturally, no precise mathematical weight can be given to the relevance of population in the outcome of the First World War. It was without doubt a testimony to German industry, courage and organisation that Germany came so close to winning. Yet in the end, where advanced industrial powers came face to face, numbers told, and numbers were decisively in favour of the Allies, who managed to mobilise nearly 46 million men in the course of the war compared with fewer than 27 million raised by the Central Powers. Excluding the United States, which was only beginning to make the impact of its manpower felt by the time the war ended in November 1918, the ratio of the men mobilised on either side over the course of the conflict (1.75 to 1 in favour of the Allies) was almost exactly the same as the ratio of the populations of the principal powers at the outbreak of war (1.73 to 1 in favour of the Allies).[43] The cradles of the 1880s and 1890s had proved decisive. If the population of Britain was being overshadowed by that of Germany, then Britain had won by calling into play the still larger battalions of Russia and the vast forces of its imperial offspring, the Dominions, and ultimately of that imperial daughter, the United States of America. The balance of forces which played out and determined the outcome of 1918 hinged critically on the demographic developments we have been charting. Beyond the particular balance of forces, the very nature of the war was shaped not only by mass industrialisation but also by mass armies the likes of which the world had never seen before; and neither of these phenomena would have been possible without the population explosion of the preceding years.

Population affected not only the outcome of the war, but also its causes. Population growth meant that Europe's societies, particularly Germany's and Russia's, were young. These countries experienced what would now be called a 'youth bulge', which has been associated with aggression and war. Politically and diplomatically, meanwhile, Britain feared an ever-rising and growing Germany, Germans feared an ever-rising and growing Russia, and this drove both, it could be argued, to rashness in July 1914. Without the sense of challenge (felt by Britain with regard to Germany) and doom (felt by Germany with regard to Russia), cooler heads might have prevailed that summer.

As for Russia, although it turned out that it was not yet developed enough in 1914 to sustain a war against Germany and Austria, even when the Central Powers opposed to it were fighting on a second front, the great boom of Russian population then under way would underpin Russia's rise as a great power. It ensured that, in the subsequent world war, despite the human losses endured by Russia under Bolshevism, the Germans were unable to resist Russia's seemingly endless reserves of manpower. Russia's demographic rise, coupled with economic and industrial growth, ensured its eventual emergence as one of two superpowers and its ability, during its demographic heyday, to dominate large swathes of the world during the cold war. In all these momentous events, demography was in the driving seat, disrupting the settled order and determining the outcome of conflicts.

Relevant too was the sheer youth of this booming Europe, a continent very different to the peaceable and greying continent of today.

There is a proven link between the youthfulness of a society and its proclivity to go to war.[44] It was large, young, enthusiastic populations that backed and egged on the most bellicose politicians; the young who flocked to the streets to celebrate the outbreak of war; the young who eagerly signed up, in so many cases sealing their fates as well as the fate of their continent. Demographic fears had helped feed the conflict. Demographic facts helped determine it.

5

The Passing of the 'Great Race'

Ensconced in his headquarters in the first months of his campaign against the Soviet Union in the second half of 1941 and early 1942, Adolf Hitler was convinced that his forces had secured the great spaces of the east, which had been his obsession for at least twenty years. Holding a social Darwinist ideology, itself with Malthusian roots and built on a foundation of racial hatred and anti-Semitic fantasy, Hitler saw life as a struggle between the races for land, their means of subsistence. His Table Talk monologues – a series of late-night ramblings and musings – reveal a mind obsessed by matters of ethnic demography.

Hitler felt an urgent need to increase the number of Germans in order to be able to compete with the other world powers, particularly the Americans:

> I hope that in ten years there will be from ten to fifteen million more of us Germans in the world . . . The essential thing for the future is for us to have lots of children . . . One hundred and thirty million people in the Reich, ninety million in the Ukraine. Add to these the other states of the New Europe and we will be four hundred million compared with one hundred and thirty million Americans.

Besides wishing to outnumber the Americans, Hitler was worried about the rising numbers of non-whites globally:

> I read today that India at present numbers three hundred and eighty-three million inhabitants, which means an increase of fifty-five million in the last ten years. It's alarming. We are witnessing the same phenomenon in Russia. What are our doctors thinking of? Isn't it enough to vaccinate whites?

Ultimately, he mused, demography would be destiny: 'The fall in the birth rate, that's at the bottom of everything . . . It's the feeding bottle that will save us.'[1]

The First World War had among other things been caused by fear and suspicion based on mutual dependence and competitive demography, Britain and France fearing Germany's growth, Germany fearing Russia's growth and its own dependence on British goodwill for food supplies. The Second World War was in turn in no small measure the result of Hitler's obsession with population, although his views were hardly unique. Between these two wars Europe's population growth picked up and then began to slow, and although Europeans continued to look at each other with fear, they also began to sense that their collective global supremacy was shaky and would be fleeting.

War, Flu and Population

One of the abiding consequences of the Great War is that a generation of boys never came home. In Britain, the figure was 700,000 (excluding the colonies); in Germany it was 1.75 million; in Russia it was almost 2 million and a million and a half each for Austria-Hungary and France. Overall, the war dead approached 10 million men. This entailed a shortage of husbands, and in an era when birth outside marriage was rare, women who never married usually remained childless. The impact, however, was reduced because women adjusted the age of the men they married and because fewer men emigrated.[2] The British economist John Maynard Keynes wrote a famous book, *The Economic Consequences of the Peace*. *The Demographic Consequences of the War* was never written, but the consequences themselves were seismic across Europe and were still reverberating long after the problems of reparations and trade that so troubled Keynes had been forgotten.

But population *was* receiving more attention. In 1919 Keynes wrote that 'the great events of history are due to secular changes in the growth of population and other fundamental economic causes which, escaping by their gradual character the notice of contemporary observers, are attributed to the follies of statesmen'. Keynes saw the war as the product of an age when Europe had gone from local to global economic dependency; in 1914, a highly industrialised Germany depended on the world for its markets, its raw materials and its food in a way it had not in 1814. This global interdependence was the cause *and the result* of booming populations, and it created insecurities that themselves contributed to the war. Germany depended on the good offices of the Royal Navy for some of its food and to supply its industries, and on British Free Trade policies for access to its markets beyond Europe. This resulted in tensions that, in Keynes's view, were the most important factor in explaining the global nature of the recent conflict. Growing populations were a fundamental part of this new interdependent world in which reliance bred rivalry and suspicion.

On top of the losses of war there was the Spanish flu which followed the war, killing 25–50 million worldwide. In the recent wave of Arab uprisings there has been much mention of the Sykes–Picot agreement, which was responsible for many of the now seemingly unsustainable borders in the Middle East; Sir Mark Sykes, the British side of the duo, died of the flu in 1919, at the age of just thirty-nine. Walt Disney (aged just sixteen) and Franklin Roosevelt survived it, going on in their different ways to make their mark on the coming era. The British writer Anthony Burgess recounted how in early 1919 'my father, not yet demobilised, came on one of his regular, probably irregular, furloughs to [our home in] Carisbrook Street to find both my mother and my sister dead. The Spanish influenza pandemic had struck . . . I apparently was chuckling in my cot while my mother and sister lay dead on a bed in the same room.'[3] The scope of the flu was global. In a remote corner of Canada a girl of eight survived her parents and two siblings, keeping herself alive by burning Christmas candles to melt the snow: a local clergyman, coming upon her, reported that 'the huskies now began to eat the dead bodies and the child was a spectator at this horrible incident'.[4]

Nonetheless, the population of Europe, North America and indeed the world continued to grow. When the human tide is in full flow, when mortality drops and fertility holds up, the underlying force for growth can be so strong that it offsets the losses from all but the most murderous calamities. War losses of 10 million represent little more than 2% of the population of Europe at the outbreak of the conflict in 1914. For a population growing at the pace of Russia's before the war, making up a loss of 2% of the population would take little more than eighteen months; for a population growing at the pace of, say, Yemen's in the early 1990s, making up 2% would take less than six months.

So Europe's population carried on growing, albeit at a much reduced rate. When things returned to 'normal' at the close of the war, those forces of modernisation which had brought down the death rate and extended life expectancy first in Britain continued to spread across the Continent. However, the forces which then depressed childbearing and population growth also began to spread, and in the 1930s the growth of Europe's population slowed.

In the first part of the nineteenth century, the European population was growing at just under 0.7% per annum, quite fast from the long historical view up to that point. It accelerated to 0.9% in the last thirty years of the century and then to slightly over 1% in the years immediately before the First World War. (It should be borne in mind that a sustained rate of over 1% was historically remarkable at a national, never mind a continent-wide level.) In 1913–20 the rate of growth was still positive despite the war, albeit at less than a third of its previous level: not even the First World War and the flu pandemic had been enough to reverse or halt the human tide, although they had certainly slowed it. Europe's population growth revived in the 1920s – which was not surprising given the period of war – but was more than a tenth below its early twentieth-century level. In the 1930s it slowed further.[5] The war had disrupted what would probably have been a gentler trend of slowdown for Europe as a whole, and this trend from a very high peak resumed in the war's wake. Gentle though the trend may have been at a continental level, it was sharper for some countries than others. This growth trend was in fact the product of three factors: a sharp reduction in births, a steep fall in deaths, and a near halt in emigration, the latter two more than compensating for the first. Given that a population's size can be determined by only three things (births, deaths and the balance of migration), how exactly were the first two 'natural' changes playing out in what would become known as interwar Europe?

Europe's Great Slowdown

In the late nineteenth and early twentieth centuries the demographic revolution which had struck Britain was widening its scope to Germany, Russia and beyond. As the tide began to ebb in Britain it was still flowing in Germany, and as it began to ebb in Germany, it was still flowing in Russia. Each of these successive tides was more pronounced than the last. Germany's population growth was more rapid than Britain's, but then it fell more rapidly. Russia's population rise was more rapid than Germany's but fell more quickly in turn.[6] The reasons for this are clear. The pioneer moves tentatively along an uncleared path, while the better trodden the path, the more rapidly successors can follow. The techniques of public and personal health can be more rapidly adopted when they are understood, tried and tested. This means that death rates, the key driver of population growth, can fall more quickly. In this, demography is like economics. Britain's industrial take-off in the nineteenth century was fast by previous standards but slow by the standards of those who came later and were not painfully cutting a new path but following one already charted, adopting techniques and technologies already adopted elsewhere.

Britain as ever was the leader of the pack, the first to experience explosive modern population growth and the first to witness a falling fertility rate and flagging population growth rates. By the eve of the First World War, fertility rates were down to below three children per woman and falling. After the First World War, British fertility rates continued to fall. Fertility sank to around two in the late 1920s and during the 1930s to below two. This is below what is today called 'replacement level', the level required to keep a population stable in the long term, which is slightly above two. It is striking that in the era immediately before the Second World War, British fertility rates were quite similar to what they are today, nearly eighty years later (there have been some fluctuations in between).

Before the First World War, German fertility rates were tumbling too, albeit from a higher level. Afterwards, Germany's fertility rate also slumped further, likewise falling below two children per woman by the early 1930s. My own family – who were living in Germany until the late 1930s – is a typical example of this: my great-grandparents, born in the middle of the nineteenth century, were mostly part of large families of around six children; my grandparents, born between the early 1880s and the period immediately before the First World War, had one or two siblings; and my parents, born in the 1920s and 1930s, were in one case a single child and in the other one of a pair. The perpetually fertile German over whom French writers and military planners had fretted a couple of decades earlier turned out to be a phantom. Concern about the low birth rate spanned the political spectrum; the left-wing SPD agreed 'unequivocally that maternity was a woman's social task' and that 'women had a duty as protectors and rearers of the species'.[7]

French women, meanwhile, were carrying on much as normal. French fertility rates in the interwar years fell only slightly, from a little under two and a half to a little over two. Not having been very high in the first place, French fertility rates did not have so far to fall. France's birth rate benefitted in this respect from the country's remaining relatively rural in an era when it was urban areas in which fertility was declining and country areas in which it remained high. Whereas in the UK in the 1930s around three-quarters of people lived in urban conurbations, and in Germany well over two-thirds, in France it was barely half. Along with matters of mortality and migration discussed below, this meant that France's perennially slow population growth in contrast to the UK's and Germany's was much diminished. Whereas prior to the First World War France's population growth was a fraction of Germany's and the UK's, during the interwar years the margin was much smaller.

If the UK was the leader of the pack, Germany a close follower and France an exception, then Russia was an extreme case. Russian fertility had been higher in the early twentieth century than it had been in the UK or Germany at their peaks (more like seven children per woman than five or six), so the fall, when it came, was faster than further west. By the late 1920s Russian fertility was down to six children per woman and by the eve of the Second World War down again, to around four and a half. This was still very high and a major contributor to continuing population growth, but the speed of the fall was the harbinger of what was to prove a very low Russian fertility rate. That fertility rates fell so fast in Russia should not be a surprise; the country was undergoing a forced, rapid, top-down transformation. Many of the goals closest to the heart of the new Soviet regime – general and particularly female literacy, urbanisation and the participation of women in the workforce – are now understood to be closely associated with lower fertility rates. The ideal Soviet woman was politically conscious (and therefore, almost by definition, literate), living in a town or city and probably employed in a factory; she was bound to have fewer children than her illiterate peasant mother. Elsewhere in Europe the pattern was similar. Italian women, who were bearing more than four children before the First World War, were bearing fewer than three by the outbreak of the Second.[8] And although the image of the large Italian family lived on long into the second half of the twentieth century, it was by then nothing more than a myth.

At a national level, data on declining fertility disguises some underlying patterns and regional variations. Within a particular country, the pace of development and therefore its position in the demographic transition was often variable. Channels of communication, cultural association and religious belief were particularly important in impacting regional trends, with low fertility rates spreading from France to Catalonia and Piedmont but not to more distant and less industrialised parts of Spain and Italy.[9] Protestant and industrial areas in Germany had the lowest fertility rates in the country, while peripheral and agricultural areas had the highest. In central Europe low fertility rates seemed to spread down the Danube to areas most accessible to the influence of Viennese modernity, while Upper Austria and the Czech lands were somewhat more resistant to the trend towards smaller families. In the Balkans, the areas which had fallen within the Austro-Hungarian Empire in Romania and Yugoslavia witnessed faster falling fertility than those areas which had been outside the Hapsburg lands before the First World War. In Russia, too, rural areas retained the highest fertility rates, as would be expected.

Part of the story of the fall in fertility is the fact that a large share of populations moved from the high-fertility countryside to the low-fertility town or city. Meanwhile, a remarkable development in

Europe was the increasing collection of data, which afforded a more detailed and reliable picture of what was happening on the ground. This was partly thanks to the existence of the League of Nations, which was able to gather standardised information on births and deaths. Precisely how lower fertility was achieved is not entirely clear, just as in earlier times, but contraception was becoming more widely known about and available. In Britain, Marie Stopes championed 'planned parenthood', publishing *Married Love* in 1918, offering advice on contraception, and opening family planning clinics across the country; and while she certainly met resistance, it was by now far less than the earlier generation of Charles Bradlaugh and Annie Besant had encountered. However, the methods of contraception available were not always cheap or reliable, as the following ditty suggests: 'Jeanie, Jeanie, full of hopes / Read a book by Marie Stopes / But to judge from her condition / She must have read the wrong edition.'[10]

The fertility slowdown certainly had the effect of reducing population growth but on the other hand, mortality was still falling in many parts of Europe, and this had the effect of propping up population growth. Life expectancy in England was just under fifty-four years at birth in 1910 and by 1930 had risen to over sixty. Fewer people joined the population through birth, but fewer left through death. This was achieved through rising living conditions and better access to health care, particularly for children. In France, life expectancy rose over the same period from slightly over fifty to a little short of fifty-six, and in Germany from forty-nine to over sixty-one, just surpassing England. The data at this time is less dependable for Russia, but it is known that life expectancy increased from thirty-two years in 1910 (for Russia) to sixty-seven (for the Soviet Union) between 1910 and 1950, a quite extraordinary increase against the background of terror and famine.[11] Just as the human tide, when in full flow, could not entirely be held back by war or pandemic, neither could it be held back by one of the most murderous regimes in history.

Expressed in terms of deaths per thousand, death rates were below ten in some parts of north-western Europe. If these seem remarkably low today, it is thanks to the retreat of disease and early death, but also thanks to the fact that recent population growth had given rise to a young population. The elderly in a population of recent expansion are a small percentage of the total, and so their demise is statistically small within the wider society. At this point, with its recent fast population growth, Europe had a young population that resembled a school more than a home for the aged – life expectancy was rising sharply, and mortality rates were exceptionally low.

Staying in Europe

The third determinant of population change, alongside birth rates and death rates, is of course migration. The decades before the First World War had seen the greatest ever outflow of Europeans, predominantly to the Americas. At its peak in the early years of the twentieth century, European migration overseas reached almost 1.5 million a year, people predominantly leaving for the United States and overwhelmingly for the Americas as a whole, Canada and Argentina being attractive destinations for people from Britain and Italy respectively. During the First World War emigration out of Europe fell rapidly (men who might have gone were conscripted, transatlantic shipping was tied up bringing supplies to the Allies, and some of the countries which had been sources of emigration came to be at war with the US), and it never recovered.

In the 1920s the doors of the United States were progressively closed and the outlets for European emigration limited. American politicians were eager to restrict emigration, particularly by those whom they considered of 'unsuitable stock', and they did this by implementing quotas based first on the pre-war balance of the immigrant population, then on the basis of the pre-war balance of total population, favouring those considered Anglo-Saxon in the widest sense of the word or at least from a background more conducive to assimilation, and discriminating against those who had come from Italy and eastern Europe – mostly Catholics, and those who had come from Russia – largely Jews.[12] Catholics were associated in the minds of many in the American establishment with the alcoholic riff-raff of the big cities, particularly in the north-east, and there was a distinctly Protestant tinge to the Prohibition movement, which banned alcohol during the 1920s and early 1930s. As for Jews, widespread and continuing prejudice kept the doors of the United States largely barred just when entry was most desperately needed.

Emigration out of Europe fell in the years before the Second World War to a couple of hundred thousand a year. To some extent this was not only the result of US immigration policies but also of changed circumstances in Europe. In much of Europe, the 1920s were years of opportunity and economic growth, reducing the desire to seek the good life beyond the Continent's shores. The loss of millions of young men in the war, callous though it may sound to say it, opened up opportunities for the boys left at home, whether in terms of career advancement or available women. Emigration had tended to be a rural phenomenon, and European societies were becoming decreasingly rural; for many, migrating to the town or city was the alternative to leaving Europe altogether. When the economic slump hit in the early 1930s, not only were American immigration restrictions very tight, but the economy of the USA was also in depression and unemployment high, making it an unattractive destination for emigration. Indeed, some poor souls – recent Finnish immigrants – were persuaded to 'return' to the Finnish parts of the Soviet Union: few survived long, dumped in the icy wastes of Karelia or, as suspect foreigners, deported to Siberia.

In national terms, the exception to the emigration slowdown was the UK, which continued to have a large overseas empire looking for recruits. In the early 1920s, British and Irish emigration rose to nearly 200,000 per annum, only slightly lower than the pre-war figure. Thereafter, however, British emigration too fell off rapidly, and less than a third the number left in the 1930s as had in the 1920s. For the rest of Europe, the drop-off was dramatic.[13] Italy, by far the greatest exporter of people in the early years of the twentieth century, was an extreme case. Around 400,000 Italians had left Italy in the peak year of the first decade of the twentieth century; by the late 1930s annual emigration was barely 25,000. The lands of Austria, Hungary and Czechoslovakia, the core parts of the Austro-Hungarian Empire before the war, had seen total emigration of around a quarter of a million a year in the first decade of the century. Restrictions changed this, as did the Great Depression – central Europe suffered badly from the economic downturn, but unlike in previous slumps, the United States, suffering its own economic problems, no longer offered the prospect of prosperity or even employment – and by the 1930s emigration from lands of the former Austro-Hungarian Empire had fallen to a negligible 5,000–6,000 per annum. All the main recipient countries – the USA, Brazil, Canada and Argentina – witnessed correspondingly steep reductions in inflows.[14] The great movement of Europeans to the New World was over.

The reduction in people leaving Europe – along with falling death rates – helped to offset the Continent's falling fertility rates and reduce the impact of its decline in demographic growth, so that even with fewer children being born, the population continued to grow because fewer people were leaving, either in a coffin or on a boat. Meanwhile, while fewer people were leaving Europe, more were moving between its countries. Europeans had always moved between European countries, Britain being an exception due to its relative isolation. Before the First World War movement was not on a very large scale. The biggest intra-European movement between states had been of persecuted Russian Jews, many fleeing to the USA, some to destinations such as Canada, Argentina and South Africa but many staying within Europe and arriving in the relatively tolerant atmospheres of Western Europe, particularly France and the UK. After 1918, movement within the Continent became more widespread. This was mostly westward, and its preferred target was France, in part thanks to encouragement by the French government. Put simply, the west of Europe was freer and more prosperous than the east, and so it acted as a magnet. In 1931 there were more than 3 million European immigrants living in France – twice the number living in Germany and three times those living in the UK – a figure which represented more than 7% of the French population.[15] The greatest sources were Poland, Italy and Spain.

There was also much movement within countries, generally from poor, rural, peripheral areas to industrial centres: in Italy from south to north; in Spain into the Basque and Catalan regions; within the British Isles from Ireland and Scotland to the English Midlands and south-east. Much of this movement was driven by economics – the search for a livelihood – but some was politically motivated, such as the movement of around 400,000 Jews from Germany and Austria in the 1930s or the flight of half a million or so Republicans from Spain to France in the wake of their defeat by Franco.

These bare numbers should not numb us to the human triumphs and tragedies often involved. For many, arrival in Western Europe was as liberating as emigration to the United States had been for a previous generation. However, German Jews who fled to France were interned after the outbreak of war in 1939, and handed over to the Germans when France fell in 1940; few survived the war. The philosopher Walter Benjamin, fleeing Nazi-occupied France for Spain in 1940, committed suicide when he came to believe that he would be turned back (a monument in his memory stands at Portbou, the town at the French–Spanish border on the Mediterranean). The great cellist Pablo Casals, having fled in the other direction the previous year, for decades avoided playing in countries which recognised Francoist Spain, which he had left for Roussillon, in French Catalonia (a statue and museum in his memory stand in Prades, on the French side of the border but under the shadow of the same mountain where Benjamin died). It was in the interwar years that the intellectual Isaiah Berlin, the banker Sigmund Warburg, the psychologist Sigmund Freud and the architectural historian Nikolaus Pevsner arrived in the UK, along with the father of the later leader of Britain's Conservative Party, Michael Howard, and the parents of recent Labour Party leader Ed Miliband, all of whom were fleeing from conflagrations further east.

Race, Pessimism and Policy

Between the wars Europe went through what Britain had experienced before 1914, namely a steep fall in fertility rates and a sharp decline in population growth. As yet there wasn't a complete understanding of what is now called the 'demographic transition', whereby a population will stabilise at a higher level once it has experienced growth as it moves from high birth rates and high death rates, through high birth rates and falling death rates, to low birth rates and low death rates.

Before the First World War, besides the worry about rival nations' population growth, there was concern about domestic fertility decline in the UK. US President Theodore 'Teddy' Roosevelt railed against 'wilful sterility – the one sin for which the penalty is national death, racial suicide'. Roosevelt was at least in this a man of deed as well as word – he himself had six children. At the end of the First World War, German futurologist and prophet of doom Oswald Spengler forecast that Europe's population would go into a 200-year-long decline, blaming wealth and female emancipation, while British writer G. K. Chesterton fretted in 1930 that 'if the recent decline in the birth rate continued for a certain time, it might end in there being no babies at all' and the French demographer Alfred Sauvy worried that Europe would be full of 'old people in old houses with old ideas'. In 1935, Keynes warned that 'a change over from an increasing to a declining population could be very disastrous'.[16]

The sentiment of interwar demographic pessimism was captured in 1937 by G. F. McCleary, a prolific writer on matters relating to population and a one-time senior official at the UK's Ministry of Health. 'People are beginning to realise that [the decline in the birth rate] cannot indefinitely be counteracted by reductions in the death rate,' he wrote.[17] Infant mortality was already fairly low and its further reduction, while desirable, would not have a material impact on population. As interwar demographer Dudley Kirk succinctly put it: 'death can be postponed but never eliminated'.[18] Life expectancy might continue to lengthen, but would do so only steadily. By contrast, the reduction in the number of births appeared rapid and alarming.

The developing sense of a decline in population growth and the prospect of falling population was now quite general. Malthus had been turned on his head, at least for the time being. Whereas before the First World War demographic concerns were mostly about how one's own nation stood in relation to a rival nation, in the interwar period there was an increasing appreciation that what had started in Britain was going continent-wide and also impacting the peoples of European extraction beyond Europe's shores, particularly in the Americas. This was an era when racist attitudes we find horrendous and astonishing today were quite normal, reflected in both public discourse and policy. Anti-Semitism was taken for granted, as was the idea that people of African and Asian origin were inferior. Sometimes concerns about slowing population and ethnicity led to tensions between the quantitative and what was considered the qualitative. On the one hand, a large population was seen as a 'good thing' for a country, particularly given the need to make up numbers from war losses and a fear of the 'next round'. On the other hand, not just any numbers would do, and some people were infinitely to be preferred to others. The eugenics movement, proposing active measures to improve the 'quality' of the population 'stock', was closely associated with the birth control movement. Marie Stopes, for example, urged the forcible sterilisation of those deemed unfit for parenthood and propagation of the race.

Concerns for the supposed quality of the population were particularly prevalent in the United States, where immigration restrictions rolled out after the First World War explicitly aimed to preserve the country's ethnic mixture and were in particular focused on reducing migration from southern and eastern Europe, which had been so predominant at the turn of the century. Although population growth did indeed decline as a result, it was still almost 1.5% in the 1920s although it dropped to half this rate in the 1930s.

Even for those permitted to enter, the United States was not always an attractive place to be.[19] Congressman Albert Johnson, co-originator of the 1924 Johnson Act imposing strict controls on immigration, opined that the 'day of unalloyed welcome to all people, the day of indiscriminate acceptance of all races, had definitely ended . . . Our hope is a homogenous nation . . . Self-preservation demands it.' In the debate on the Act, a senator from Maine called for a 'racially pure country' while a congressman from Maine suggested that 'God intended [the US] . . . to be the home of a great people, English speaking – a white race with great ideals, the Christian religion, one race, one country, one destiny'.[20] A congressman from Indiana was even more explicit, arguing that there

> is little or no similarity between the clear-thinking, self-governing stocks that sired the American people and this stream of irresponsible and broken wreckage that is pouring into the lifeblood of America the social and political diseases of the Old World . . . we cannot make a well-bred dog out of a mongrel by teaching him tricks.[21]

The background to both the debate and the anti-immigration legislation was fuelled by pessimism and racial prejudice. The two most notable interwar polemics foretelling the doom of the white race as a whole were not by Europeans but by Americans, namely Madison Grant's 1919 *The Passing of the Great Race, or The Racial Basis of European History* and Lothrop Stoddard's 1920 *The Rising Tide of Color Against White World-Supremacy*. The two authors' focus was different, although their underlying ideology of obnoxious racial prejudice was similar and Grant wrote the preface to Stoddard's work. Grant was more interested in 'racial science' than in demography; although stressing the importance of 'primary races', he distinguished quite sharply between those of different European origin and concluded that

> if the Melting Pot is allowed to boil without control and we continue to . . . blind ourselves to all distinctions of race, creed and color, the type of native American of Colonial descent will become as extinct as the Athenian of the age of Pericles, and the Viking of the age of Rollo.[22]

Stoddard, too, worried about the 'Mediterranean' versus the 'Nordic' element within the white race, fearing that the industrial revolution had stimulated the growth of the former type even in England, where the evolutionary selective processes favouring the Nordics were growing less strong as the country became less rural: 'The small, dark types in England increase noticeably with every generation.'[23] Yet his concerns were essentially pan-European in nature. He may have had his preferences *among* Europeans, but he was more worried about their collective fate in the face of the rise of people of non-European origin. He noted and lamented the impact of the First World War in Europe on population, fearing the 'Chinese braves [*sic*]' of Lenin and their destructive, Asiatic influence on Russia and calling for 'white solidarity'.[24] A mixture of Bolshevik agitation, Japanese ambition and sheer Chinese and Indian demographic weight threatened to topple European domination of the globe now that the Europeans had so weakened themselves by their lethal internecine squabble. It comes as no surprise that Stoddard was a member of the Ku Klux Klan and that his work is thought to have contributed the idea of the *Untermensch* or 'subhuman' to the Nazi lexicon.

The works of Grant and Stoddard encouraged works in a similar vein, such as John Walter Gregory's 1925 *The Menace of Color*. They also entered the popular consciousness through works such as Scott Fitzgerald's *The Great Gatsby*:

'Civilization's going to pieces' broke out Tom violently . . . 'Have you read "The Rise of the Colored Empires" by this man Goddard? . . . The idea is if we don't look out, the white race will be utterly – will be utterly submerged. It's all scientific stuff; it's been proved.'

Although Tom's attitude seems somewhat mocking, Fitzgerald's own attitude to Stoddard's ideas was probably quite sympathetic. Recent research has shown how editors stripped much of his work of open racism and anti-Semitism.[25]

However, not all Americans took the same pessimistic view of the prospects for whites, although their 'optimism' was no less charged with unpleasant racial prejudice. It was not that those like Edward M. East, author of *Mankind at the Crossroads*, were eager to express any cosmopolitan views; rather, that their interpretation of the data was different. East noted that globally there were more 'Whites' (550 million) than 'Yellows' (500 million), 'Browns' (450 million) or 'Blacks' (150 million). He conceded that the 'Others' might collectively outnumber whites and this was 'indeed a terrifying sum total from the white point of view'.[26] However, he challenged the pessimists' growth figures and suggested that the white population in North America had a demographic profile allowing it to double every fifty-eight years and that in Europe to double every eighty-seven years, while the other races would take well over one hundred years to double in the case of blacks and well over two hundred years in the case of south and east Asians.[27] By global and longer-term historical standards, the growth rate of peoples of European origin was still strong, and by and large, non-whites had not yet had a demographic 'awakening'.

Comparing population growth figures of the different races, East insisted that 'anyone who sees white stagnation . . . needs a pair of spectacles'; although fertility rates were falling, so were mortality rates, and this was supporting population growth. 'The Stork may have become less active, but the inertia of Death has more than made up the difference,' he wrote. The reason for the pre-eminence of whites and their falling death rates was the existence and persistence of empire: 'The white race is increasing rapidly. Why? Simply because it has political control of nine-tenths of the habitable globe.'[28] In a virtuous circle, East said, demographic strength would maintain empire and empire would sustain demographic strength. The blacks were no threat at home any more than the coloured races were abroad; the ratio of white to black in the United States had been 7.9 to 1.8 million in 1820; in 1920 it was 94.3 to 10.5 million. US blacks had gone from being 22% of the white population in the USA to 11% over that century, the result of massive white immigration in the intervening years.[29] East waxed lyrical, even biblical, albeit voicing some slight concern about Africa:

> The sons of Japheth ... have increased and multiplied; they have progressed beyond belief ... Looking to the north, the east and the west, the horizon is unlimited ... Only in the south appears a little cloud ... This is the direction in which to double the guard.[30]

Voices as optimistic as East's were harder to find among Europeans who remained in Europe. The ratio of whites to blacks in the United States was of little consequence to British administrators worrying about how to defend Australia from the threat of Japanese incursion, or from the perspective of French military planners observing a still growing gap between the generational sizes on either side of the Rhine, or indeed from the perspective of the German military planners watching the still faster growth of Russia's population. While the Americans could afford the luxury of a global view, Europeans, at least those of Western Europe, had to concern themselves with the ongoing viability of their extra-European empires and, as before the First World War, their perceived demographic weaknesses relative to that of their continental neighbours.

The British, while continuing to worry about the situation at home, were to some extent comforted by the falls in population growth across the North Sea. On the other hand, they now began to worry about demographic trends in the colonies. Seventy-seven million people in Japan shared 261 thousand square miles, while a white population in Australia just 7% of the size of Japan's enjoyed an area more than ten times larger.[31] It was in the light of such growing awareness of the demographic weight of Asia that the White Australia policy developed, excluding Asians from Australia, just as they had been excluded in the late nineteenth century from the USA. Fear of Asians in Australia can certainly be dated to the pre-First World War period and was particularly strong on the political left. William Hughes, Labor Party leader and later prime minister, had written in 1896 that on

> our northern border we have a breeding ground for coloured Asiatics, where they will soon be eating the heart's blood out of the white population, where they will multiply and pass over our border in a mighty Niagara, sowing seeds of diseases which will never be eradicated, and which will permanently undermine the constitutional vigour of which the Anglo-Saxon race is so proud.[32]

Legislation was passed in Australia, as in New Zealand and the United States, to exclude non-European and particularly Asian immigration, and as the Second World War approached G. F. McCleary, denying that this amounted to a 'dog in the manger attitude' on the part of the white Australian, stated resolutely: 'He [the white Australian] means to make full use of his manger, but to use it in his own way – to people his country without racial admixture, conflict and disaster.'[33] Concern was not expressed about the demographic fate of Canada, which had also passed legislation against Asian immigration, for no non-European elements were deemed to be lurking there. In contrast, Australia posed a particular worry because of its proximity to what French academic Étienne Dennery had referred to as 'Asia's teeming millions'. His book *Asia's Teeming Millions and its Problems for the West* had been published in English in 1931, and in a section entitled 'The Expansion of China', Dennery noted that there were a total of 8 million Chinese outside the country and over 400 million at home (he was perhaps making a deliberately provocative reference to Seeley's 1883 book *The Expansion of England*, just as the French writer Henri Andrillon had done in 1914 with *The Expansion of Germany*). He also noted the expansion of Indian emigration to east Africa, to the Caribbean and to south-east Asia, insisting 'there is a real danger for Western nations and the future peace of the world in these hapless masses of Asia, cramped on the narrow confines of their tiny rice field or their little strips of land'.[34] Talk of the 'Yellow Peril', which had started before the First World War, was now more resonant. It was pointed out, for example, that Asian immigration of 100,000 a year into Britain's antipodean colonies would do little to relieve the overcrowding of Asia but 'would demoralise everything in Australia and New Zealand'; it was essential that the ethnic homogeneity of the colonies be retained.[35]

Unsurprisingly, while Europeans may have worried about Australia's ethnic demography, Australians themselves were even more concerned. The legislation they brought in had, in the first instance, been driven by a labour movement with economic reasons for keeping out cheap workers, but motives became increasingly racial. Indeed, the legislation was somewhat watered down, at least in its presentation, under pressure from Britain not to give offence to the Asian powers and in particular to preserve good relations with Japan.[36]

The adventure novelist and agricultural reformer Henry Rider Haggard also worried about the demographic fate of the colonies. His contribution to the topic is to be found in an edited volume on the subject of controlled parenthood to which Marie Stopes also contributed. On the one hand, Haggard argued, Australia and Canada were wide and open, and if they were not peopled by those of British origin, they would ultimately be lost. On the other hand, the mother country was overcrowded and should not be populated beyond its ability to feed itself in a crisis. The answer had to lie in continued emigration to the colonies; without such a flow, the colonies would decline or fall into foreign hands. Inflows of people from other countries could not be relied on, as they would eventually 'water away [the] . . . original blood' until the Anglo-Saxon character of the Dominions was lost.[37] Haggard's own mixed Jewish and Indian ancestry did not seem to prevent him sharing the general opinion of the time on both sides of the Atlantic, that the Anglo-Saxon was the finest specimen nature had ever created.

British concern for the Dominions and particularly for Australia can be seen as a specifically national worry that the pre-war demographic weaknesses of the UK were now being manifested in its colonial offspring. Nevertheless, now that the threat was deemed to come from non-Europeans as well as from Europeans, the language was specifically racial, even more so than it had been before the war, when the worry had been more about German than Japanese cradles. It was noted that the annual increase in population in Australia had fallen from over 2% per annum to 1.5%, and in New Zealand from just under 2% to 1.25%.[38] Before 1914 British commentators had been worrying about British decline in relation to the rest of Europe; now they also worried about general European decline in relation to the rest of the world. Indeed, they saw an analogy between the two: just as Britain would have been imperilled during the Great War with a smaller population, so now its population weakness threatened the empire; as Haggard put it: 'Where, for instance, should we have been and where would our Allies have been if, during the late war, Great Britain had possessed half her present population?' Likewise, the empire might be imperilled for lack of people: 'Sixty million persons of our blood are not too many to rule over some three hundred and seventy millions of native peoples.'[39]

McCleary, writing in 1938, compared the birth rates of England and Wales, France, Italy and Germany in the early 1880s with those of the mid 1930s, and found that they had fallen by 56%, 37%, 39% and 52% respectively. It was the absolute numbers rather than the growth in numbers in areas further to the east which were alarming. Haggard spoke of Russia's supposed 180 million people and the devastation they might wreak 'if directed and organised by German skill and courage and aided by other sinister influences',[40] and as late as 1945 (and as yet unabashed by the discrediting of racial language through its association with the Nazis) McCleary published a work entitled *Race Suicide?* in which he saw the problem of falling European fertility as being not so much a symptom of the 'biological decadence of nations' as it was of excessive individualism and what he called 'the cult of self-development'.[41]

In Britain there continued to be an intra-European as well as a colonial aspect to population concerns, with the latter sometimes expressed in terms of 'the white race', which somewhat contradicted the worries closer to home. It was not always clear whether the falling birth rate in Germany, the low birth rate in France and the first signs of reductions in Russia were to be greeted as a reduction in the menace posed by European rivals or regretted as part of a general white decline. So far as Asian peoples were concerned, the Chinese and Indians represented 'teeming millions' while the Japanese represented a special threat since they had shown how rapidly Asians might adopt European practices and both expand their populations further and deploy European military technology and organisation against the Europeans. Sir Leo Chiozza Money, an Anglo-Italian, one-time parliamentary secretary to Prime Minister Lloyd George and a government minister, feared 'the possibility of Europe perishing through the employment by the coloured races of its own scientific methods'. He noted that the birth rates of other European countries were falling fast. Japan added 700,000 people a year as against a quarter of a million in England and Wales. From this he drew the explicitly pan-European conclusion that it 'is suicidal to encourage racial scorns, racial suspicions, racial hatred among the small minority that stand for White Civilisation'.[42] Such pan-European sentiments were not general enough, however, to prevent a second European conflagration.

The French, meanwhile, continued to fret about their demographic weakness even if the gap between their birth rate and that of Germany had diminished. In the years immediately before the First World War, great tomes had been published with titles such as *La Dépopulation de la France* and *Patriotisme et paternité*, the latter pointing out and indeed warning that in 1907 France had only 286,183 conscripts compared with 539,344 in Germany the following year.[43] This theme was continued after the war with works like *La question de la population* by Paul Leroy-Beaulieu, which argued, perhaps not very persuasively, that the key problem of France's weak population situation was not so much military or economic, important though these factors were, but ultimately moral.[44] This was, in a sense, a precursor of McCleary's worry about excessive individuality, a premonition, perhaps, of the 'second demographic transition' which was, half a century later, to see fertility rates across much of Europe plunge far lower than anything experienced in the interwar years.

It is not by chance that France turned out to be by far the most welcoming place to immigration in Europe between the wars, with nearly a million coming from Italy, over half a million from Poland and over 300,000 from over the border in Belgium. Although hardly free from racial prejudice, the Enlightenment and revolutionary traditions of France tended to a universalism which accepted that anyone – or at least anyone white – could in time become French. France was particularly keen to encourage immigration of the 'right sort of stock', ideally Latin in culture and language, Catholic in background and easy to assimilate into French society – for which purpose, as well as to boost the birth rate, the Alliance Nationale pour l'Accroissement de la Population Française (National Alliance for French Population Growth) was established.[45] The Alliance can be seen as an early case of combining 'hard demographic engineering' with 'soft demographic engineering', an attempt to shore up weak population numbers through first encouraging immigration and then encouraging a shift in identity to the prevailing host culture.[46] With a more flexible attitude to the relationship between ethnicity and nationality, what might be called civic nationalism, France was able to bolster its numbers in ways which were not open to its more ethnocentric neighbour across the Rhine, particularly after 1933.[47]

Immigration and integration were only part of the French demographic armoury; the other arm was pro-natalism, which was given a boost by the civic society La Plus Grande Famille. Long obsessed by demography, the French were more willing than other democracies actively to promote the birth rate. Significantly, even though La Plus Grande Famille was founded in 1915 and one might have expected it to have been more fearful of populations over the Rhine than over the Mediterranean, its founder put its mission in racial terms: 'If the white race restrains its birth, who will guarantee that the yellow race will follow? Who will assure us that the black race will sacrifice its fecundity which, to cite one example, is a cause of anxiety for whites in the United States?'[48] And so birth control and abortion were highly restricted in interwar France, while motherhood was promoted by benefits and medals.[49]

Demography and the Dictators

After the First World War there was a retreat in classic liberalism. The ideal of the minimal state and the predominance of the individual lost currency. Classic liberalism had passed its zenith in the face of growing state intervention even in the UK in the later decades of the nineteenth century, but the process accelerated during the Great War as the state's involvement in the economy became necessary for the war effort. As a result, the notion that the state should adopt demographic goals and implement policies to advance them became more widely accepted. This was true of the democracies but even more so of the dictatorships that were spawned between the wars. Although generally pursuing the goal of large populations for the sake of prestige and power, dictators did not necessarily follow their goals consistently or rationally. After all, the practice of wholesale murder, whether committed by Communists or Nazis, is hardly consistent with the professed aim of increased population growth. Yet while killing people with impunity, dictators were generally keen to see their numbers replaced by births, either by a new generation whose views could be suitably moulded (Communists) or by those who fitted the right ethnic, racial or national criteria (Fascists and Nazis).

The Soviet attitude to population underwent a change that is perhaps best mirrored in their attitude to art. Just as the early years of the revolution adopted an artistic policy that favoured experimentalism and what might be called a revolutionary spirit, so attitudes to family and reproduction were what today might be called 'progressive'. Marx and particularly Engels had, after all, condemned the family as a facet of capitalism and marriage as little more than a socially recognised form of prostitution. Over time, however, more conservative forces kicked in, and just as the Party preferred the conformity of 'socialist realism' in art, so it came to adopt more conventional attitudes to the family. The tensions were there from the beginning: Alexandra Kollontai, the most senior Bolshevik woman at the time of the revolution, opined that 'the sexual act should be recognised as neither shameful nor sinful, but natural and legal, as much a manifestation of a healthy organism as the quenching of hunger or thirst'.[50] Lenin disagreed.

The Soviet state was the first in the world to legalise abortion, but contraception remained generally unavailable and unused in part because of its expense (even in the more prosperous West it was still largely the preserve of the middle classes). At this stage in the life of the Soviet state, abortion was justified on the grounds of personal choice and women's welfare. As one worker from a factory staffed mostly by women reported months before the legalisation: 'Within the past six months among 100–150 young people under age 25, I have seen 15–20% of them making [sic] abortions without a doctor's help. They simply use household products: They drink bleach and other poisonous mixtures.'[51] The abortion legalisation decree stated:

> For the past ten years, the number of women having abortions has been growing . . . The legislation of all countries struggles against this evil by . . . punishing women who opt for abortion and the doctors who perform it . . . It drives the operation underground and makes women the victims of greedy and often ignorant abortionists.[52]

The predominantly peasant population still had a high fertility rate, but this was beginning to fall as more of the population was urbanised and became literate. Under Stalin, social revolutionary attitudes waned and the Soviet Union was faced with a dilemma: there was a need for female labour in the fields and, increasingly, factories, but also a desire to ensure a large population for the strength of the state. There was also a growing distaste for abortions which, in some cities, surpassed the number of births.[53] In 1935 Stalin declared 'man the most precious resource' and the following year abortion was outlawed in all but exceptional circumstances. As usual, the more junior officials parroted the new party line. Aaron Soltz, an Old Bolshevik and sometimes referred to as the conscience of the Party, insisted that in the new 'Socialist Reality', abortion was no longer required: 'Our life becomes more gay, more happy, rich and satisfactory. But the appetite, as they say, comes with the meal. Our demands grow from day to day. We need new fighters . . . We need people.' He talked of 'the greatest happiness of motherhood'. Others compared mothers to Stakhanovite workers and justified punishment for abortion on the grounds of the need to 'protect the health of women' and 'safeguard the rearing of a strong and healthy younger generation'.[54] Yet despite the newly minted pro-natalism of its Communist leadership, Russia's fertility rate continued to fall. The human tide could not even be held back by Stalin 'the Great Architect', and it turned out it was easier to determine the output of steel or tractors than of children. Nevertheless, the Soviet Union's population continued to rise sharply thanks to the fact that, although falling, fertility was high and, despite the famine and purges, life expectancy for the population as a whole continued to lengthen, while emigration was largely forbidden.

Whereas Soviet Russia wavered somewhat in its attitude to motherhood and childbearing, attitudes in fascist Italy were more consistent when it came to traditional sexual morals and the role of women more generally. Despite his initial differences with the Catholic Church, Mussolini supported the Church's teaching on contraception and abortion in making population one of the country's four national 'battles' (the others being for land, grain and a stronger lira). In 1927 he declared: 'I assert that a prerequisite, if not a fundamental aspect, of the political power of a nation, and so of its economic and moral power, is its demographic strength . . . Gentlemen! In order to count for something in the world, Italy must greet the second half of this century with no fewer than 60 million inhabitants.'[55] This represented a 50% increase on the population size at the time. Bans on abortion and contraceptives were enforced, bachelor taxes increased and loans offered for families. Despite these policies, the impact on the Italian population was not dramatic, with Italy continuing to follow a path quite common to European countries. The population did rise from 37 million in 1920 to 47 million by 1950, but this was well short of Mussolini's target, representing an annual growth over the period of around 1%. And the gain was not achieved through any victory in the 'battle for births' – fertility rates fell from over four children per woman before the First World War to three by the late 1930s – but by a falling mortality rate and lengthening life expectancy – from forty-seven in 1910 to sixty-six by 1950 – and by a dramatic fall in Italian emigration to around 6% of the level it had been before the First World War by the late 1930s.[56]

Hitler was obsessed by demography. His genocidal views stemmed from a perception of population *quality*, but we should not overlook

his views on the *quantitative* issues more commonly concerning political leaders at the time. Half a million Germans had flocked into the
country from the lands ceded to Poland after the First World War and
another 132,000 from Alsace-Lorraine, but by the outbreak of war in
1939 hundreds of thousands of Jews had fled the country. There were
already pro-natalist elements within the Weimar Republic, but these
came to the fore with the Third Reich, where Mother's Day became
an official holiday and some assistance as well as encouragement was
given to those prepared to bear large families. The Mother Cross was
instituted for women having more than three children (bronze), more
than five (silver) or more than seven (gold). Abortion was made a
capital crime during the Second World War. In 1934 Hitler declared:
'German women want above all to be wives and mothers . . . They
do not yearn for the factory nor the office nor for Parliament. A cosy
home, a dear husband and brood of children is closer to their hearts.'[57]

The Nazis wanted to expand the population base and were prepared
to do this by pro-natal policies and propaganda and indeed by incor-
porating the Germans of Austria and Czechoslovakia, but they were
more than happy to exclude those not considered suitable. Motherhood
was encouraged only among those who were 'worthy of bearing life'.
Numbers counted, but for the Nazis purity of the race meant more
than numbers. On the other hand, when the war economy required
it, millions of those who were considered ethnically impure were
permitted to enter the fatherland to work, often as slave labourers.[58]

In reality, Nazi population policies were confused. There was
tension between traditional morality on the one hand and policies to
propagate those deemed most racially valuable on the other; such
policies included encouraging those going off to battle to have children, outside wedlock if necessary. Hitler believed that Germany's
survival depended on reversing a disastrous demographic decline,
itself supposedly the result of decadence, individualism, homosexual-
ity and over-urbanisation.[59] Yet at the same time he believed that the
existing German population was too great for its territorial resources,
hence the need for *Lebensraum* (living space). Whether the ultimate
problem was too little space for the existing population or too few
people within the existing space was not entirely clear or resolved,
and this gave rise to all sorts of contradictory as well as extraordinarily

inhumane demographic policies both during the occupation of Poland and during the occupation of large parts of the western Soviet Union.

Overall, Hitler's greatest impact on the population size of Germany – quite apart from his devastating impact on the population of Europe as a whole – was the loss of around 7 million Germans during the war, both military and civilian casualties. Underlying this calamity, however, were the fundamentals of Germany's demographic trends, which resembled Italy's and were in line with general European patterns. Nazi pro-natalist policies had a modest impact, with births per woman picking up from a little below two in the early 1930s to a little above two by around 1939, still well below where they had been in the early 1920s not to mention before the First World War. Life expectancy, a little short of fifty-four in 1920, had grown to nearly sixty-four by 1950. Fantasies of millions more Germans comfortably settled in the Ukraine and the Urals over the bones of the local Slavic population never came to pass. Nevertheless, in numeric terms, German losses from the First World War were made up in fairly short order.

The End of the Great European Powers

The second volume of Leonard Woolf's memoirs, covering his work as a colonial administrator in Sri Lanka in the first decade of the twentieth century, contrasts sharply with George Orwell's *Burmese Days*, reflecting his own experiences in a similar capacity in Burma between the wars. Despite Woolf's later (and possibly even contemporary but personal) anti-colonialism, the impression Woolf gives is of an empire full of confidence, expecting to last for the foreseeable future. Orwell's empire is tired, apprehensive and full of a sense of its own doom. Not too much should be read into the works of just two individuals, but they do give us a sense of a changed attitude to empire and particularly to its likely lifespan.

To some extent interwar imperial exhaustion had demographic underpinnings, and it was not limited to Britain. Concern about the decline in the birth rate and growth in numbers of people of European origin as a whole was widespread and included French, Americans and Germans. The days when someone like Rhodes or Seeley could foretell a world dominated by whites, let alone by Anglo-Saxons, was over, and in no small measure because they acknowledged the sheer numbers of non-whites, their potential to grow in number and the fall in growth of Europeans. Already Britain had lost most of Ireland. Now movements for self-rule were on the rise from Egypt to India and beyond. Europeans no longer believed that they could easily overcome such movements.

Although always outnumbered in their Asian and African colonies, Europeans had been buoyed by a sense of their own demographic momentum and dynamism in contrast to the apparent stagnation of their non-European subjects. But precisely the same pattern which had thrust Britain forward in contrast to its European nations, then seen Britain slip back relative to those nations, was about to be played out on a global scale. From the interwar perspective there was no reason to anticipate a post-war baby boom and plenty of reason to assume that European birth rates would remain low or even continue falling. On the other hand, the eventual growth of non-European populations through the same processes that had once driven forward population growth in Europe was all too evident. It was not for nothing that Hitler worried about how improved material conditions and medical care were raising the numbers of Indians as well as Russians.

In the meantime, while the threat of eclipse from the colonies loomed on the horizon, it became increasingly apparent as the Second World War progressed that the traditional European powers had been eclipsed by the United States and the USSR. They were ambiguously or only partially European in different ways – the former because of its location on another continent, despite its population being overwhelmingly European in origin, the latter because of its location on the edge of Europe and indeed stretching beyond it, and because of its Orthodox culture with origins not in Rome but in Byzantium. The rise of these two semi-European powers came at the expense of the European core. The role which demographic trends played in this is unquestionable. The German assault on the Soviet Union was ultimately defeated by an abundance of Russian troops and Russian space (and, of course, Russian weather). Millions of Russians were killed,

millions captured and yet millions more came and ultimately overcame. As German General Manstein complained, the Russian Army
was like a hydra: cut off one head and two appeared in its place.[60]
When frozen German troops outside Moscow at the end of 1941 or
their desperate comrades trapped at Stalingrad a year later noted how
the Russians just kept coming, regardless of how many had been
captured or killed, they were observing the simple playing out on the
battlefield of deep demographic trends.

The Soviet Union's ultimate victory would have been less likely
without the burgeoning of the Russian population and the slowdown
in Germany's. In the first forty years of the century, Germany had
managed an average of only a little over 0.5% population growth per
annum, while Russia, despite the ravages of civil war and Communism,
had experienced nearly 1.4% per annum.[61] Thus while at the turn of
the century the German population had been a little over half that of
Russia, by the time of the German invasion of the Soviet Union, it
was not much more than a third. Superior German organisation,
which had overcome Russian numbers even when simultaneously
fighting a full-blown war in the west in 1914–18, was already being
overwhelmed by the weight of Russian numbers before the Western
Front was opened in 1944. There were other important and sometimes offsetting factors such as the rapid industrialisation of Russia
between the wars, Stalin's initial mismanagement of the military
campaign, Hitler's interference with his generals and the failure of
Germany properly to equip its troops for winter warfare. The ability
of Hitler and Stalin to alienate the non-Russian populations of the
western Soviet Union also played an important role. Yet none of this
can take away from the fact that the eastern front in the Second World
War was to a considerable extent a brutal game of numbers. In the
course of the war, Russia had more than 34 million men under arms,
all fighting on the one front. Germany had 13 million stretched across
various theatres.

The same point can be made in regard to the United States during
the Second World War. Its economic might was to some extent the
product of its population size, but that size was also highly significant
in its own right. The inexhaustible supply of men as well as machines,
of human as well as material resources, made the United States

effectively unbeatable from the German perspective. Again, it is instructive to compare the population sizes of the two countries: at the turn of the century the population of Germany had been almost three-quarters the size of the United States; by the time the US entered the Second World War it was facing a Germany with a population less than half as large as its own.

With America's population reaching a multiple of that of any European power, the dominance of the European powers was ended not only militarily but also economically. With a larger market and greater potential for economies of scale, the US was able to outclass the UK in terms of per capita income, but even more decisive than the absolute size of its economy was its population size. In 1870 the US population had been almost one-third as large again as that of the UK and its economy about the same size. By 1950, with a population three times larger than that of the UK, the economy of the United States was four and a half times larger than the UK's. The relative positions of the two economies had been reversed on a per capita basis, but a much more significant factor in their changing relative sizes was the changing relative sizes of their populations.

The bipolar superpower world of the US and Russia could perhaps have been predicted from the demographic reality of the interwar years, when the Soviet Union and the United States, with their vast spaces and potential to support expanding populations, started pulling away from the countries of Europe. Indeed, the emergence of Russia and the United States as the world's leading powers had been predicted by the French political theorist and traveller Alexis de Tocqueville more than a hundred years earlier: 'each of them,' he wrote, 'seems marked out by the will of Heaven to sway the destiny of half the globe' – and precisely on the demographic grounds of their fast-growing populations and an ability to sustain population growth which the traditional European powers could not rival.[62]

Without economic and industrial growth the demographic giant of China continued to slumber, but where population growth and industrial development went hand in hand with demographic growth and scale, a fundamental shift in world power and the global system was unavoidable. The decline of Europe's empires was not just a matter of waning European demographic predominance, though; the antagonistic ideology of Woodrow Wilson at Versailles in 1919, forcing the League of Nations on the Europeans as well as 'mandates' in place of 'colonies', had origins going back to the American War of Independence. However, the fact that Wilson was in a position to impose his ideas reflected the triumphant growth of America's population. It foretold a world not fully to be born until after 1945, in which the United States had completely ceased to be an appendage of 'the West' and had become its embodiment. This was a new world created by the human tide – the wax and wane of which would shape the half-century to come.

Over the course of two world wars, whole populations were mobilised in ways that would have seemed unimaginable earlier. Jane Austen's heroines had lived their lives famously oblivious to the Napoleonic Wars engulfing Europe at the time, an event they only seemed to notice when presented with an opportunity to meet the odd dashing soldier or sailor. A century or so later, their female descendants were busy as land girls, digging for victory and ensuring the country was fed, or working in armaments factories, keeping the front line supplied with shells or tanks. The invention of the aeroplane and subsequent bombing meant that even in their island fastness they could not escape direct experience of the conflict. And when societies were able and willing to call up their whole populations to the war effort, the numeric size of those populations counted more than ever.

After 1945 the West entered a quite different phase. Its wars were once again fought in distant lands, having little direct impact at home. New social and economic trends came to the fore, and now the trendsetter was the most populous country of the West, the United States.

6

The West since 1945

From Baby Boom to Mass Immigration

Living in Surrey in the early nineteenth century, and seemingly oblivious to the revolutionary changes occurring in the industrial heartland a few hundred miles to the north, the Reverend Thomas Malthus was describing a vanishing world. It was a world in which the capacity of land to support people rose only gradually, while growth in human numbers might grow exponentially and would be kept in check, one way or another, by the limitations of slowly growing food production. Yet while Malthus was expounding his theory in various versions of *An Essay on the Principle of Population*, his agrarian assumptions were being undermined as a whole new society was being born around Manchester and other new industrial centres in England's north and Midlands.

In this new world, where furnaces replaced furrows and rows of tenements replaced country cottages, it was possible for vastly larger populations to manufacture goods and trade them with the rest of the globe in exchange for huge quantities of food, which could be produced from vast new tracts of territory in distant continents cleared of their indigenous peoples and placed at the service of feeding the mother country. New forms of transport unimaginable to Malthus, the railway and the iron steamship, would move food across the globe, adding innumerable 'ghost acres' to England and then to other industrialised countries. Malthus lived too early in the nineteenth century, and too far away from the heart of the action, to see how the system he had described was being ripped up and replaced by a new one which could support vastly more people than he believed possible.

After the Second World War something strange happened. A generation of statisticians and social scientists living a century after

Malthus had reasonably theorised and described the post-Malthusian world. Less well remembered than Malthus, the American Frank Notestein described what would come to be known as the 'demographic transition'. Rather than existing in a state of eternal Malthusian constraint, a country would start with a high fertility, a high mortality rate and a small population, then its mortality would fall, causing the population to grow rapidly; next, fertility would decline, resulting in continuing but slower growth; and finally, fertility and mortality would be back in balance, with the population stable again but at a much higher level.

Broadly speaking, Notestein got it right – this is what had happened earlier in Britain, America and across Europe – but as with Malthus, precisely as he was describing the system, it was changing. The advanced industrial societies of North America and northern Europe were supposed to have reached the final stage of the journey, with around two children per woman, low death rates and large and more or less stable populations, and the human tide's course had been charted to what was supposed to be its end. But what in fact happened, against all expectation, was a baby *boom*, with young women across the developed world for the couple of decades after the end of the war bearing significantly more children than their mothers had. Just as population turned out to be more unpredictable than Malthus had thought, so Notestein was likewise wrong-footed. Again, just when the study of demography appeared to have identified a settled pattern, it took a new form.

The Birth of the Baby Boomers

On 10 March 1964, a mild early spring day, a forty-one-gun salute was heard in the heart of London.[1] Winston Churchill was in his final year of life and Alec Douglas-Home – the last aristocrat to hold the job of British prime minister – was installed in no. 10 Downing Street. The event being marked by the salute was the birth of Prince Edward, third in line to the throne at his birth behind his two elder brothers Charles and Andrew but ahead of his sister Anne. After this fourth birth the Queen – by then in her late thirties – had no more children, but she had notched up precisely twice as many children as had her mother. Once again, the British royal family matched their genera-tion and their age, typifying trends which went well beyond the gates of Buckingham Palace – where Prince Edward had been born – and well beyond the narrow confines of the British Isles. And in turn, the current Queen Elizabeth II's four children have gone on to typify their generation, none of them having more than two offspring, reverting to the more limited childbearing habits of the interwar generation to which their grandmother had belonged in terms of small family size.

When we think of the archetypal nineteenth-century family, it may be Queen Victoria and her brood which come to mind, the children posing regally or playfully around their adoring parents. But by the mid twentieth century, the action had moved west, both in terms of power and money, and when we think of the post-war baby boom, it is the United States which comes first to mind. The United States was now the demographic powerhouse of the Western world, a land noted since Malthus's time for high fertility rates and strong population growth. Yet births per woman were already falling before the First World War and continued to do so in the interwar era – the Great Depression of the 1930s helping to discourage childbirth and family formation.[2] Unemployed men on both sides of the Atlantic, struggling to support their families, either delayed marrying and plan-ning for children or, if already married and with children, avoided adding to their family. Contraception was increasingly known about, affordable and starting to be practised even among the poorer members of society, for whom it had once been out of reach. (It was celebrated, somewhat jovially, as the epitome of modernity by the British novelist Evelyn Waugh in *Black Mischief*, a novel published in 1932; twenty years earlier, the topic would have been hard to imagine in print.)

The most common form of contraception was some kind of sheath. Such devices had been known in ancient times and had certainly been in fairly widespread use in eighteenth-century London, as the diaries of James Boswell show. Rubber, which was used from the nineteenth century, became cheaper in the early twentieth century, making sheaths more affordable. Often distributed discreetly in the UK, condoms were supposedly offered to customers by barbers who would ask, 'Anything for the weekend, sir?' From immediately before the First World War onwards, IUDs or coils became available for women, and these too became increasingly available in the interwar years. For many people, however, especially the poor and the less educated, withdrawal, abstinence and primitive and illegal abortions continued to be the way in which family size was limited. Unreliable and (in the latter case) dangerous though these may have been, they worked with sufficient reliability to bring down fertility rates to a third of the level of the 1860s.

Between the wars the fertility rate in the US fell from a little over three children per woman to a little over two.[3] This fall has been attributed in particular to lower fertility among immigrants, a rise of the urban population (with its traditionally lower fertility rate) as people left the countryside to come to the towns, and finally to a convergence of rural and urban fertility rates. A smaller share of the population was living in the countryside, and increasingly behaving more like urban dwellers when it came to childbearing and family size.[4] This meant the growth rate of the population declined, but it did not much bother commentators or policy makers; the population was still growing overall, pulling away in terms of size from potential rivals on the international stage. Much of the establishment in the US was generally more interested in reducing immigration and preserving America's white Anglo-Saxon identity than it was with population growth.

By the 1930s the population of the US was growing at less than 1% per annum, low by historical standards for the country. This was no longer the America of Emma Lazarus, whose poem adorns the Statue of Liberty, drawing to it the huddled masses: with the ever more stringent immigration controls ushered in during the 1920s, the US was making it clear that the huddled masses were no longer welcome. Nor was it any longer the America of Thomas Jefferson in which fertile young settlers with endless access to fresh lands (taken, of course, at the expense of indigenous Americans) could double their numbers every twenty-five years through fecundity alone.

Then from 1945, against all expectation, everything changed. With the war behind them, US GIs returned wanting homes, brides and families. At first this might have been put down to an immediate post-war catch-up, with plans for marriage and family formation, postponed by the war, finally coming to fruition. However, the trend turned out to be more than short-lived. Total fertility in the United States, which had fallen to a little over two before the war, rose to well over three and a half by the late 1950s.[5] Nothing in Frank Notestein's demographic transition theory had prepared anyone for this near doubling of fertility once the transition to low mortality and low fertility had been achieved. With hindsight it is clear that Notestein's model of demographic transition, while not exactly upturned, was in need of refining .

The total number of births per annum in the latter part of the 1930s had been a little over 2 million across the US, but by the late 1950s it was twice this number.[6] Annual population growth now, even in the continued absence of mass immigration, was double its 1930s level.[7] By 1960 the United States had around 180 million citizens compared with a little over 100 million barely forty years earlier. Between the mid 1940s and mid 1960s it appeared that the America of Thomas Jefferson − in which large families fuelled population growth − had returned, even if the America of Emma Lazarus − in which hundreds of thousands or even millions of immigrants converged on the US − had not. The maternity wards opened even as the gates stayed more or less shut, at least for the time being.

Population trends are the aggregate result of millions of private decisions taken by individuals and couples. Perfect knowledge of why they occur is never possible. Understanding the human tide, unlike the maritime tide, can never be an exact science. However, it is possible to speculate about the reasons for the post-war baby boom in the US. There was, as we have seen, the move to catch up after the war and to some extent the depression. As one commentator has written: 'When the boys came home from "over there" they married, proceeded to get jobs, buy homes and have babies.'[8] Yet this does not explain why the baby boom was still going − indeed reaching its peak − around fifteen years after the war ended, when those GIs yearning to settle down had long done so. To some extent trends like this gather their own momentum. Early marriage and larger family sizes become the norm, and people emulate what they see at the cinema and on television and observe among their friends.

A more compelling reason for the long duration of the baby boom is economic. Population growth and economic boom become self-reinforcing under the right circumstances. More marriages and more children meant a need for more homes and for more of the goods which were increasingly expected in or around the home – the fridge, the washing machine, the telephone, the television and above all the motor car. Providing for this demand in an era when the US still manufactured most of its own consumer goods fed back into the climate of optimism, further encouraging family formation and births. It was the golden era of the American corporation, of rising wages and job security, exactly the circumstances under which young couples were prepared to take the plunge, get married and start a family, or feel confident enough to have that extra child. To some extent, it was a final throwing off of the Malthusian constraint. In a more chaste society than ours, delaying marriage often meant sexual abstinence and frustration. As economic opportunity opened up to young men, many felt they could risk getting married and having children earlier than their fathers had during the depression years. (As a relation of mine told me of the 1940s: 'In my day, marriage was the only way you could have sex with a nice girl.') Home ownership among those in their late twenties and early thirties in the US had, by 1960, risen to twice the level at the start of the century, and the average age at which women had their first child fell.[9] Whereas in an earlier era restraint, late marriage and small families had been typical of those pulling themselves up, now early marriage and larger families were a sign of financial success.

The baby boom was no more limited to the United States than was the post-war economic boom; rather, it was widespread across the West. In Canada, where the trend was stronger than in the US, by the early 1960s fertility rates were not far short of four children per woman, making Queen Elizabeth more typical of her Canadian subjects than her British ones. In part, this was due to continuing high fertility rates among the French-speaking Quebecois, whose fidelity to Catholic teaching on birth control persisted longer than elsewhere (and – by the evidence of the birth rate – much longer than in their home country of France). Australia and New Zealand more or less tracked the American experience, while the UK, which had experienced fertility rates of barely two by the late 1930s, saw a rise to nearly three by the early 1960s – the peak was reached in 1964, the year of Prince Edward's birth. Germany, too, saw a rise, although never above two and a half children per woman, accompanying the country's post-war economic miracle and reconstruction from the ashes of 1945. Finally, northern Europe was to some extent an echo of the American phenomenon; here fertility rates certainly went up above their pre-war levels, but not to quite the same heights.

Southern Europe differed from North America and northern Europe as, before the Second World War, it was still relatively unindustrialised, had a much larger rural population and a higher although falling fertility rate, and was still in the process of completing its demographic transition. In Spain, under the authoritarian rule of Franco and the domination of the Catholic Church, fertility rates rose from two and a half to three, while in Italy they remained more or less flat at two and a half. Irish women remained Europe's champion childbearers, with around four children per woman by the early 1960s, another late triumph for the Catholic Church, but Ireland remained a small country in population terms; its continuing struggle to develop much beyond the agrarian stage meant that high birth rates continued to translate into high emigration, much as it had done a century earlier. Ireland's children continued to spread from Boston, Massachusetts, to Birmingham, England, and Brisbane, Australia, following the now well-travelled pathways of exile in search of economic opportunity. By 1970 the population of the Irish Republic, despite its high birth rate, had hardly grown since the end of the Second World War.

The baby boom had a big impact on societies, which were now flooded with young people. Nineteen fifties North America and Western Europe saw the dawning of the era of the teenager (the term 'teenager' may have its origins in the interwar years, but was properly born in the decades following the Second World War), the era of rock and roll, the era when, for the first time, there was something that could meaningfully be called mass youth culture. The countries of the West were young, with large cohorts of children rising to young adults outnumbering the cohorts that went before, and able to influence social practices and conventions.

At the climax of the baby boom in the 1960s, the children born immediately after the war were coming of age while the last boomers were being born, and teenagers displayed a blend of adolescent rebelliousness and consumerist conformity; it was the period of student rebellions from California to Paris, of blue jeans, The Beatles and the Rolling Stones. This was a confident and influential generation because it was a large generation. When the young are much more numerous than the old, it is not surprising that conventions are increasingly questioned, challenged and in some cases overturned. The ongoing popularity of the culture of the 1960s testifies to the size of that cohort and to its continued impact, although today its members are less likely to be protesting for free love and against the Vietnam War and more likely to be protesting against a cut in pensions or a rise in the retirement age.

'Rock and Roll is Dead', the Lenny Kravitz song of 1995 proclaims. The timing is perhaps no coincidence, for at this point the cohort of baby boom Americans reaching teenage was at its nadir, the fertility rate having bottomed out about a decade and a half earlier; and it can certainly be argued that there has been a general retreat in youth culture and assertiveness since then, based on deep changes in society's age structure. Whereas in 1965 under twenty-fives represented not much short of half the population of the US, by 2015 they constituted less than a third. The late 1950s and 1960s were the height of the era in which youth predominated.

Baby Bust

In their prime the baby boomers were accused of undermining the fabric of Western civilisation. In their approaching dotage, they are accused of milking the economy, feathering their own nests and undermining the welfare state through a sense of entitlement.[10] These accusations may be justified and often have political ramifications. The UK general election of 2017 provides an example. The middle class, once heavily Tory, split almost evenly between Labour and the Conservatives. No longer was class the great predictor of voting behaviour; now it was age which determined the likelihood of voting one way or the other. The Conservatives were thirty points ahead among the over sixty-fives and fifty points behind among the under twenty-fours disillusioned by high house prices, diminishing economic prospects and Brexit.

Around 1965, the contraceptive Pill, which came to be known universally as 'the Pill', was made generally available. It arrived just as fertility was starting to fall and it undoubtedly contributed to that fall. If one wants to suggest father figures for the Pill, they would have to be Carl Djerassi and Gregory Pincus. Djerassi had fled Europe in his teens, arriving in the US on the eve of the Second World War, and eventually became a Stanford professor. Pincus was the scion of an earlier and larger group of Jewish refugees to America, his parents having been part of the great wave of eastern and southern Europeans who reached America's shores in the decades before the Second World War. Pincus ended up at Harvard, Djerassi at Stanford. Djerassi's motivations were clear:

> The overwhelming fact is that at my birth there were 1.9 billion people in the world. Now there are 5.8 billion and at my 100th birthday, there are likely to be 8.5 billions. That has never happened in world history before that during a person's lifetime, the world population more than quadrupled. That can never happen again.[11]

In turn, it's possible to suggest two mothers of the Pill: Margaret Sanger, the birth control pioneer who organised, coordinated and inspired the effort, and Katharine Dexter McCormick, the biologist and agricultural equipment heiress who funded it.

Their work bore fruit when the US Federal Drugs Agency approved the Pill's use in 1960. The following year it was introduced into the UK – initially for married women only – and its use spread rapidly across the West except where the Catholic Church managed to hold it at bay (until the mid 1970s in Spain and until the 1980s in Ireland, for example). Other forms of contraception such as condoms and IUDs had by the 1960s been generally available for some time, otherwise the low fertility rates of the 1930s would never have been achievable on a mass scale. Even nineteenth-century French peasants had managed to curtail their fertility, presumably not by entirely curtailing their sex lives. Yet the Pill's sheer simplicity, reliability and cheapness (often, along with other forms of contraception, provided free by the welfare state) meant that the link between sex and birth was finally and irrevocably broken. At least sex without the risk of conception was now universal.

The unexpectedly high post-war US fertility rate, which had peaked in the late 1950s, thereafter began to tail off. At first the fall was relatively modest, from just under three and two-thirds of a child per woman in the second half of the 1950s to a little under three and a half in the early 1960s. The fall was then more rapid, to barely one and three-quarters in the late 1970s. Thus, in the twenty years from the late 1950s to the late 1970s the total fertility rate of the United States more or less halved from nearly four to fewer than two children per woman. Thereafter, it flattened out and recovered somewhat, hovering at or slightly above two children per woman from the early 1990s, close to if not quite at what is generally considered to be replacement level and thus only a little below its pre-war level, and most recently there appears to have been a reversal down to somewhat below two. Speaking generally, then, the United States can be seen as having reverted to the norm of the final stage of the (first) demographic transition, and is now somewhat beyond this point.

Against this backdrop, the post-war baby boom can be seen in retrospect as an aberration – a kink – in the demographic transition, rather than a reversal. The virtuous cycle (virtuous at least to some) of new families creating demand for new goods, boosting the economy, boosting economic prospects and encouraging the formation of new and larger families could not go on forever. New social forces and norms came into play, among them feminism, as a generation of women who themselves had been born in the baby boom more commonly aspired to higher education and careers rather than simply to marriage and motherhood. Smaller and later families accompanied the changing attitudes of and towards women, their broadening horizons and rising educational opportunities; this turned out to be the case almost everywhere in the West. Of all women in the US in their early twenties, those who were college-educated rose from 20% to nearly 60% between the 1960s and 1990s.[12]

The Pill made contraception massively more convenient and simple and it changed sexual practices and attitudes profoundly, but demographically it was not transformational, for although the forms of contraception used before the war – the condom and IUDs – were less convenient and at that stage less accessible and affordable, they still managed to facilitate a fall in fertility rates across many Western countries to replacement level. So it turned out that you did not need to educate women in order to lower the fertility rate, although lower fertility would almost certainly be the outcome if you did. Female education and families of six or eight children may go together in individual cases, but not at the level of a whole society. A more negative attitude to marriage and childbirth, probably always around but never articulated on so wide a scale, was expressed by Marilyn French in her 1977 feminist classic, *The Women's Room*:

> Years of scraping shit out of diapers with a kitchen knife, finding places where string beans are two cents less a pound, intelligence in figuring the most efficient, least time-consuming way to iron men's white shirts or to wash and wax the kitchen floor or take care of the house and kids . . . these not only take energy and courage and mind, but they may constitute the very essence of a life . . . I hate these grimy details as much as you do.[13]

No: the baby boomers were not going to create their own baby boom.

The Second Transition

What was being born – or indeed, ironically, what the baby boomers were giving birth to – was another unforeseen phase of modern demography. Quiet progress towards low fertility and low mortality, which had been achieved across much of the industrialised world in the 1920s and 1930s, was not the final word, but neither was the post-war baby boom. Instead of reverting to the interwar era, birth rates in many places undershot the level of two children per woman, representing a whole raft of social trends from later marriage to the very questioning by the LGBT movement of what it means to be a man or a woman. This can be described as the second demographic transformation.

With monarchies increasingly rare and arguably archaic, in the contemporary era political leaders are perhaps better exemplars of the age, and in this respect it is notable how many are women – in 2018, most notably the Chancellor of Germany and the Prime Minister of the United Kingdom, neither of whom has any children (despite Angela Merkel being known affectionately as *Mutti* ('Mummy')). Hillary Clinton, who came close to becoming the most powerful person in the world, has one daughter. And while it is true that combining political life at the highest level with child-rearing is diffi-cult, it is notable that an earlier era of famous female politicians – Golda Meir, Indira Gandhi and Margaret Thatcher – each managed to have two children (although Margaret Thatcher, with characteris-tic efficiency, minimised the time over which they delayed her polit-ical career by having twins).

The turn-around in fertility and ending of the baby boom was soon noticed, for by now the gathering of statistics and statistical techniques had greatly improved. By the early 1970s the neo-Malthusian concerns of US President Richard Nixon about too large a population at home, expressed as late as 1969, appeared outdated.[14] Other changes were taking place too, besides feminism. Society was undergoing a secular-isation in which, for example, the share of Catholic women using methods of birth control not approved by the Church appears to have risen from less than one-third to more than two-thirds.[15] By the early 1970s the fertility rate of Catholics and Protestants in the US had more or less converged as the era of the famously large Irish and Italian family came to an end.[16] The average age of childbearing for a woman in America has risen from around twenty-six for several decades after the war to a little over twenty-eight. Abortion law was being relaxed and social acceptance of abortion was increasing. The unexpected rise in post-war fertility appears essentially to have been driven by economics. Its reversal was largely the product of technological progress (the arrival of the Pill), which mediated changing social attitudes and female educational attainment. These patterns became

THE WEST SINCE 1945

prevalent throughout the developed world; what marks the United States out from other parts of the developed world is that, for a long time at least, US fertility rates fell to, but not very much below, replacement levels, a fact that possibly reflects the persistence of religious belief and practice in the US more than Europe. This elevated level of fertility was a Protestant, not a Catholic, phenomenon. Irish and Italian Americans were no longer following the Church's advice to avoid the use of contraception, and as a result they were no longer having larger families, so it was not the Catholics who were maintaining a high national birth rate; rather, the birth rate in the US was held back from complete collapse thanks to traditional attitudes towards family and the role of women that clung on in the Bible Belt. At the extreme end of this tendency is the Quiverfull movement, which urges women to 'relinquish their wombs for God', who should be left to determine the number of children they have, and which bases its pro-natalist teachings on biblical texts commanding man to be fruitful and multiply, condemning Onan (and by extension Onanism) and extolling the man with a 'quiverfull of sons'.[17] The Church has used the Bible's condemnation of Onan as the basis both for condemning masturbation and the withdrawal method of prevention. While the Quiverfull group is small and unusual, it is a manifestation of the link between religiosity and fertility which can be seen among other religious sects with particularly high fertility, such as the Jewish Haredim in New York and their satellite communities, the Mormons concentrated in Utah, and the Amish of Pennsylvania and Ohio.

Another factor boosting US fertility was the arrival of large numbers of people from Latin America, where largescale childbearing remained the norm. This migration began precisely as the general fertility rate began to fall in the US – that is, in the mid 1960s. Normally fertility rates of immigrant groups from high to low fertility countries fall within a generation or two, and this has certainly happened with Latinos in the US, but before they converge the immigrants boost the birth rate. Taking into account the Bible Belt and the arrival of Latinos, then, it is understandable that even at its lowest, the US fertility rate has not yet fallen below one and three-quarters children per woman. It is noteworthy that nine of the ten states with the lowest fertility rates are in the north-east, outside the Bible Belt and for the most part outside the areas of higher Latino immigration. The current relatively low figures for US fertility as a whole reflect both the continuing convergence of immigrant child-bearing practices and local practices, and a decline in religious belief, reducing the size of those populations with religiously elevated birth rates.

The absence of an equivalent Bible Belt and – at first – lower levels of migration from the developing world meant that elsewhere in the West the collapse of childbearing was more dramatic. It was also, in most cases, starting from a lower base. Canada moved, from a fertility perspective, into the new paradigm of the second demographic transition more convincingly than the US, enjoying a fertility rate of over three children per woman already in 1945, and seeing that climb to almost four by the early 1960s; for the immediate post-war decades, the country consistently outbred Americans. Yet the 1960s was a decade of rapid social change in Canada, similar to what was happening south of the forty-ninth parallel but accentuated by the impact of the large number of Catholic French Canadians who underwent rapid secularisation. Their birth rate has fallen at the same time as their falling church attendance, once over 80% and now less than 10%. By 1970 the fertility rate of Canada was somewhat lower than that of the US, and since this point Canada has experienced a consistently low fertility rate, not much above one and a half children per woman in the early part of the twenty-first century, while Australia and New Zealand have been somewhat closer to replacement fertility and the American pattern.[18]

The developed countries of northern Europe, which for our purposes here includes France, had a post-war baby boom similar to that of the US although a little less pronounced. In the UK, as in the US, fertility rates fell from the mid 1960s. In the UK women were having around one and two-thirds children by the early years of the current century, although this has picked up slightly since then. The picture is similar in Scandinavia. In France, fertility also fell, then picked up a little, but has never gone much below two children per woman. Part of the pick-up in recent years has probably been due to the growth of immigrant communities with higher (but falling) birth rates, as with Latinos in the US; this seems likely but is partly conjecture, as the gathering of statistics on ethnic lines is difficult in France.

Part of the modest rise in fertility across some of the developed world since the last years of the twentieth century has also been due to what demographers call the 'tempo effect': this is when social attitudes change and women start to acquire an education and careers, and so delay childbearing. During this period, fertility appears low. However, to some extent what they are doing is not having fewer children but having them later. A cohort's fertility often picks up somewhat in its later years, partly but not fully compensating for not having conceived earlier. This may seem like a technicality – and of course it is – but it means that a recent modest rise in recorded fertility in a developed country does not necessarily signal a long-lasting or meaningful rise in the birth rate but simply the end to an upward drift in age of childbearing. The human tide is capable of deceiving rips and hidden surges.

The tempo effect and variations of fertility rates across Europe may appear like minor wrinkles on the face of a generally low-fertility and ageing Europe, but they are worth examining because they make a difference. Germany, for example, has one of the lowest fertility rates in Europe, and the most dramatic fall was in East Germany. The collapse of Communism, the end of the comfortable certainties and support for working women and the lure of moving to the West for the young meant that the number of births in the territory fell from 200,000 in 1989, the last year of the German Democratic Republic, to 80,000 five years later. But the problem is not confined to East Germany. Since the early 1990s Germany's fertility rate has at least stopped falling, but has levelled out at around one and one-third children per woman, perhaps beginning to pick up to around one and a half. This will have potentially serious implications for the long term.

In southern Europe the story has been somewhat different, characterised by a generally higher starting point but in recent decades by a universally low level of fertility. It was not just in the suburbs of New York and Boston that Italian mammas with their large broods have long ago become a thing of the past; it is just as true of Milan and Rome. Southern European societies were less developed industrially than their northern neighbours before the Second World War, and so the post-war social transition has been more radical. Spain saw a post-war rise then fall in fertility, with a late but heavy drop in the 1980s, since when fertility has generally been even lower than Germany's. In Italy, fertility rates barely rose after the war and have fallen to persistently low levels. 'We are a dying country,' said the Italian health minister in 2015 when it was revealed that at barely half a million, Italy had had fewer babies born in 2014 than in any year since the country's unification more than a hundred and fifty years earlier (when, it should be noted, a larger crop of babies was produced from a population notably smaller than half its current size).[19]

As in the United States but a little later, Catholics in Europe were starting to have smaller families than Protestants.[20] While delayed childbearing may give rise to some recoveries among those countries with the lowest fertility rates, such as Germany and Italy, the effect will be limited at best; completed fertility for recent cohorts, a definitive indicator albeit one measurable only in retrospect, shows 1.5 children per woman for Germany and 1.6 for Italy, somewhat above current total fertility rates but well short of replacement level.

It is noteworthy that at mid-century the highest fertility rates in Europe were Catholic countries (France, Spain and Italy) and the lowest predominantly Protestant (Sweden and the United Kingdom), but that since then the situation has been reversed, with the lowest fertility rates found among Catholic countries. The reason for this seems to lie in varying attitudes to women, marriage and birth. Births outside marriage in the UK and Scandinavia have become common-place, but this has not been the case in Catholic southern Europe. While fertility rates within marriage do not vary markedly in various parts of Western Europe, fertility as a whole is supplemented by extra-marital birth in less traditional areas and not in countries such as Italy and Spain.[21] The lowest fertility, it seems, is experienced in societies caught on the one hand between modernity, individualism and female emancipation, which are associated with a delay in or indefinite post-ponement of marriage, and on the other hand by the traditions which frown on birth outside marriage.

Compare Denmark with its near replacement fertility rate and 45% rate of childbirth out of marriage with Spain where until recently only 12% of births were outside of marriage, or Greece, where the tally was 4%, and bear in mind that in both Spain and Greece fertility rates are around half a child less than in Denmark.[22] The experience of east Asia is similar to that of the Catholic countries of southern Europe and produces equally low fertility rates: indeed, it was as if, collectively, women had found themselves in the position of saying 'We will have only so many babies within marriage; the rest we will either have outside marriage or, if you do not approve of that, we will not have them at all.' Fertility rates, therefore, are especially low in countries where women are encouraged to get an education and a career but where birth outside marriage is frowned upon. They are much better in countries where attitudes to women in the workplace are more positive and provision is made to allow both female and male workers to combine careers with parenting.

It is often in countries such as Italy and Spain, where women are encouraged to get an education but attitudes in the workplace are less advanced, that fertility is lowest. When the Italian government launched a campaign to encourage women to have more children, and to have them earlier, there was an outburst of protest from women holding placards saying '*Siamo in attesta*' or a play on 'we are expecting' and 'we are waiting', referring to their expectations of enhanced facilities for combining work and maternity, while a Facebook group complained: 'The government wants us to have children – and fast. Lots of us don't want to, and in fact, we are waiting. For nurseries, welfare, salaries, benefits.'[23] The IMF has marked Italy down as one of the countries where least has been done to encourage women into work. Whereas once this might have been associated with higher fertility rates, now where women are given educational but not employment opportunities, or where it is made difficult for them to combine work and childbearing, they do not tend to bear children.

While the difference between various countries of the West can appear acute, the longer view reveals that their experiences conform to a pattern of resurgent then falling fertility in the post-war years. For example, there is around half a child difference in the fertility rates of say Germany and the Republic of Ireland, representing respectively the highest and lowest rates in the group, and whilst this difference will be material if sustained over the long term, these differences should nevertheless be seen within an overall picture of strong general movement into the last phase of the first demographic transition and, at least in some cases, beyond it.

Those countries in central Europe that became part of the West (specifically those that joined NATO and the EU) after the collapse of Communism have universally experienced falling and then very low fertility rates since 1945. The largest of these countries by population is Poland, where women were bearing nearly four children in the early 1950s but are today bearing fewer than one and a half. Again, these countries, from Bulgaria to Lithuania, are stuck in the middle ground of high female education levels and labour force participation but traditional notions of family and difficulties for women who try to combine careers with childbearing. Indeed, within Europe there is a very low fertility rate almost everywhere except the British Isles, Scandinavia, France and the Low Countries. Catholicism has no more spared Lithuania or Slovakia from this fate than it has saved Italy or Spain.

The Greying of the Whites

In January 2015 an unusual job advertisement appeared in the British press: the Queen, fast approaching her ninetieth year herself, was looking for someone to help her with sending the customary congratulations to those amongst her subjects in the UK who had reached the age of 100. 'You will be responsible for dealing with the requests from the public to ensure all eligible recipients receive the Queen's congratulatory card.' When the Queen first ascended the throne in 1952, only 3,000 such greetings were sent, but by the time of the advertisement, this had more than tripled.

Those living to over 100 are still a rarity in every country. There are around 15,000 centenarians in the UK today, a number that has tripled in a decade. The UK population aged over ninety also tripled between 1984 and 2014, reaching well over half a million by the latter date. Super old age was once an overwhelmingly female domain, but in the UK, whereas in the late 1980s there were four and a half women over ninety years old to every man, today that ratio is more like two and a half. More women are living to an exceptionally old age, but *many* more men are. And of course, the rise in the number of the very old is not limited to those entitled to receive Her Majesty's congratulations. Relative to their populations, Germany and the United States are not far behind the UK and Spain, while Sweden, France and Italy are ahead of it.[24]

So while the fertility side of the story has had some surprises along the way, with an upward bump after the Second World War and then a sharp fall in the last fifty years across most of the West, the mortality side of the story has not, with people living longer and longer whether in Europe or North America. Indeed, much of the ageing in developed societies today is the result of the baby boom, with the large cohort born immediately after the Second World War now in their seventies. This should come as no surprise. Decisions about family size depend on a range of social, cultural, economic and religious factors, so are highly variable, but in every society most people want to live longer. The extension of life therefore becomes almost ubiquitous as a goal of individuals, governments and society. The provision of health care to extend life has become one of the most central, if not *the* most central, function of government in the eyes of many of its citizens, and lifestyle advice and choices centre on healthy living and ways in which to delay the onset of mortal disease. In developed societies, fewer and fewer people die of contagious diseases such as flu or cholera, and private and public health care succeeds in minimising or eliminating these threats to life. More and more of us, meanwhile, die of the diseases generally associated with age.

These advances were already well under way in the more advanced countries of Europe well before the Second World War. The poor described by George Orwell in the 1930s 'in their row after row of little grey slum houses', however hard their lot, enjoyed a much higher level of material prosperity and longer lives than their ancestors portrayed by Charles Dickens. Their health was better, their life expectancy longer, they had fewer children and those they did have were much more likely to survive into adulthood. The process was extended after 1945 across the West: housing improved, education improved (almost always associated with longer life expectancy), and incomes and living standards rose across the board; finally, universal free or subsidised health care became the norm.

The most frequently used measures of a society's age look at its life expectancy at birth and its median age. US life expectancy rose from a little short of seventy to a little short of eighty between 1950 and 2010. Europe's record has been more impressive still. A number of European countries, such as France, Austria and Belgium, starting in 1950 with life expectancy not much above sixty-five have now surpassed eighty. The greater provision of the European welfare state and socialised health care, whatever else may be said for or against it, and perhaps healthier diets and lifestyles, have meant that the average west European outlives the average American by a couple of years.[25]

As in the United States, so in Europe lengthening life expectancy by a decade or more since 1950 has to some extent helped to offset the impact of slowing population growth – or even population decline – which would have resulted from falling fertility alone. The consistent lengthening of life expectancy has in recent years become patchy in the West; there are sub-groups in the US, for example – specifically lower-class white men – where it has ground to a halt or even slightly reversed itself. There was a very slight reduction in US life expectancy between 2014 and 2015, the result of drugs, alcoholism and what are known as 'diseases of despair'.[26] Widespread and growing obesity is not helping either. It is too early to say whether such a reverse will become significant, widespread and long lasting. It seems unlikely – the inexorable march to longer and longer life expectancy is so often thought of as an absolute given of demography – but once again, the human tide could be about to take an unexpected turn.

The general lengthening of life – even if there have been some recent small reversals – and fall in birth rates has meant that Western societies have aged, as can been seen from the median age. Whereas the median age in the United States from 1950 to 2015 went from thirty to thirty-eight, the rise was sharper in many European countries, which have experienced a sharper rise in life expectancy and a sharper drop in birth rates. In Spain, for example, it rose from twenty-eight to forty-three and in Italy from under twenty-nine to forty-six. In Germany too it has reached forty-six, the world's highest along with Japan. Probably for the first time in history, societies are emerging which are middle-aged and growing old. Today the average German – with decades of life ahead of him or her – has reached an age by which his or her great-grandparents could at birth have expected to be dead. Spaniards, Italians and most other people in the West are in a similar position.

Longer life expectancy and a higher median age are in many ways to be welcomed. People want to live longer, so it should be recognised that when on average they do, it is a good thing, enriching lives and opening opportunities and vistas for changes in work and for leisure once unimaginable for most people. Whole industries, such as leisure cruising, have grown up to give those in retirement adventures and experiences that their grandparents could only have dreamed of. What was once viewed with terror – growing old and sick and dependent on others – has become for many a golden sunset. The gains are social, not just individual. Older populations tend to be more peaceful and the societies in which they predominate are less crime-ridden, compensations perhaps for a reduction in the energy and creativity which comes with youth.

There is a proven link between ageing societies and falling crime, and crime rates have indeed fallen over the last few decades across much of the Western world. But there are two main and related concerns. The first is that an increase in the elderly population will give rise to an increase in the need for personal and health care that will over-tax the manpower resources of societies in which it is occurring. This became a central issue during the UK election campaign of 2017, when Prime Minister Theresa May proposed reforms to the current systems of social care and was then forced to back down, crucially losing her reputation for being 'strong and stable'. A lack of young people locally to meet these needs is likely to give rise to demands for further immigration, with further consequences to follow. Immigration is in any case probably only a temporary palliative for ageing; immigrant populations age and the flow of young people will dry up well beyond Europe. Besides, there is no reason to think that Europe will forever have the economic clout to draw in young immigrants from beyond its shores, even if it wanted to.

The second concern related to ageing is that where the elderly receive generous state benefits in retirement, these will be increasingly difficult for a shrinking workforce to bear. When, in 1889, Chancellor Otto von Bismarck first introduced old-age pensions for German workers living beyond the age of seventy, the chances of ever benefitting from them were slim. German life expectancy at the time was well short of fifty, so a worker living beyond the age of seventy was a lucky and fairly rare individual. What was put in place was real insurance – specifically, insurance against the poor living too long. Retirement ages since then have come down while life expectancies have soared, and this has placed intense pressure on the intergenerational compact which underpins the welfare state in many European countries. With a large ratio of young workers to the dependent elderly, as was the case in the early years of the welfare state, it was not difficult to finance old-age provision through transfer payments, even if they decreasingly resembled genuine insurance (since most expected eventually to enjoy their rewards).

This changes as more and more people live well beyond retirement age and the pool of young workers dries up. In order to stabilise government pensions spend as a share of GDP, it is estimated that benefits would have to be reduced by more than one-third in Germany and by over 40% in the Netherlands and the US. The alternative would be to increase the retirement age, by as much as seven years in the Netherlands for example.[27] Either of these options or a combination of them will be politically difficult, but with many European states already heavily indebted, it is not obvious that governments will for long have the option to postpone the problem by increasing debt. The spectre of poverty in old age and state bankruptcy is haunting Europe, with the United States not far behind.

The Mexican Wave

With persistently low birth rates and an insatiable appetite for labour, the developed countries of Europe and North America have hoovered up populations from the developing world over the past decades. Immigrants have come from societies with booming fertility – as we will see later – and in many such countries the departure of thousands of people has not prevented their own populations from growing rapidly. Culturally and demographically, the impact has been greater on the receiving rather than the sending nation, not only preventing what would otherwise have been plummeting labour-force numbers in the host nation but also changing its ethnic complexion. In the case of the United States, the bulk of that immigration has come from Latin America and in particular, at least until recently, from its immediate southern neighbour, Mexico.

In the 1920s, when immigration controls were imposed in the US, the debate in Congress made it quite transparent that the objective was to 'defend America's white majority', to keep America as white and as Anglo-Saxon as possible, with as few as possible coming from southern or eastern Europe and ideally none at all from anywhere in Asia or Africa, and for the ensuing forty years this was the view informing US immigration policy. Then in the mid 1960s, along with the liberalisation of views on families and the role of women, a change in attitudes to race meant a complete overturning of US immigration law. Suddenly the gates were open again and this time those best positioned to take advantage were not those from the British Isles or Western Europe (they were enjoying their own post-war economic boom), nor those from eastern Europe (they were locked in the Soviet empire), but those to the US's immediate south, the poor of Latin America and particularly Mexico, their numbers swelling through their own demographic transition and the tantalising prospects of the American dream just a river away. Conveniently, this coincided with the nosedive in the US fertility rate.

America's population continued to expand towards 300 million (and beyond), but now this growth was driven upward not by the arrival of the huddled masses from Europe at Staten Island, nor by arrivals in the maternity wards, but rather by arrivals from over the Rio Grande, from Mexico and other Latin American countries and, to a lesser extent, from Asia. Today's America has been shaped by the choices of people since the 1960s to have fewer children and by big shifts in social attitudes to race, as a result of which the doors were opened wide to non-European immigration. People from across the world were eager to take advantage of the opportunity and embrace the American dream.

There was already a Mexican population in place when the US annexed what was then the northern half of Mexico in 1848, although it was probably not much greater than 100,000 and many of these left.[28] Yet despite this and the repatriation and deportations of the depression era, the Mexican population grew steadily, and by 1970 the census showed over 9 million Latinos in the US, of whom around half were Mexican.[29] At this stage the number began to rise sharply: by 1973 there were already 6 or 7 million Mexicans in the country. By 1980 there were nearly 15 million Hispanics, representing more than 6% of the population, of which around 60% were Mexicans, the next largest group being Puerto Ricans (15%) and Cubans (12%). The latter were given open immigration rights as part of the government's anti-Castro policy.[30] Growth continued well into the twenty-first century. According to the 2010 census, Hispanics as a whole were over 16% of the population, outstripping the traditional largest minority, blacks, who comprised below 14%, while at 50 million, Latinos, two-thirds of whom are now Mexican or of Mexican origin, had grown more than fivefold in forty years; those self-identifying as fully white were now below two-thirds of the total and as fully or partly white little more than three-quarters.[31]

While most of the growth of the Latino population since the 1960s was driven by immigration, it was also partly 'natural': with a young demographic profile and high fertility, the Hispanic birth rate was half as high again as that of whites and for Mexicans in particular higher still.[32] Indeed, in the early twenty-first century, with immigration slowing, births to Mexicans in the US outstripped arrivals of Mexicans.[33] This great migration to the US may not have been as large in relative terms as the migration at the end of the nineteenth and early twentieth centuries: back then, the foreign-born population of the US peaked at around 14% while in the late 1990s it was around 8%.[34] However, in absolute terms it has been the largest inflow the country has experienced. Furthermore, it made the US by far the largest global recipient of migrants.[35]

Yet there are signs that the great Mexican inflow into the United States is abating. Just as demography and economics drove migrants inward, so improvements in the Mexican economy and sharply falling fertility rates in Mexico (now not much above replacement level) and associated falling population growth – nearly two-thirds down on its peak level – have reduced the flow out of Mexico. At the same time the post-2008 economic downturn in the United States has reduced the demand for cheap labour, which many of the latest Mexican arrivals were satisfying, and one estimate suggests that from 2010 there were half a million fewer Mexicans in the United States than in 2007.[36]

The changing complexion of the new America was nowhere more dramatic than in California, where the share of the population classi- fied as white European fell from 70% to 40% in the thirty years from 1980 to 2010. This shifting ethnic demography has had political conse- quences of two sorts. First, the minority vote has come to matter more as it has grown. Second, the still dominant white vote has to some extent reflected a backlash against rapid ethno-demographic change. Based on the white vote alone – which was still dominant until quite recently – Barack Obama would not have become president in 2009. Meanwhile, many see Donald Trump's emergence and triumph as a last-gasp effort not so much to 'make America great again' but to 'keep it white for as long as possible'. Whether or not cosmopolitan elites wish to see it (or are comfortable discussing it), a number of serious studies of contemporary populism suggest that it is not, in essence, the cry of the dispossessed or of those losing out as a result of globalisation, but rather the protest of a single ethnic group that has long been retreating from global predominance and now sees itself declining at home. As the British newspaper the *Independent* argued, noting the rapidity of ethnic change in the US: 'Racial anxiety is deep in white American ethnicity. Now Trump has weaponised it.'[37] Areas most unsettled by mass immigration were the ones most likely to back Trump, while rapid ethnic change rather than Rust Belt economic resentment is a better explanation of populism in the US, when median wages are at last rising and unemployment is below 5%. Trump's most iconic pledge was not to reopen the coalmines but to build a wall to prevent Mexican migration, and the reasons behind it were not poor economic performance or youth unemployment, even if these have additionally contributed to the frustrations fuelling the growth in his support.

Donald Trump's famous Mexican wall, the characterising theme of the 2016 presidential election, is perhaps best conceived as a demographic wall, designed to ward off the consequences of past fertility choices that have led to the numbers of WASPs stagnating while those of Latinos boom. Yet as noted, more Mexicans have *left* the US in recent years than arrived, itself the result of a waning in the birth rate in Mexico (where it is now below twenty per thousand, whereas in the early 1970s it was over forty) as well as of rising economic prospects back home.[38] In parallel, many Latinos are fast assimilating into American life with the third generation even ceasing to speak Spanish. Nevertheless, their presence has transformed vast swathes of the United States and American life. (It is notable that Trump's closest rivals for the Republican nomination in 2016 – Marco Rubio and Ted Cruz – are either fully or partly of Latino origin and the next runner up, Jeb Bush, is married to a Latina.)

The Rest of the West Follows Suit

The demographic fate of the rest of the West has largely resembled the United States, with a post-war baby boom ending in the mid 1960s and eventually being followed by mass immigration from the global south. This has been true of Canada, Australia and New Zealand and Western Europe. The immigrants to Europe have generally come from former colonies or from non-European countries with which the host nation has been associated: from south Asia and the Caribbean in the case of the UK, north Africa in the case of France, and Turkey (a German ally before and during the First World War) in the case of Germany. Spain has had its own arrival of Latin Americans.

As in other matters demographic, the UK has been at the forefront of developments. Until the post-war era the only significant inflows from outside the British Isles since the Norman invasion had been of Europeans, perhaps 50,000 Huguenots in the sixteenth and

seventeenth centuries and perhaps 200,000 Jews in the decades immediately before the First World War.[39] The former had integrated
entirely into British society, to the point where speaking of 'Huguenot
communities' would be meaningless. The latter, themselves increasingly intermarrying and assimilating into the local population, represented even at their demographic peak never more than 1% of the
total population. Individuals had appeared from the colonies from
time to time, but had never created demographically sustainable
communities.

Small black populations in some ports, particularly Liverpool,
merged into the wider population. This changed after 1945, starting
with an inflow from the Caribbean. By 1971 there were over 300,000
West Indian-born people in the UK and by the mid 1970s the
community had reached around half a million.[40] A larger wave of
immigrants came from the Indian subcontinent, either direct from
India and the newly created state of Pakistan (and later Bangladesh) or
from the descendants of south Asian migrants to east Africa. Often
the former were men who came in search of work: in 1961 there were
more than five Pakistani-born men in the UK for every Pakistani-
born woman. Yet in due course family reunions were more common
than returns to the homeland. Further migrations have occurred from
a wide variety of sources in recent decades, often in the form of
asylum seekers and economic migrants or involving movement
within the EU. The scale of immigration in the post-war era now
looks modest by comparison to the early years of the twenty-first
century. In some twelve-month periods since 2000 more people were
arriving in Britain than had been the case in the whole period
1066–1950.[41]

The impact on the ethnic make-up of the UK of this turn of the
tide has been profound. While in the immediate post-war era those
of white British and white British/Irish origin would have made
up almost the entire population, by 2011 those defining themselves as
white British had declined to just over four-fifths. The number of
whites overall fell from 91.3% to 86% of the population of England and
Wales in a period of just ten years. Asians were over 7% of the population and those identifying as black (Afro-Caribbean, African or black
British) were more than 3%.[42] People of non-European origin made up

40% of the population in the UK's largest cities and in London outnumbered whites in every age group up to twenty.[43] The population of immigrant origin is much younger than the indigenous population; proportionately, there are twice as many under tens in the Bangladeshi and Pakistani communities as in the white British one. Although fertility rates of minorities have tended to converge downwards to those of the white British population (indeed Indian fertility rates may be lower), with continuing inflows of immigrants, the population of white British origin may be heading to below 60% of the total by the middle of the twenty-first century in the UK, while non-whites will rise over half a century from around 10% to around 30%.[44] The balance will be made up of people of continental European extraction.

The picture in France and Germany is similar. In both countries a mixture of heavy immigration flows from beyond Europe (plus significant inflows from within Europe) and the low fertility rate of the indigenous population over an extended period has radically reshaped the ethnic demography. France had already experienced – indeed encouraged – immigration from other parts of Europe before the Second World War, and this continued subsequently. It has received over 2.5 million Italians, 1.5 million Spaniards and over a million Portuguese. Since 1945 it has hosted a vast influx from north Africa, initially of *pieds-noirs* fleeing an independent Algeria but increasingly those indigenous to north Africa and to other parts of former French colonial Africa, a total of around 3 million.[45] As with Pakistanis in the UK, initially many immigrants from north Africa were men who had come alone to work, but increasingly they managed to bring their families as well. France continues a tradition of 'assimilationist Republicanism' and lacks official data on minorities, but it is estimated that more than 10% of people living in France in the early part of the twenty-first century were foreign-born and a somewhat lower proportion were Muslim. Again as in the UK, the population of immigrant origin is younger than the indigenous French population, and this suggests future growth even without further immigration.

In Germany, with its exceptionally weak fertility rate, the numbers are also striking. One source believes that as much as 30% of the population was either born abroad or is descended since 1945 from immigrants.[46] As in the case of France, migrants to Germany have come both from southern Europe (often the Balkans, particularly Yugoslavia or the former Yugoslavia) and from the Muslim lands further south (particularly Turkey). Initially, Turks came as guest workers, but as elsewhere, families have followed. The gaining of citizenship has been more difficult in Germany than in Britain and France, with rights depending more on origin than place of birth or residence, although this has changed somewhat in recent years. The pattern of immigrant groups being younger and having higher fertility, already noted in France and the United Kingdom, appears to apply to Germany as well. This was the backdrop to the swell of immigrants trying to get into Germany in 2015, many but far from all fleeing from the Syrian civil war. Chancellor Angela Merkel insisted 'wir schaffen es' – 'we can cope', 'we can get it done' – but the backlash from a large number of her citizens suggests that there is far from a consensus on this matter.

In addition to arrivals from the south, since the fall of the Berlin Wall and expansion of the EU there has been a mass movement of people *within* Europe, from east to west. As in the US, these shifts have not only changed the ethnic composition but have been a major component in fuelling new political forces in reaction, whether UKIP and the Brexit vote in the UK, the Front National in France or Alternative für Deutschland in Germany. In France the vote for the Front National has risen steadily along with the size of immigrant communities as well as concern about their radicalisation. The slogan of Marine Le Pen, runner-up in the 2017 presidential election – '*On est chez nous*', which is perhaps best translated as 'this is our place' – is about identity and a dividing line between the 'indigenous' French and more recent arrivals. As with Trump, Le Pen's support can best be explained as a reaction to ethnic change rather than as a response to economic woes. More important than worries about economic inequality, today's populism in the developed world can only fully be understood in its demographic context. For example, there is a clear correlation in the UK between changes in the ethnicity of a local district in the decade prior to the European referendum, and the share of voters opting for Brexit. Attitudes to immigration correlate more closely to an 'out' vote than to any other factors, other than to the EU itself. Moreover, support for Germany's far-right AfD surged after the highly publicised mass migrations of Syrians in the summer of 2015.

Without its early lead in the demographic transformation, Britain could not have exported its people to run an empire on which the sun never set. Without the sharp drop in fertility rates that followed – and the simultaneous rapid expansion of populations in lands where Britain had once ruled – mass immigration and the arrival of a more multicultural society would almost certainly not have happened. If one wishes to understand why Californians speak English or why there are five times more Muslims than Methodists in the UK, consider the great forces of population change in recent times.

Just as the United States had implemented policies to preserve its (predominantly north-west European) ethnic character, so Australia introduced a 'white Australia' policy early in the twentieth century, specifically to stave off Asian immigration. As with the United States, so in Australia, a change in attitudes to race and ethnicity meant that these policies were relaxed in the post-war era. By 2011 a quarter of Australians had been born overseas and a further fifth were the children of at least one overseas-born parent. The UK continued to be the largest single source of immigration, although immigrants from the UK represented only a fifth of the total of foreign-born Australians, with 15% coming from various Asian countries (mostly China, India, Vietnam and the Philippines). Reporting ancestry (where some people cited more than one ancestor), only 55% claimed to be of English, Scottish or Irish descent while 35% claimed to be of 'Australian' origin (very few of whom, it can be assumed, were fully or even partly of Aboriginal descent). Those descended from Italians, Germans, Dutch and Greeks totalled 13% of the population, while Chinese and Indians represented a still modest but fast-growing 6%.[47] Australia's essentially Anglo-ethnic character, which once seemed insuperable, is rapidly waning.

Is the European in Retreat?

Declining fertility of people of European origin, whether in Europe or in demographically 'Europeanised' lands, along with the great inflow of non-European peoples into these lands, has changed the world in ways that would have been unimaginable at the peak of European ascendancy in the late nineteenth century.

The peoples of what would become the West were, until the fifteenth century, not particularly significant on the global stage. Their collective religious dream of imposing themselves on the Holy Land had been defeated by the Muslims and they were hemmed in by Islam to the south, by the ocean to the west, by Arctic seas and wilderness to the north, and by wide expanses peopled by often hostile nomads to the east. In retrospect, perhaps the seeds of Europe's rise were visible, but it might not then have been expected that the people of this small peninsula would come to dominate the globe. By the start of the twentieth century it was difficult to imagine anyone but the Europeans as overlords of the planet.

Europe's people had subdued vast areas of the Americas. The same was true of Australasia and might have been in the process of coming true in southern Africa. Where Europeans had not settled, they held political control by means of their empires in most of Asia and Africa, and where they did not incorporate territories formally, such as in China, they still held great sway. Economically, the industrialised areas of the world were almost exclusively European (including Europeanised America) and lands beyond the US and the European heartland (including parts of eastern Europe and Russia) were of global economic significance only for their provision of raw materials and in some cases as markets. None of this, the human tide shows us, would have been possible without an essentially demographic base. Although Europeans started to circle the globe in the fifteenth century, it was not until the nineteenth century, with their dramatic population explosion and expansion, accompanied by technological and industrial advances, that they were able to dominate it.

We are perhaps too close to events to see what a dramatic reversal the twentieth century has been for the peoples of western European origin. The end of formal empire was a largely political event, and initially did not seem to end the European economic and military dominance of the globe. Yet there was no inherent reason to believe that the technologies that had facilitated European demographic growth and economic and political dominance would forever remain the exclusive domain of Europeans. Signs of the end of European domination came even before the outbreak of the First World War: the resistance of the Boers, albeit people of European extraction, shook the British Empire. The defeat of Russia by Japan in the Russo-Japanese War of 1904–5 dispelled – or should have dispelled – any illusions of the supposed invincibility of the white man.

Today Europe and the United States and the wider traditionally white Anglosphere continue to be relatively prosperous societies by global standards, but that relative prosperity is no longer anything like a monopoly. Highly prosperous societies have emerged in east Asia and are emerging elsewhere. Demographically, even after accounting for the large inflow of non-Europeans, the West has waned significantly when compared with other regions and cultures. On the basis that the overall size of an economy is nothing other than the product of the per capita income and size of the population, this has inevitably meant the waning of Western economic dominance.

In 1950 the United States and the rest of what was then the developed world represented between a fifth and a quarter of the world's population; today it comprises below 15%, and by mid-century it will be barely a tenth. In power purchasing parity terms, the West commanded around two-thirds of the world's economy in the middle of the twentieth century, but this figure is likely to be around 40% by the middle of the twenty-first.[48] Having triumphed in the cold war, the West still dominates the world militarily; effectively, here, 'the West' can be defined as the United States, assisted by its NATO allies. It is debatable how long this will continue with challenges from the world's other great civilisations, particularly China, whose economy is already believed to have surpassed that of the US on the above basis.

However, comparing the demography of the US to the demography of its current or erstwhile global rivals, Germany, Japan, Russia and China, it is the US which is in the best shape.[49] Large powers such as China and Russia, and potential powers such as Brazil, India and Indonesia, are experiencing either low or fast-falling fertility rates. Both their flagging demographic expansion and the institutions of international order may limit the ability of these powers to challenge established Western global hegemony. Meanwhile, areas of population explosion in the Middle East and Africa, which we will investigate in later chapters, lack economic development and are experiencing fragmentation. Before we come to look at today's prospective rival for global hegemony, however – namely China, or the Middle Eastern and African lands of demographic explosion – we must first examine a recent rival, namely Russia, along with members of the erstwhile USSR and the rest of what was once the Eastern bloc. Russia, always ambiguously partly in, partly out of Europe, was a late but rapid adopter of the European demographic transition in the late nineteenth and early twentieth centuries, and after 1945 once again the human tide turned east.

7

Russia and the Eastern Bloc from 1945

The Demography of Cold War Defeat

On 11 March 1985, hours after the death of Party secretary Konstantin Chernenko, the Politburo of the Communist Party of the Soviet Union elected Mikhail Gorbachev Chernenko's successor at what was, by Soviet standards, the tender age of fifty-four. Chernenko had held the position for only a year, inheriting it in a state of terminal illness from Yuri Andropov at whose funeral he could barely even raise a salute (and at which, according to Gorbachev, Margaret Thatcher's doctor was able to forecast the date of Chernenko's own demise to within a few weeks).[1] As Gorbachev surveyed his realm he was, as he put it later, 'immediately faced with an avalanche of problems'.[2] The USSR may well have been one of only two global superpowers, a nuclear power, the largest country on earth by surface area, and the centre of a socialist camp stretching from Germany to Vietnam, but signs of severe ill health were showing.

Many of the problems Gorbachev described as descending on him like an avalanche had deep roots in the demography of the country, as was being borne out in the ageing of the party leadership, whose enfeebled senior cadre had elected in Chernenko a man within thirteen months of death. For just as we can learn much from Britain's demography by understanding the family life and fertility of its queens, so we can learn much about the Soviets by seeing how their leadership aged. The gerontocracy which, until Gorbachev, had been running the country, was representative of a demographic retreat at the heart of the Soviet Union. Indeed, a decade earlier Gorbachev had commented to Andropov that most of the members of the Politburo running the country already had one foot in the grave.[3] The young, Red revolutionary avant-garde of 1917 (even the most senior Bolshevik, Lenin, was under fifty, and most were much younger) had turned into a greying establishment, mouthing tired revolutionary clichés nobody any longer believed. The greying of the establishment was symbolic of the greying of the country as a whole, or at least of its Slavic heartland.

Just as rapid population growth had been a precondition of Russia's emergence as a superpower by the middle of the twentieth century, so population decline was fundamental to the issues with which Gorbachev had to wrestle. True, a grossly inefficient command-and-control economic system lay at the heart of the country's economic problems; the queues which formed for the most basic provisions, the sloth and decay in factories, the slapdash approach to health and safety which caused the Chernobyl nuclear disaster – none of this can simply be put down to demography: but whatever the changing needs of the economy, a drying up in the flow of new Russian workers, a reflection of an earlier slowing of the birth rate, made it harder and harder to disguise the underlying problems. Whereas in the past an endless flow of fresh workers allowed economic inefficiency to be patched over and created an impression of economic dynamism and growth, now there were as many hands retiring from the factories or fields as entering them, and this made it difficult to sustain the mirage of economic growth.

Gorbachev's problems were not limited to an underperforming economy at home. As he looked across his southern border he could see a war in Afghanistan in which Soviet troops had been bogged down for years. Here casualties were mounting as Soviet troops failed to exert control over the country and prop up the puppet regime in Kabul against its Islamist adversaries. The Soviet Union's problems in Afghanistan were no more purely demographic in nature than were its economic problems back home. The topography of the country and the famously resistant culture of its people played a major part in Moscow's headache, not to mention the support the rebels received from the West; but all of this was made much more difficult for the Soviets by the fact that their own army could no longer draw on an ever-growing cohort of recruits from the Slavic heartlands but instead had to rely more and more on the polyglot youth of the Caucasus and central Asia, whose own loyalties were suspect and

whose lack of command of the Russian language made the management of the campaign more difficult.

The inability of the Soviets to master Afghanistan had many causes,
but some basic demographic data tells us an important part of the
story and this has to do with the demography of Afghanistan and not
just the USSR. By the time the Soviet Union collapsed, Afghanistan's
population was growing nearly ten times as fast as Russia's. (As
recently as the mid 1950s it had been growing more slowly than
Russia's.) The median age in Russia was thirty-three; in Afghanistan,
it was below sixteen.

As ever, we need to be careful with historical counterfactuals, and
to be aware that the picture for the Soviet Union as a whole was better
than for Russia alone (although, as discussed, this itself gave rise to
problems of military reliability and uniformity). Nevertheless, despite
the challenges of the terrain and enthusiasm for supporting the rebels
from Reagan to Riyadh, we should wonder whether, had the demography been the other way around, had Russia been young and growing and Afghanistan experiencing feeble population growth and
ageing, the shoe might not have been on the other foot. Just as positive
Russian demography had stood the country in good stead as it faced
the ageing Germans, so negative Russian demography let it down
in the face of the demographically vigorous Afghans. A young,
growing population, even if smaller in size, is difficult to defeat on its
home patch, as the West itself was to learn in Afghanistan and Iraq.
Perhaps Gorbachev was only partly aware of it, but as he wrestled
with the problems of the Soviet system and Soviet society – from
ossified Leninist orthodoxy to alcoholism, from Afghan mujahideen
to the newly self-confident leadership of the West of Thatcher and
Reagan – he faced the fact that history had dealt him an almost impossible demographic hand.

Russian Retreat

Gorbachev might have complained of his problems, but when the
Bolsheviks had come to power in 1917 the problems were of a quite
different order of magnitude. A still 'backward' country with a

predominantly peasant population, Russia had been severely damaged by four years of war, was warding off German and Austrian military advances and was running short of supplies. Meanwhile a civil war was looming, which made matters worse still.

Yet from a population perspective, things were in good shape, and the legacy of positive demography would see the Communists through many a decade of military and economic struggle. In the late tsarist period, it will be recalled, women had still been having exceptionally large families, averaging around seven children, mortality rates were falling fast with the arrival of rudimentary education and health care, and the population was growing rapidly – much like Britain's experience nearly a hundred years earlier, although because it was happening later, it was happening faster.

Russia then experienced a classic case of demographic transition, with falling mortality rates followed by falling fertility and the gradual slowdown in the growth of the population. From the mid 1920s to the mid 1940s fertility halved from six to three children per woman – a drop which had taken Britain twice as long to achieve in the late Victorian and Edwardian periods. As women became more urban, better educated and were given opportunities to enter the industrial workforce, so they chose to have fewer children, a pattern which had already been seen in the UK and Germany and which would sweep the wider world. And whatever the other shortcomings of the Lenin and Stalin regime – and they were legion, with their oppression, their terror and their gulags – credit should be given for efforts to emancipate women. Between 1897 and 1939, female literacy rose from one in five to four in five.[4] This alone tells us much: literate women simply do not, en masse, carry on having broods of six or seven.

After the Second World War fertility rates for the USSR as a whole continued to drop, reaching replacement level during the 1970s, after which they continued to fall. Urbanisation and female education can explain much of this, but there are also specifically Soviet aspects to the decline. In contraception, as in many other fields, the Soviet Union did not succeed in providing consumer choice or the quality of consumer goods that were available in the West. Long after the average worker in West Virginia or Westphalia could assume the easy availability of a car or the Pill, Soviet consumers were still relying on broken-down buses and abortions. Family planning was no different in this respect from anything else. Abortions, legalised again in 1955, were for most women the only easily available form of contraception. It is estimated that in the later Soviet period the average Soviet woman was having an average of six or seven abortions in the course of her life,[5] and the number of abortions per annum during the 1980s fluctuated around the 7 million mark.[6]

Abortion was never an easy choice and was invariably a highly unpleasant experience. Olga from St Petersburg, who had already had seven abortions and expected to have to undergo seven more, reported her experience in the later days of the Soviet Union:

> Then it's your turn, and you go into a hall splattered with blood where two doctors are aborting seven or eight women at the same time; they're usually very rough and rude, shouting at you about keeping your legs wide open . . . if you're very lucky they give you a little sedative, mostly Valium. Then it's your turn to stagger out . . .[7]

Meanwhile childbearing was little more attractive, one mother recounting:

> The doctors keep screaming at you 'Get on with it.' The treatment is inevitably rough, impersonal; we're treated as if sex and birth are a big crime. There was so much pain that I had nightmares about it for years afterward – the brutality of our maternity wards are the best contraceptive method we have; very few of us *ever* want to go through it again.[8]

Despite falling fertility rates in the 1950s and 1960s, however, the USSR's population was still growing fairly rapidly just as Britain's had done during the Edwardian period thanks to a phenomenon known as 'demographic momentum'. Births per woman may have been slowing, but thanks to earlier population rises, there were plenty of young women having children while the elderly and therefore those mostly likely to die were a small share of the population. What should have constituted a powerful demographic momentum, however, was blunted by the huge losses Russia incurred as a result of the wars, famines and purges between 1914 and 1945. There is much debate about precisely how many deaths in the Soviet Union were directly due to Stalin and Hitler, whether through famines, the purges, the *Einsatzgruppen* or deportations of nationalities deemed 'disloyal'. What is not in question is the sheer scale of the disaster, suffering and loss of life that took place between Tsar Nicholas II taking Russia to war in 1914 and Stalin seeing off the Nazis thirty-one years later. These events all took place against the backdrop of such a strong inbuilt demographic momentum however that, through it all, the population of the Soviet Union kept growing. Despite Lenin, Stalin and Hitler, in the face of two world wars, a civil war, famines and terror, the human tide kept rolling on. The population of what would become the USSR was one hundred and twenty-five million in 1897; by 1970 it had nearly doubled to not much short of a quarter of a billion.[9] By the time of its demise, the Soviet Union boasted nearly 287 million people. Robust population growth to 1939 had been hugely set back by the war, but then picked up again after 1945 and continued into the 1960s. However, as it then sank, declining growth was by now built into the population just as it was into the economy. In the face of low fertility, demographic momentum eventually weakens. In the 1970s and 1980s, the average annual growth rate of the Soviet Union was below 1% and falling, and while this was not in itself catastrophic, the ethnic picture which underlay it was worrying for many in the Soviet establishment, as we will soon see.

Besides the cataclysmic course of history, the other factor which restrained Soviet population growth was the failure of life expectancy to increase significantly even once the wars were over and the terrors diminished. Life expectancy for Russian men was a little over sixty in the late 1950s and by the late 1980s had only increased to just under sixty-four, a rise barely a third of what was achieved across most of the West.[10] In fact, disastrously, this was to be a high point of Russian life expectancy and after the fall of the Soviet Union, far from catching up with the levels achieved in the West, it went into reverse and at the start of the twenty-first century was back to its 1950s level. (Since then there has been some improvement, but in 2017 male life expectancy had barely exceeded its late 1980s peak.)

Unlike Britain or the United States, Russia in the Soviet period was largely a closed system of population, with little immigration and little emigration. The walls of the Soviet Union were high and it was difficult as well as unattractive to get in, and almost impossible to get out. In the 1970s a campaign was launched for the right of Soviet Jews to emigrate to Israel, but in the whole period up to Gorbachev less than half a million left, which was significant for Israel perhaps but a drop in the ocean for a Soviet Union with a quarter of a billion people.

The overall numbers, meanwhile, do not tell us what was happening beneath the surface and specifically at the level of individual nationalities. Russia was officially, of course, the Soviet Union, on paper a state with many equal nations, many of which had their own Soviet republics or at least autonomous regions. Russia might have hosted the capital city and its people might have been lauded as the instigators of the first successful socialist revolution, but formally the state had no preference for one national or ethnic group over another. All were supposed to be brothers, united in bonds of fraternal internationalist solidarity.

The reality was different, and this shows markedly in demographic terms. Russia may have seemed materially 'backward' to West Europeans (notwithstanding its unquestionable cultural and scientific achievements), but from the perspective of the outlying regions, Russia's great cities were metropolises and its people sophisticates. The great industrialised regions, whether the Donbas in eastern Ukraine or the rapidly assembled factories in the Urals, were mostly in regions inhabited by the Slavic core – either Russians, Byelorussians or Ukrainians. These were the first populations to urbanise and become fully literate, and were also, as would be expected, the areas first to experience the demographic transition – with attendant population expansion – while the Caucasus and central Asia were still stuck in the Malthusian trap. In addition, there was a degree of pressurised and possibly phoney Russification, such as the recategorisation of between 3 and 4.5 million rural Ukrainians between 1926 and 1959.[11]

From the vantage point of the mid twentieth century, it is not surprising that within the Soviet Union it felt as if the future belonged to Russians and their related people. But as the Russian population growth started to slow, so the outlying areas, particularly those in which Muslims predominated, began to undergo their own modernisation. This was no longer just socialism in one country; it was multiple stages of the demographic transition in one country. As ever, infant mortality serves as an excellent indicator of social and economic progress. Fewer than sixty babies per thousand were dying in Russia by the late 1950s – great progress versus earlier periods but still very high – while in Tajikistan the rate was nearly three times as high and other central Asian and Caucasian republics were experiencing similar levels. By the early 1990s infant mortality had fallen across what was by then the former Soviet Union, but whereas by then in Russia an extra thirty-seven babies per thousand were making it to their first birthdays compared to the 1950s, in Tajikistan it was an extra sixty-three.[12] Infant mortality was still much higher in central Asia than in Russia – three times higher in Uzbekistan, for example, in the mid 1970s – but the fall in infant mortality had been much greater in the more backward areas, and its sharper fall contributed to their faster population growth.[13]

It was not just that more of the children in central Asia and the Caucasus were surviving than in the past; more were being born when compared with Russia. By the early 1990s Tajik women were still on average having more than four children. By then, Russian women were having barely one each.[14] The fertility rates of Uzbekistan remained at least two and a half children per woman higher than in Russia throughout this period and at some points was three and a half children higher.[15] Uzbekistan was fairly typical of the other republics with predominantly Muslim populations, including what were eventually to become the independent states of Azerbaijan in the Caucasus and Kazakhstan in central Asia. In fact, the data at republic level understates the case at nationality level, since there were non-Russians in Russia increasing Russia's fertility numbers while there were ethnic Russians in Uzbekistan reducing its fertility. There were Muslim minorities within the Russian Republic (RSFSR) which showed the same characteristics: between 1926 and 1970 the Russian population grew 60% while the number of Tartars more than doubled.[16]

With a slowdown in Russian population growth and a rise in the growth among the minorities, the Russian share of the population inevitably started to wane. The shifts were at first fairly modest:

between the 1959 census and the 1970 census, the Russian share of the population fell a little over one percentage point and the Turkic and/or Muslim share rose by nearly two percentage points.[17] This might appear to be a small shift, but until this point it had been assumed that Russification was an ongoing process, somehow tied to progress and socialism; the 1970 census therefore came as something of a shock to Soviet officials.[18]

The trends continued after 1970. The Russian population as a share of the total Soviet population outside the RSFSR (that is, outside the core Russian areas which were to become the Russian Federation) fell from nearly 18% in 1959 to around 14% in 1979.[19] It felt as if the great outward movement of Russians, after centuries of aggressive expansion, was reversing itself. In the last thirty years of the Soviet Union the ethnically Muslim population doubled while the Russian population grew by little more than a quarter. The republics of the Soviet Union with Muslim majorities saw their populations rise from just under 13% of the population in 1959 to just under 20% in 1989,[20] and it was projected that Russians would be not much more than a third of the total Soviet population by the middle of the twenty-first century.[21]

Meanwhile, in addition to their numerical rise there was effective de-Russification taking place among the populations of the central Asian and Caucasian republics. Surveys of the population of the Soviet Union outside the Russian core suggested that fewer and fewer were competent in the Russian language.[22] In part this may have reflected the attitudes and aptitudes of indigenous nationalities, but it also reflected the ending of significant migration of Russians to central Asia, and of its partial reversal. This followed Khrushchev's Virgin Lands policy in which official policy had been to boost agricultural production by settling Soviet citizens (predominantly from the Slavic core) in peripheral areas judged to have agricultural potential. By the early 1960s the policy was clearly failing and the movement of young Russians to the outlying areas was over. The waning Russian presence in the periphery threatened to reduce the unity and coherence of the state and suggested a reversal of what had once seemed an unstoppable trend of Russification, cultural and demographic.

Like the Anglo-Saxons in America and the English and Afrikaners in South Africa, the Russians were discovering that the advantage to those first out of the Malthusian trap of unconstrained population growth was only temporary; it was only a matter of time before others caught up. The inevitable rise and rise of the Great Russians (i.e. those belonging to the 'core' Russian nationality and not related Slavonic ethnicities such as 'Little Russians'/Byelorussians or Ukrainians) was no more inevitable, it turned out, than the triumph of socialism: Russians were no more destined to fill the earth than the Anglo-Saxons had been; they were not even destined to fill the Soviet Union's periphery.

As ever, we have to be a little sceptical of the data and in particular of the classifications which were used. Anthropologists today would blanch at the cut-and-dried approach often taken in the Soviet Union in relation to what constituted a 'nationality' and who was to be defined as what. Categories of ethnicity in the Soviet Union were no more 'perennial' or 'natural' than anywhere else. The distinctions were in some cases arbitrary or at least debatable (e.g. the designation of Jews as a nationality), and in the cases of non-European peoples, often imposed, along with systematised and regularised languages and folklore. To some extent, despite the Marxist-Leninist rhetoric, Soviet ethnology was not very different from the European approch taken by powers beyond Europe and was at least in part constructed the better to organise and manage the subject populations.

Political Responses

The Soviet Union was not a land in which matters were supposed to take their own course – it was a planned society. For Soviet ideologues, society and the economy were to be run to meet specific goals. With effectively no free market or private property, the state was supposed to provide everything for its citizens from education and a home to a job and a holiday – not to mention a maternity ward and a funeral, the archetypal 'cradle to grave'. It should come as no surprise, therefore, that demography was not going to be left to chance. But while it turned out that the state could not arbitrarily determine how many children would be born or how many people in any year would die, and therefore it could not entirely control the population's size and make-up, it could and did react to population trends in the country.

The pressures on Soviet policy makers were numerous and conflicting, and this perhaps explains the slow and relatively ineffective nature of policy making. First, party doctrine was always pro-natalist. Marx had been explicitly anti-Malthusian, arguing that constraints on population were not 'natural' but rather the product of oppressive, exploitative and extractive political and economic systems. Malthus, as far as Marx was concerned, was an apologist of the bourgeoisie for the impoverishment of the peasants and workers, dressing up their poverty as an inevitable consequence of biology and ecology rather than the outcome of an outdated political economy no longer in line with the requirements of the age. For Marx, then, population control was unnecessary; under socialism, there would be plenty for all. From the perspective of doctrine, therefore, the Soviets favoured a large population. Moreover, a large, young, growing population proved the virility of the Soviet model and the life-affirming nature of socialism. Waves of young men – and indeed women – had staved off the invading Fascist hordes in 1941. A large and growing population was also required to ensure the workforce continued to expand and make its economic contribution in fulfilment of the plan.

There were, however, countervailing pressures at work which tended to make Party bosses less keen on large families. These included the need to keep Soviet women in the workforce: while encouraging their childbearing would help meet future requirements for the workplace, it detracted from the more immediate requirements of the day. Childcare facilities could be put in place to encourage childbearing and prolong workforce participation, but there were other demands on resources. Particularly in the early days, the Soviets tended to associate large families with backwardness and the habits of peasants. Educating women, urbanising them and giving them a place in a modern industrial economy was not compatible with their having six or seven children.

Although the fertility of central Asians and people of the Caucasus contributed to the overall fertility of the country, the reduction in the predominance of Russians in particular and Slavs in general gave rise to concerns which again ran counter to nominally internationalist

Marxian orthodoxy. First, there was no doubt a degree of racial prejudice on the part of many in the Party and state establishment, some of
whom remained at heart Great Russian patriots if not chauvinists
(sometimes disguising or justifying this in Communist terms by reference to the leading role of the Russian people in the revolution).
Second, there was concern in some quarters about the loyalty of
Muslim and Turkic peoples to the USSR, and a suspicion that their
disloyalty might manifest itself in bonds of ethnic and/or religious
sentiment, for example, with the Muslims of Afghanistan, many of
whom are ethnically close to those of central Asia. Third, from a
purely economic perspective, the areas providing population growth
were providing people of relatively low educational achievement and
low economic productivity: the marginal Russian or Ukrainian
would add more to the economy than the marginal Uzbek or Tajik.
In short, all Soviet babies were equal but some were more equal than
others. A Russian baby was, at least in the eyes of many officials,
probably inherently more desirable and certainly more likely to make
a loyal and productive citizen than a baby born in Azerbaijan or
Turkmenistan.

The problem for the Soviet Army was particularly acute and
reflected a more general problem. Loyalty mattered more directly
among soldiers than among citizens as a whole. Poorly educated
soldiers from the central Asian republics were less effective and, as the
Hapsburgs had discovered, it was difficult to organise a modern mass
army on multilingual lines. By the final years of the Soviet Union up
to three-quarters of recruits from central Asia could not speak
Russian.[23] Furthermore, while the general data above shows the rise of
Russia's Muslim population at an aggregate level, this was seen more
acutely among eighteen-year-old recruits than at the level of the
population as a whole. The Muslim population was disproportionately
young and so the young population – which was being recruited into
the military – was disproportionately Muslim.

From the 1970s the debate within Soviet academic and policy
circles focused particularly on the tension between the need to have
a growing population and the wish to ensure its 'quality' or (when
code was not used) its Russianness. The first concerns of an ethnic
nature came to the surface after the 1970 census, which suggested that

the Russian demographic high tide had passed. Voices began to be raised in favour of a 'differentiated' population policy, encouraging more births in Russia and in the Slavic republics and fewer in those of the Caucasus and central Asia. The debate became polarised between 'differentiators' favouring discriminatory pro-natalism and those denouncing it as being contrary to the spirit and ideology of the country. Among the latter were 'non-differentiators' from central Asia arguing that a differentiated policy was tantamount to being discriminatory, even if it was dressed up as an attempt to even out fertility rates by lowering them where they were high and raising them where they were low. The anti-differentiators cited General Secretary Leonid Brezhnev as suggesting that the large families produced in the peripheral republics were seen as a source of delight, not of concern, and an Uzbek politician (perhaps somewhat tongue in cheek) praised the 'leading role' of the Uzbeks in boosting the Soviet population. ('Leading role' was a term usually reserved for describing the Party's job in directing society.) The debate continued up to the Twenty-Sixth Party Congress in 1981 when, however, it was resolved in favour of the differentiators, Brezhnev acknowledging that the problem of demography had 'become more acute of late' and announcing policies such as paid leave and a shorter working day for mothers.[24] It was left for his colleague Nikolai Tikhonov to clarify that the new policies were to be rolled out 'step by step', republic by republic, effectively meaning that they would be implemented in Russia first and only later, if ever, in central Asia and the Caucasus.[25] In fact, they were first introduced in the Soviet Far East and in Siberia, areas in which Russia has traditionally wished to boost its sparse population.[26] They never reached the Muslim periphery.

Demography and the Collapse of the Soviet Union

Demography played a role in the demise of the Soviet Union both economically and ethnically. Economically, the reduction of the growth in the workforce was an important component in failing Soviet economic growth rates, or put another way, an inefficient economic system had been buoyed up by exceptionally high growth rates in the key input of labour; once this failed, the system failed. This was accentuated by the fact that the growth in the labour force was increasingly coming from areas where educational and productivity levels were poor. Perhaps even more important, the breakdown of the Soviet Union into its component parts and the rise of nationalism can be seen as a reflection of the waning of the ethnic Russian demographic presence.

The Soviet Union, despite its nomenclature, can be seen essentially as an extension of the Russian imperial state. For it to hold together, it needed the presence of a dominant language and culture. The ideology of Marxism–Leninism and the centralising institution of the Communist Party were simply not enough. Although the most prominent challenges to Russian hegemony came from places like the Baltic states, which posed no demographic threat, Russian confidence in its ability to hold the state together was sapped by its waning presence in the periphery of the country and the rising and uncontrollable ethnic tensions and conflicts in places like Nagorno-Karabakh. Add to this the problems of holding together an increasingly ethnically and linguistically diverse army and it becomes clear that many of the pressures which brought down the USSR had at least partially demographic roots. It was in the increasingly de-Russified Caucasus that the failure of Soviet control first became evident. Clashes between Armenians and Azeris broke out in early 1988, nearly three years before the Soviet Union's formal demise.

For Russia, the collapse of the Soviet Union meant a retreat from territories it long considered core. For non-Russian nationalities, it meant the opportunities and challenges of independence, more or less to be circumscribed over time by proximity to Russia and the latter's sense of their being part of the 'near abroad'. For the world, it meant the end of the cold war and, specifically, the triumph of the United States and its allies over the Eastern bloc.

Just as the fall of the Soviet Union had more than purely demographic causes, so the West's cold war triumph had more causes than just the fall of the Soviet Union – including its own dynamism in contrast to the moribund nature of the economy and society in the countries of the Warsaw Pact. Nevertheless, some have claimed that if the Soviet Union had been as ethnically homogeneous as China, it would still be in business.[27] Cuba and North Korea, lacking real ethnic cleavages, have continued to pursue Soviet-style policies of central planning and no or very limited private property which continue to impoverish their peoples, yet their regimes cling on a generation after the Soviet collapse. That the Soviet Union was not ethnically more homogeneous was due, ultimately, to demography and specifically to the differential timing of the demographic transition between the very different areas of what was the world's largest country.

Is Russia Dying?

In 1991 the USSR was formally dissolved and its predominant Russian component, the RSFSR, became the Russian Federation. Since then the country has gone through the chaos of the Yeltsin years and the more orderly if less liberating Putin years, with its economy first buoyed by the high price of hydrocarbons and then hit by their fall. Meanwhile the demographic problems carried over from the Soviet era – low fertility, poor life expectancy and the waning of Russians as an ethnic group – have continued to dog the country, although with some signs of improvement.

According to the United Nations, Russia's total fertility rate stood at a little over one and a half children per woman in the early 1990s and fell to one and a quarter in the latter part of that decade, since when it has recovered somewhat to around one and two-thirds children per woman.[28] This recovery is material but does not mask the fact that Russian fertility rates are low, if not among the world's lowest. The shock of the collapse of Communism and the ensuing chaos and financial difficulties are generally seen as important causes of the low levels of the 1990s. Shortages of housing in urban areas are often cited too, while in addition the child benefits of late Soviet times have been swept away in real terms by rampant inflation. More intangible and difficult to quantify is an anti-natal culture which is not a recent phenomenon. For some, anti-natalism can be expressed as a horror of large families, and the association of such families with the rural peasantry and the uneducated. Of course this attitude is not a singularly Russian phenomenon but can be seen in many societies which have recently undergone a process of modernisation.[29]

Although superficially Russia's low fertility rate bears similarities to the fertility rates experienced in southern and central Europe, there are some notable differences. During the Soviet period, when the Russian fertility rate was already low, Russian women had not adopted the tendency of women further west to delay childbirth. Around the time that the Soviet Union ended, the average age of first childbirth was just short of twenty-two. Although this began to change in the New Russia, the change was only gradual: by 2004: the average age of the mother at the birth of her first child was not much over twenty-three.[30] This is good and bad news for Russian fertility rates. On the positive side, it means that the recovery of fertility in the recent decade or so has been *despite* the (admittedly modest) tempo effect of women delaying childbearing, in contrast to a recovery of fertility in northern Europe which has been largely attributable to the ending or slowing of the tempo effect. This may mean that the underlying vigour of the jump in the total fertility rate is slightly greater than it appears. The bad news is that, with childbearing occurring so early in the life of the average Russian woman, there is plenty of potential for the tempo effect to kick in. In other words, if Russian women decide to delay childbearing until their late twenties or early thirties, the period during which they do so will witness depressed fertility.

There are several other noteworthy characteristics of Russian fertility. One is the continued tendency for women to have only one child. In other countries with low fertility there is a wide spread between women having no children and women having several. In Russia, one child per woman has been very common and childless women have been fairly rare. This was markedly the case in the Soviet era (although there are now some indications that it is beginning to change and that the number of childless women is starting to grow).[31] Thus low fertility in Russia essentially stems from women choosing to stop childbearing after one child. Where a second child is born, the gap between the first and second child is larger in Russia than in the West.[32] In other ways Russia continues to be fairly unlike those countries of the West which have undergone the second demographic transition: premarital cohabitation has, at least until recently, remained relatively unusual and marriage (as well as first childbearing) remains fairly early.[33] Abortion rates have however halved since Soviet times, presumably because of the wider availability of affordable contraception.[34]

Meanwhile it is worth noting what has been happening to fertility in the rest of the former Soviet Union since its demise. The Baltic states all witnessed declines after the end of the USSR but have seen some modest recovery, like Russia to around or slightly above the one and a half children per woman level. A similar pattern can be observed in Belarus and Ukraine. In the former Muslim republics, fertility has dropped sharply, in line with developments in the wider Islamic world which will be investigated later. Azerbaijani women have shifted from bearing just under three children to a little over two children since the collapse of the USSR, and even Uzbek women, once the childbearing champions of the Soviet Union, have reduced their fertility from around four children in 1990 to two and a half at the latest count.[35]

While life expectancy in the Soviet Union after 1945 was paltry compared to what was achieved in the United States and, even more so, in Western Europe, as noted above, in the post-Soviet era the divergence widened. Life expectancy for Russian men fell from sixty-four in 1989 to fifty-eight in 2001. This bears extremely poor comparison not only to what had been and was still being achieved in the West by way of lengthening life expectancy, but also in growing parts of the developing world. In the same year India, with a per capita income less than one-third of the Russian level, achieved male life expectancy of two years longer.[36] The gap between male and female life expectancy in Russia is exceptionally high. In 2008, when male life expectancy had recovered to the age of fifty-nine, the life expectancy of Russian women was seventy-three,[37] and the most recent UN data suggests that while male life expectancy is recovering it is still only back to where it was fifty years ago. The extraordinarily wide gap between male and female life expectancy in Russia (three or four years is normal for most countries, but the latest UN data suggests more than a decade for Russia) indicates that Russia's mortality problem lies essentially with its men.

The most often cited problem related to low life expectancy is alcoholism. Here, although Russia's alcohol consumption per capita is not much higher than that of some west European countries, in

Russia it seems to be concentrated among men and in drinking bouts. Interestingly, a drop in alcohol consumption in the mid to late nineties was accompanied by a modest fall in mortality.[38] Another contributing factor to poor life expectancy is the fact that Russia's suicide rate is one of the highest in the world; it was the cause of over 50,000 deaths in 2000.[39] The atmosphere of morbidity in the immediate post-Soviet era was captured by one correspondent:

> The deaths kept piling up. People – men and women – were falling, or perhaps jumping, off trains and out of windows; asphyxiating in country houses with faulty wood stoves or in apartments with jammed front-door locks; getting hit by cars that sped through quiet courtyards or ploughed down groups of people on a sidewalk; drowning as a result of diving drunk into a lake or ignoring sea-storm warnings or for no apparent reason; poisoning themselves with too much alcohol, counterfeit alcohol, alcohol substitutes, or drugs; and, finally, dropping dead at absurdly early ages from heart attacks and strokes.[40]

Beyond alcoholism and suicide, there would appear to be a number of other factors contributing to Russia's higher mortality and low life expectancy. The death rate from infectious and parasitic diseases stands at more than double the level experienced in the EU, and death from cardiovascular disease appears to be at near twice the level which would be expected given Russia's GDP. Overall levels of spending on health care in Russia are low even relative to GDP, and the levels of service may be worse than they were in Soviet days.[41]

Although there has been some modest improvement (in part thanks to lower suicide rates and some reduction in alcoholism), Russian male life expectancy is no further ahead than it was in the late 1960s, since when the world as a whole has witnessed an improvement in life expectancy of a decade and a half. This means that Russia lags behind countries such as Egypt and Pakistan.[42] Because Russia's infant mortality rate is not particularly bad, the picture of life expectancy at age fifteen is even worse when compared to others. However, the result is that Russia does not have quite the same ageing problem as most countries in Europe. Falling childbearing tends to increase the average age in a society, but premature deaths of those who would be elderly has the reverse effect. At under thirty-nine, Russia's median age is a full eight years older than it was in the mid 1970s but seven years younger than Germany's.[43] It is little comfort for a society, though, that it is not ageing because so many people are dying in middle age and never reaching old age.

The great difference between Russia and central and southern Europe is that while both are experiencing a fertility rate well below replacement level, in the latter this is somewhat compensated for by rising life expectancy whereas in Russia falling life expectancy (i.e. rising mortality) has until recently compounded the impact of low fertility and resulted in a sharp natural decline in the population. In the nine years after 1992 there were more than 12 million more deaths in Russia than births.[44] Other countries have reached a similar position of natural decline, but invariably this is *in spite of falling mortality* rather than in part *because of rising mortality*.

The fact that the Russian population has not dropped as fast as the natural decrease would suggest is thanks to migration. With the ending of the Soviet Union, Russia became in population terms a much smaller entity than its erstwhile Soviet self. At the time of the break-up, the Soviet population was 287 million and Russia's population was peaking at nearly 148 million; by 2015 it was under 143 million.[45] The vast bulk of this loss is, of course, not due to birth or death rates but to the shrinkage of the state which no longer covers now independent countries from Estonia to Kazakhstan. Nevertheless, with Russia's poor balance of births and death, UN forecasts based on median fertility suggest that by the end of the current century it will have fewer than 125 million people, while some forecasts say it will sink below the 100 million mark (although recent gains in fertility rates and life expectancy make this less likely).[46] Although there are grounds for some optimism, this is a far cry from the heady days of the Soviet Union when the population was approaching three times the hundred million mark. A mixture of low fertility, high mortality and imperial retreat has made Russia a much diminished entity from the one of seemingly boundless imperial ambition at the start of the twentieth century. Unsurprisingly, this has had geopolitical consequences.

As is usual when a country's population is stagnant or falling, it is the outlying districts that feel it first. Urbanisation continues as people carry on moving from the countryside to the towns and cities, and in Russia this is particularly so because of the remoteness and inhospitable climate of so much of the country. The Soviet Union was vast and many of the peripheral areas were populated by Russians thanks only to the efforts of the state; once the state was enfeebled and less willing to direct people to places, it was inevitable that the process of settling distant areas reversed itself as people abandoned places denuded of facilities, infrastructure and job opportunities. In one village to the west of Moscow where only eight people remain, a local resident laments: 'only old people are left here. And what do we, old people, do? We die.' One in ten villages in Russia had fewer than ten inhabitants in 2010; today the number is probably considerably worse.[47]

Putin Fights Back

The newly self-confident and assertive Russia of Vladimir Putin, in contrast to the chaotic post-Soviet era of Boris Yeltsin, is not short of critics, who will point out that much of the apparent resurgence depends on a veneer financed unsustainably up to 2014 by high oil and gas prices. Whether or not such criticism is justified, Putin's efforts go beyond a military build-up, annexation of Crimea and intervention in Syria; his regime is aware of the demographic crisis and would very much like to be able to count a demographic resurgence among its achievements. A significant milestone was a major speech in 2006 in which Putin spoke of 'the most acute problem facing our country today – the demographic problem'.[48] Twenty-five years after Brezhnev spoke to the Twenty-Sixth Congress, demography had gone from being acknowledged as simply one of many national problems to being seen as the most serious issue confronting the nation.

While there was some focus in Putin's 2006 speech on the need to lower the death rate, for example by reducing traffic accidents and upgrading health care, the focus was on the need to boost childbirth. Putin explicitly linked low fertility to problems of low income, inadequate housing and poor prospects for the health care and education of children. He even suggested that parents were worried simply about feeding their children. With a fundamentally material and financial interpretation of the problem, Putin's response was a capital grant on the birth of a child and improved rights for working mothers. As ever, it is difficult to know whether these policies have been responsible for the recovery in Russia's total fertility rate or whether the recovery relates to other factors.

Before its disintegration, the Soviet Union was becoming less Russian and the Russian nationality represented a bare majority of the total population and a declining one at that. Retreating into the borders of what had been the RSFSR meant a consolidation and a demographic strengthening from an ethnic perspective within a more limited but still vast space. However, just as ethnic Russians had lived across what had been the Soviet Union and not only within the RSFSR, so there were non-Russian minorities within the new Russian Federation, some of them 'indigenous' in the sense that their presence long pre-dated the Soviet Union, others more recent arrivals, attracted by the opportunities which the metropolitan centre offered.

In thinking about the Russianness of Russia since the end of the Soviet Union, we have to distinguish between three phenomena: first, the 'return' of Russians from the 'near abroad', people preferring to live in Russia than in the newly independent republics: second, the indigenous populations of non-ethnic Russians within the republic, such as Tartars and Chechens, many of them Muslims and demonstrating the relatively higher fertility rates of their central Asian co-religionists, and third, the influx of non-ethnic Russians into the Federation, generally from the former non-Russian republics of the Soviet Union and mostly to the major cities. The first of these phenomena has had the effect of strengthening the Russian composition of the population (while continuing to diminish the Russian presence in the 'near abroad'), the second and third of diluting it. A fourth phenomenon can also be considered, and that is the emigration of non-ethnic Russians since the end of the Soviet Union, particularly of around 1 million Jews to Israel and 500,000 Germans to Germany, which although numerically limited and essentially a one-off, nevertheless has had some impact in increasing the Russianness of Russia by reducing minorities within its borders.

The best way to disentangle these various strands is to investigate the ethnic composition of Russia as a whole. In 1959, the population of the RSFSR was more than 83% Russian.[49] In 2002 the population of the Russian Federation was around 80% ethnically Russian, a modest but material drop. By 2010 the Russian share was down to below 78%.[50] The largest minority, the Tartars, comprised around 4% of the population.[51] Although there appears to be a solid Russian majority, there are trends which should be worrying to Russian ethno-nationalists. In 1989–2002, while the ethnic Russian population of the Russian Federation had declined from just under 120 million to just under 116 million, the number of Chechens had grown from less than 1 million to more than 1.33 million – this despite a vicious war and alleged genocide in Chechnya. In Russia as a whole at that point, the median age was just over thirty-seven whereas in Chechnya it was under thirty-three.[52]

Meanwhile, the influx of central Asians and people from the Caucasus into the large Russian cities is transforming their ethnic make-up: Moscow, for example, is believed to be around 20% Muslim.[53] Although the leadership of the Russian Federation proclaims a multi-ethnic and multi-faith rhetoric, it nevertheless tightened its citizenship laws in 2002, making it more difficult for those of non-Russian origin to obtain Russian citizenship than had been the case under the laxer 1991 law, essentially adopting *jus sanguinis* or rights depending on 'blood' or ethnic origin.[54] Moreover, while the primary demographic concern of the Russian authorities continues to be the low fertility and high mortality rate for the country as a whole, it appears that they are aware of the long-term likelihood of a shifting ethnic mix in Russia as well, and have taken action which, if it has not stemmed the inflow of non-Russians into Russia, has at least reduced their rights to Russian citizenship. Thus as the multi-ethnic rhetoric continues to hold at the level of the national leadership, this is not always the case at local level. Moscow, now believed to have the largest Muslim population of any city in Europe of perhaps as many as 2 million people, has only six mosques despite requests to build more (Moscow's mayor has described the number of Muslims in his city as 'excessive' and 'harmful' – a statement which would be totally rejected from a mayor of a major city in Western Europe; indeed London's mayor *is* a Muslim).[55]

The Orthodox World Beyond Russia

Until the end of the 1980s the USSR was often thought of as part of a more or less single entity alongside the rest of the Soviet bloc, a political grouping that included countries which were neither linguistically Slavic nor religiously Orthodox (e.g. East Germany and Hungary), Slavic but not Orthodox (e.g. Czechoslovakia and Poland), Orthodox but not Slavic (e.g. Romania) and both Slavic and Orthodox (e.g. Bulgaria). The Orthodox world since 1991, with the ending of the Communist enterprise, can arguably be located culturally and developmentally alongside Russia. It is worth noting that, with the collapse of Communism, the collapse of fertility in the former Communist countries in the late 1980s and early 1990s, from an already low base, was quite general. For example, the birth rate in the German Democratic Republic fell from thirteen per thousand in 1988 to five and a half per thousand in 1992, an extraordinary drop in such a short period.[56] As in Russia, the general disruption and economic hardship were in part to blame, as well as a significant movement of young women of childbearing age to the West.

There is convincing evidence that nations and ethnic groups which can be grouped together as 'civilisations' have a tendency to behave in a similar fashion demographically as well as in other ways, and that this indeed is something which defines them *as* a civilisation. The West, meaning the US and Canada plus Western Europe and Australia and New Zealand, has followed a broadly similar pattern of post-war baby boom then falling fertility rates and mass immigration from less developed countries, all accompanied by steadily rising life expectancy. Similar broadly uniform patterns, albeit with local variations, have occurred in the Far East, the Middle East, Latin America, south Asia and sub-Saharan Africa. Indeed these similarities have allowed this book to be organised along civilisational lines for the post-1945 period. The same is also the case for what can be described as the Christian Eastern Orthodox civilisation (called 'Orthodox' even if, after 1945, it was ruled by Communist regimes and its churches were for the most part marginalised or persecuted). Most Orthodox countries had by 1950 completed a large part of their demographic transition with only Russia and Serbia reporting a fertility rate of above three children per woman, and both were witnessing a rapid decline below that level by the mid to late 1950s. While the path these countries took has varied – with an unusual spike in the case of Romania – all have ended up at a point of exceptionally low fertility at the start of the twenty-first century. In all cases except Serbia, fertility dropped to well below one and a half children per woman, although in most cases there has been some recovery to or somewhat above that level in the last decade or so. (Unlike Russia, most Orthodox countries have experienced extending lifespans, so population declines from sub-replacement fertility rates have to some extent been counteracted.) Still, this is well below replacement level. The reasons for this are similar to those affecting Italy, Spain and Portugal: a mixture of modern attitudes to female education and aspiration alongside continuing traditional views on birth outside marriage.

The Romanian Spike

The late 1960s spike in Romanian fertility rates, however, is an example of a remarkable (and often tragic) contra-flow in this trend. Noting the decline in fertility rates in the 1950s and early 1960s, the authorities worried that this would slow the growth of population which it, more than other regimes in the Eastern bloc, regarded as a measure of prestige as well as a source of economic growth. The dictator Nicolae Ceausescu was ahead of his socialist colleagues elsewhere in the Soviet bloc in identifying demography as an issue, declaring that the 'most important problem is that of a steadier population growth – an essential factor of the dynamics and of the productive forces of society . . . by the end of the next decade, Romania may number twenty-four to twenty-five million inhabitants'.[57]

So, overnight and unexpectedly, the regime outlawed abortion (with limited exceptions) in 1966. This was justified by the need to balance personal freedom on the one hand with the national require-ment for 'natural' population growth on the other.[58] Until that point, as in Russia, abortion had been the most common form of birth control; for example, in the year before the abortion ban, there had been four abortions for every birth. Not surprisingly, the fertility rate rose from two to three and a half children per woman almost imme-diately.[59] For the late 1960s as a whole, however, the fertility rate was three, indicating that by the end of the decade the impact of the ban on fertility was wearing off. The one-off shock to the system had had an immediate effect, but the population began to find its way around the ban, either through illegal abortions or through alternative means of contraception. By the mid 1980s the fertility rate of Romanians was back to that of the country's civilisational peer group.

Nevertheless, the policy had an impact for the best part of twenty years. Apart from resulting in a population larger than it would otherwise have been, it is likely that it also gave rise to the culture of unwanted births and under-resourced and neglectful state orphanages which so shocked Westerners after the fall of the Communist regime. As for Ceausescu's population targets, they were not met. The population of Romania did rise a little above 23 million in the 1980s, but has since slipped back to below 20 million. The Romanian experiment is an interesting case study in the limitations of even the most authoritarian governments in manipulating demographic trends.

There is another aspect of the Romanian story that is worth noting with respect to the subject of demographic engineering or the deploy-ment of demographic strategies by ethnic groups or states in conflict. The Romanian government was more transparently nationalist than some of its East European neighbours, and it pursued a patently ethno-Romanian strand in its demographic policy. It was markedly more relaxed than was the Soviet Union in allowing Jews to emigrate from Romania to Israel from the late 1960s, albeit in exchange for cash payments, while it is suggested that the abortion laws were less strictly implemented in the case of ethnic Hungarians and of Roma than for ethnic Romanians.[60]

The Yugoslav War

At the close of the cold war, most previously Communist countries managed a largely peaceful transition to capitalism, whether this involved remaining within the same boundaries (e.g. Poland, Hungary), splitting up (e.g. the Czech and Slovak republics) or merging (e.g. East Germany with West Germany). Most of these countries had been more or less ethnically homogeneous, at least since the massacres of the Second World War and the forced migrations which followed it, and had populations which were ethnically stable. This was not the case in Yugoslavia, however, and here demography played a role in a defining conflict of the 1990s.

Like the Russians, Serbs experienced a falling fertility rate after 1945, an experience shared by their fellow Yugoslavs of Christian heritage (Balts, Ukrainians, Moldovans and Byelorussians in the case of the Soviet Union; Croats and Slovenes in the case of Yugoslavia) but not by those of traditionally Islamic background (Caucasians and central Asians in the case of the Soviet Union; Bosnian Muslims and Kosovo Albanians in the case of Yugoslavia). The result was a diminishing proportion of Serbs within Yugoslavia, particularly in areas where they lived alongside Muslims. In Bosnia-Herzegovina, the Serb share of the population fell from 44% in 1948 to less than 33% in 1981 while the Muslim share rose from less than 33% to nearly 40% between the same dates. In Kosovo (unlike Bosnia-Herzegovina, located within the Serbian republic rather than being a separate republic within Yugoslavia), the Serb share of the population was already below a quarter in 1948 but by 1981 had reduced to barely 13%, the result not only of a lower birth rate than the local Albanians but also migration of ethnic Serbs to Serbia.[61] Both these areas were sensitive so far as Serbian nationalists were concerned, the former being the area where Serb nationalists had triggered the outbreak of the First World War in 1918 by assassinating Austria's Archduke Franz Ferdinand; the latter being the location of a Serbian battle against the Turks in the fourteenth century which featured centrally in Serbian historic consciousness, and also the location of many medieval Serbian monasteries of historic importance. The aggregate population data partly disguises even more dramatic trends among the young: the share of under fourteens in the population of Serbia is half of that among Kosovars.[62]

In addition to the Serbian loss of demographic presence in these sensitive areas, there was the memory of the Second World War, when large numbers of Serbs had been massacred not only by Croats but also by Bosnian Muslims organised by the Nazi SS. The outbreak of war as Yugoslavia dissolved cannot be put down simplistically to demographic factors alone, but they certainly contributed. A careful study of where the violence took place during the war in Bosnia-Herzegovina has shown that areas of declining Serbian population between 1961 and 1991 were particularly likely to witness fighting.[63] In due course the fertility rates of Bosnian Muslims and of Albanians have fallen fast, and today Bosnia-Herzegovina (including both Serbs and Muslims as well as Croats) has, along with Moldova, the lowest fertility rate in Europe (barely one and a quarter children per woman), and even Kosovo's total fertility rate is only around replacement level.

In summary, the former Yugoslavia is an exemplary case of the destabilising impact of uneven demographic transition, striking people of different religious or ethnic backgrounds at different times.

The Demography of Disappearance

Throughout the Christian Orthodox world the same forces have been at work. After long periods of low fertility rates, it is not just that young women are having fewer children but that there are fewer young women, so both the fertility rate and the birth rate are low. In many places economic opportunities have been scarce and a chance of migration to the wealthier regions of Western Europe has been open, making for large-scale emigration with little or no compensating inward migration (the exception being Russia, which has received immigration from the former republics of the USSR). A good example is Bulgaria, which had close to 9 million people in the 1980s; in 2015 it had barely 7 million, recent declines driven not just by low fertility rates but also by EU accession and attendant emigration opportunities. As ever in such cases, rural depopulation is rife. In a village where once eight hundred people lived, one of the two remaining inhabitants laments: 'I am going to draw my last breath here. Sadly there is not a priest in Matochina. When I die they will have to call someone from elsewhere.'[64]

Nearby Moldova has lost more than 7% of its population since the early 1990s and, according to the UN median fertility population projection, will probably have lost another half by the end of the current century. By 2015 the populations of Greece and Bulgaria were among the seven oldest in the world in terms of median age.[65] In the case of the Orthodox world, it is not just a single country but an entire civilisation which, unless something quite fundamental changes, will simply non-breed itself out of existence sometime in the next century.

The revolutionary swell of human population, having exploded in Britain in the early nineteenth century and spread across Europe, including Russia, and the lands of European conquest and colonisation, had finally broken on the banks of the Black Sea and retreated.

Yet this account covers only a mere minority of the earth's surface and population. In continents beyond, far larger trends will play out at a scale and speed that far surpasses the Western experience.

PART THREE

The Tide Goes Global: Beyond the Europeans

8

Japan, China and East Asia

The Ageing of Giants

In May 1905 Aleksey Novikov, a twenty-four-year-old peasant from southern Russia, found himself sailing into the Sea of Japan on board the battleship *Oryol*. Having previously been dismissed from the tsarist navy for political unreliability, he had been allowed to return at the outbreak of war the previous year. The fleet had left the Baltic in October 1904 and taken more than six months to reach its destination. On arrival in the Far East, Novikov and his comrades found themselves outmanoeuvred and outgunned by the Japanese navy, who disabled the squadron and sank several of the ships without themselves sustaining any more damage than 'if they had been engaged in target practice'.[1] Novikov was fortunate. After a relatively short period as a prisoner of war he returned to Russia where he resumed his revolutionary activities and eventually took up writing. Around 70,000 of his comrades did not survive the war: Russia lost eight battleships and many smaller vessels, losses which dwarfed those of the Japanese.

This was not how it was supposed to be. The Europeans were surely the masters of the globe, able to exert their will and expand their empires where they chose. True, the Boers had proved difficult for the British to suppress a few years earlier, but they were, after all, of European extraction albeit established in Africa for generations. Non-European peoples were not supposed to fight back, and certainly not supposed to win. Tsar Nicholas II's cousin Kaiser Wilhelm II had urged him to take on Japan in defence of Christianity and the White Race; instead, the outcome of the war fuelled the paranoia of the kaiser and others at the 'Yellow Peril'.

The Russo-Japanese War was a shock not just to the Russians but to all Europeans who thought that their inherent superiority would give them eternal world domination. Japan's triumph was not signifi-cantly demographic – Russia had a much larger population than Japan – but rather strategic. Nevertheless, there was a demographic component, and it was this: Japan was on the rise, its people the first non-Europeans to escape the Malthusian trap. Along with the modernisation of the military and the navy came a modernisation of industry which allowed Japan to construct a Russia-beating fleet. Along with Japan's entry into the modern world came precisely the kind of demographic take-off and population expansion which had accompanied similar developments in the heart of Europe. It is no coincidence that the first non-European people to escape pre-modern demography were the first in modern times to give a European great power a bloody nose.

Japan, China and east and south-east Asia make up an area which today holds almost one-third of the world's population, and comprise a region which has in large part successively undergone the same transformation experienced by Europe and North America – a trans-formation pioneered by Japan. Beyond this familiar tale, in Japan and China the region contains two countries which are unprecedented from a demographic point of view: Japan because it was the first non-European country to break through the Malthusian bonds into demo-graphic transition and now has the world's oldest population; China because it has a larger population than any other country in the world's history. Both countries had ancient histories, long-established institutions and complex societies before they were forced into close contact with the West, and that contact was bound to be transforma-tional for both, not least demographically.

The Sun Rises: Japan's Ascent

How it was that Japan came to challenge the West is the source of much dispute. It has been suggested that speaking of a 'demographic transi-tion' is to foist a Eurocentric model on non-European peoples.[2] To do so, it is claimed, is to argue that nothing much of interest occurred in demography (or, by implication, in anything else) until the adoption of European models of economic and social organisation. To some extent this is a fair criticism, although it applies as much to Europe as to the rest of the world. Europe had its own demographic ups and downs well before the nineteenth century, not least the Black Death, which set the continent's population back for centuries. The point, however, is not that nothing happened until the demographic transition, but rather that only when modernisation, however defined, commenced did populations follow a more or less uniform and predictable path, at least for a period. The Japan that suddenly, in the middle of the nineteenth century, re-engaged with the rest of the world was the product of a long, complex historical process, and the same can be said of its population. This need not distract us, however, from the fact that what happened in the late nineteenth and early twentieth centuries, when Japan was swept by a wave of urbanisation and industrialisation, was truly revolutionary in terms of the country's history.

Part of the difficulty in grasping Japanese demography in an earlier period is the problem of data. As in most places before the industrial era, the demographic data for Japan before the early twentieth century is patchy. Many aspects are contested. Nevertheless, some broad outlines are clear. The population of Japan increased initially during the period of political stability and agricultural innovation during the Tokugawa period from the start of the seventeenth century[3] – indeed, it may have grown by around 1% per annum for much of the late sixteenth and early seventeenth centuries. At this time much of the rest of the world was suffering demographic setbacks: China was experiencing disruption caused by the transition from the Ming to the Qing dynasty, Europe was experiencing the horrors of the Thirty Years' War, and the British Isles was embroiled in civil war, whilst England's American colonies were only just starting to establish themselves and were still demographically feeble. Japan's seventeenth century was by contrast serene and prosperous, and as a result population rose. However, it then stagnated at somewhere between 26 and 33 million from the middle of the seventeenth century.[4] Even taking the lowest opening and highest closing estimates from 1721 to 1846, Japan's population appears to have grown by no more than 5% in over a century.[5]

One interpretation of the long plateau in Japan's population is that internal stability and the absence of war simply made more space for the other Malthusian terrors of scarcity and disease and that Japan was operating at the edge of its maximum population frontier by the early eighteenth century. According to this interpretation, the country had simply expanded to its productive frontier, at which its people lived in a state of Malthusian misery. Another interpretation is that the population lived above the level of the Malthusian frontier of subsistence and misery – in other words, that more could have been supported at a lower level of subsistence – but that social institutions kept the population in check, predominantly through means of infanticide and abortion.[6] (These are hardly the checks of which the Reverend Malthus would have approved; he acknowledged the possibility of communities avoiding expanding to the edge of starvation and misery, but thought the only morally acceptable way for them to do so was through the sexual restraint which comes with chastity and late marriage.) At times, infanticide might have accounted for as much as 10% of births or even 20%, in part evidenced by the male–female population imbalance in an age before the possibility of sex-selective abortion. In parts of eastern Japan in the eighteenth century, infanticide was referred to as *mabiki*, that is, the uprooting or thinning out of rice seedlings. In some circumstances it was considered virtually an obligation, with parents of large families branded as anti-social for breeding like dogs. The diary of a prosperous rural merchant records how he undertook infanticides himself, determining through means of divination which infants should live and which should die.[7]

Under the circumstances, and given the availability of the data, it is hard to disaggregate infanticide from lowered fertility. Abortion was also a common method for controlling population until it was criminalised progressively from 1870 and particularly from 1882:[8] how common it remained thereafter is uncertain. Apart from abortion and infanticide, abstinence and marital separation appear to have played a role in creating in late seventeenth- and eighteenth-century Japan what has been called a 'culture of low fertility'. It is difficult to know whether what really prevailed was fertility suppressed by sexual abstinence and contraceptive techniques or by abortion or infanticide. In any case, if this interpretation is right and by one means or another the Japanese were avoiding producing as many people as they could, and if they thereby enjoyed the opportunity to live a little better and conserve some capital, then in this respect Japan bore a similarity to eighteenth-century England.

The end of isolation and the restoration of the Meiji dynasty in 1868 was accompanied by what can broadly be termed the end of feudalism and the birth of the modern state. At first industrial and demographic progress (that is, progress through the demographic transition) was slow, but both accelerated in the late nineteenth and early twentieth centuries. Official figures for this period suggest rising birth rates, from 25.4 to 35.7 per thousand between 1875 and 1920. Other sources suggest that the birth rate was already over thirty, or even over thirty-six per thousand in 1875. Conversely, while the official sources suggest rising mortality, other sources suggest it was dropping, which would be more in line with what would be expected in the early stages of demographic transition.[9] The latter does indeed seem more likely: however basic conditions were in the cities of early industrial Japan, conditions for the peasant were probably worse and it is likely that as the Japanese came increasingly to live in towns and cities, they started living longer.

Although the picture of what underlay the rise in population is confusing, at least to 1920, there is no confusion around the fact that the population was indeed growing after its long plateau of between 26 and 33 million. By 1914 the population had risen to 52 million and by 1924 to over 58 million.[10] In the late nineteenth century, Japanese population growth exceeded 1% per annum, as the UK's had at its time of industrial take-off, and in 1915 annual population growth was not much under 1.5%.[11] This rate, which rivalled that achieved by Russia a few years earlier, reached a level of more than 1.5% per annum in the late 1920s.[12]

Memoirs and letters of Western travellers and expatriates in the decades before the First World War are revealing both for what they cover and what they do not. Diplomats' wives and missionaries, frequent authors of such works, depict Japanese flower-arranging and Japanese shrines, waxing lyrical about temples and mountain landscapes. Few, however, seemed to notice that what was going on in Japan was akin to what the UK had experienced a couple of generations earlier. Such writings are, of course, replete with jarring racist

THE TIDE GOES GLOBAL: BEYOND THE EUROPEANS

stereotyping. Basil Hall Chamberlain, Emeritus Professor of Japanese and Philology at the Japanese Imperial University – and therefore better informed than most writers on the topic – noted in 1891 that Japanese tradesmen, despite thirty years of acquaintance with the West, still had much to learn. The 'average native dealer', he observed,

> is still very backward in such matters as punctuality, a strict regard for the truth, the keeping of a promise, however trivial. He is a bad loser even of the smallest sums, and will not consider it derogatory to endeavour to get out of a contract, the fulfilment of which would entail a loss.[13]

(Perhaps Chamberlain's racism should come as no surprise: his younger brother was Houston Stewart Chamberlain, Richard Wagner's son-in-law and a man who in his final years hailed Hitler as the coming man after a transformative personal encounter with him.) However, unlike most of his competitors vying for readers with a taste for tales of lacquered vases and geisha girls, Chamberlain did at least comment on the country's economic and industrial development, noting that

> the chief progress made during the past thirty years has been in industrial development. Mines have been opened, mills erected, and new manufactures started. Japanese coal is now well-known throughout the East; copper and antimony are largely exported . . . Many articles that were formerly imported are now manufactured in the country.

Given its low cost and skilled labour, 'which requires only to be directed by competent men of business, the industrial future of Japan should be bright'.[14]

Another exception to Western commentators who overlooked Japan's rapid modernisation was Stafford Ransome, an engineer as well as a journalist, who noted in 1899: 'No more striking illustration of the wonderful adaptability of the Japanese character is to be found than that afforded by the readiness with which they have taken up Western methods of manufacturing.' Ransome observed how the modern industries of Japan are now dotting themselves about all over the country . . . Osaka now may be said to be fast developing into an industrial city pure and simple; and this is no doubt why I have heard Englishmen call it the Manchester, and Scotsmen the Glasgow, and Frenchmen the Lille, and Germans the Hamburg and Americans the Chicago of Japan.[15]

Industry and power are inextricably linked with the rise in size of Japan's population. Just as the demographic rise of the Anglo-Saxons gave the UK and US huge advantages in dominating large parts of the globe, so Japan's combination of demographic and industrial strength – the latter not sustainable without the former – propelled it into the position of being considered by Europe (especially after the Russo-Japanese War) as 'a power', a status not shared by any other Asian country. Modernisation and transformation underpinned Japan's remarkable victory against Russia in the war of 1904–5, showing that what might have been mistaken as inherent Anglo-Saxon or then European advantages were in fact simply the advantages not of race, but of a combination of population size and economic and industrial weight. Without these factors, Japan would not have been able to pursue the aggressive expansionism that would defeat Russia, overwhelm China and much of south-east Asia, take on the British Empire and the USA and expand its imperial power (albeit briefly) from the borders of India to deep into the Pacific. Japan's ability to conquer and dominate large parts of China shows that demography alone was not sufficient – China, after all, always had more people – but that a combination of Japanese demographic and industrial dynamism could defeat the Chinese demographic giant.

After the institution of the first modern census and improved data gathering from 1920, the picture developed of a *gradually* falling birth rate accompanying increasing urbanisation, a *sharply* falling mortality rate and therefore, in line with demographic transition theory, a fast rise in the population.[16] Although the growth in population was driven by improving economic circumstances, the discourse in Japan showed an alarmist concern about overpopulation. Japan was the most densely populated country in the world relative to its arable land.[17] This concern perhaps motivated and was certainly used to justify the imperial expansion of the 1930s.[18] Yet Japanese emigration – whether within the widening imperial bounds or beyond it – was on a small scale. Admittedly it was not helped by North American and Australasian immigration restrictions which remained in place right up to the 1960s, but even within areas conquered by Japan such as Manchukuo in China, emigration by Japanese made no material difference to the overall size of the population at home.[19] Emigration out of Japan was rarely above 10,000 a year, paltry compared to population growth (and of course utterly paltry when compared with European emigration rates in the period before the First World War), and by the 1930s there were more Koreans living in Japan than vice versa.[20] Manchukuo, it turned out, was not to be Japan's Canada. It was not to be heavily settled by Japanese nor to serve as an overflow for surplus population nor to serve as a breadbasket for the mother country.

In many ways the dilemma, the rhetoric and the policy of imperial Japan resembled that of Nazi Germany. Population expansion had been made possible by industrialisation, with a growing industrial population increasingly fed by imports of agricultural goods paid for by industrial exports. By the late 1920s, Japan was relying on imports for around one seventh of its rice consumption.[21] This was a situation which involved reliance on international trade and which nationalists disliked because it was seen as dependent rather than self-reliant. Nationalists both in Japan and Germany then claimed the need for additional space to feed their populations in a self-reliant manner. Both Japan's ambassador to London and its ambassador to Washington justified imperial expansion to their host countries on the basis of population growth, the latter arguing that the people of the US should recognise, in the light of the increasing number of Japan's people, 'the absolute necessity for more territory for their existence'.[22]

Yet when the Japanese imperialists conquered that space, like their German counterparts, they found it hard to fill with migrants from the supposedly overcrowded homeland. For all Hitler's desire to turn Ukraine into a German prairie and for all the appeals to the Americans that Japan needed its own 'Wild West' into which to expand, the

Anglo-Saxon model of demographic expansion going hand in hand with territorial expansion was simply not workable. On the one hand they were citing the exigencies of population pressures at home to justify expansion abroad, and at the same time they were stoking those population pressures through pro-natalist policies. In Japan, explicit pro-natalist policies were launched in 1941 when the government set a goal to boost the population to 100 million by the early 1960s, offering financial incentives:[23] two years later the prime minister said the goal was necessary for Japan's successful continued existence.[24]

Japan's industrial, demographic and imperial rise had already provoked reactions among the established powers. As early as 1895 Kaiser Wilhelm II had taken up the term 'Yellow Peril', while three years later Russia's minister of war had worried about Japan and China in terms of the armies they could field[25] and in Britain the *Spectator* fretted about 'a Japanese military caste controlling China and organising its army and navy': the same year the British prime minister expressed concern about 'great countries of enormous power, growing every year'.[26] None of this was exclusively demographic in tone and it tended to conflate Chinese scale with Japanese growth, but all of it recognised that at root it was the population dynamic of east Asia which made it seem threatening. The British response was to sign a treaty with Japan, developing its navy and using it against its rival Russia. The Russian response, determined by being closer than the British and by clashing ambitions on the mainland of the Far East, was to oppose Japan, fight it and lose. In any case, the demographic rise of Japan and the perception of the threat it posed, combined with industrial and military advance, shaped the international relations of east Asia and the Pacific from 1900 to 1945.

Japan's industrial and population expansion, like that of its European counterparts, was linked, and Japan's imperial expansion and subsequent wars were inconceivable without both the push and the resources which an expanded population offered. Japan's wartime losses of around 3 million people represent personal and historical tragedy, but in demographic terms they corresponded to no more than three or four years of peak population growth. Thus while Japan in 1945 was industrially and morally devastated, its population was still one of the world's largest. Like Russia – itself admittedly on the winning side, but having sustained huge human and material losses – Japan ended the Second World War with at least one crucial advantage: the strong demographic momentum which goes with recent rapid population expansion.

Post-War Japan: Towards the World's Oldest Country

Immediately after the Second World War Japan experienced a remarkable baby boom. Both in absolute terms and relative to the baby booms of America and Western Europe, it was notable for its intensity, but even more so for its brevity. The birth rate, which had dropped below thirty per thousand in the late 1930s, rose to 34.3 in 1947.[27] At this point (and now with reliable data to hand), total fertility in Japan was around four and a half, far above anything experienced in the West in the post-war period, after which it rapidly slumped.[28] By the early 1950s it was already down to three and by the 1960s two. There was a small upward movement from the mid 1960s to the mid 1970s, but the fertility rate never reached much above two, and then it fell again, slowly and steadily but to ever more exceptionally low levels, reaching 1.3 children per woman in the early years of the current century.[29] Today, the latest UN data suggests an improvement but an extremely modest one, with a total fertility rate still below one and a half children per woman.[30]

What had happened? The causes of this fall in fertility cannot be definitively determined in the case of Japan any more than they can elsewhere, but as elsewhere this very low fertility rate is correlated with rising income, urbanisation and increasing female education, particularly tertiary education. Compare female enrolment in higher education at below 5% in 1955, barely one-third of the male level, with around 50% forty years later, exceeding the male level.[31] Where these factors are combined with traditional attitudes to women in the workplace and to family (in Japan only around 2% of children are born out of wedlock compared to nearly 50% in the UK), the pattern, as we have already seen, is one of low fertility. And while current Japanese rates are well below replacement level, they are no lower, and indeed slightly higher, than those observed in many countries in southern and eastern Europe. Overall, the pattern of fertility change resembles that of the West but, confirming the concept of an accelerating demographic whirlwind, is somewhat faster.

The reasons for low fertility are of course impossible to establish with any certainty. Nonetheless there is much intriguing anecdotal evidence and comment on the subject. A demographer from Kobe University suggests:

[I]f you are single, it is difficult to find a good and right partner for marriage. If you are married, and if both husband and wife work like this, there's a slim chance to have a baby. No time or no energy left. If you want a baby, you (typically your wife) face a choice – continue to work or quit your job and have a baby. There's a trade-off here.[32]

As seen in Europe, in an era of female education and emancipation, cultures in which life is not made conducive for women to enter the workforce, to rise within it and to be able to combine its demands with those of childbearing and child-rearing will be countries with low fertility rates. It is hardly surprising therefore that the World Economic Forum consistently rates Japan one of the worst places in the developed world for economic equality in the workplace. One woman, Tomita, a thirty-two-year-old from Tokyo, describes an experience that may well be typical:

[A] boyfriend proposed to me three years ago. I turned him down when I realised I cared more about my job. After that, I lost interest in dating. It became awkward when the question of the future came up . . . The bosses assume you will get pregnant. You have to resign. You end up being a housewife with no independent income. It's not an option for women like me.[33]

There are suggestions that young Japanese people are increasingly turning off sex and relationships and opting for more solitary pleasures, often involving some form of electronic gaming.[34]

Besides its falling and then very low fertility rate, the second noteworthy feature of Japanese demography since the Second World

War has been the extension of life expectancy. In the early 1950s it was already over sixty at birth, itself a great improvement on the level of a little over age thirty-five in much of the nineteenth century.[35] The improvement continued with the benefits of increased urbanisation and industrialisation as the Japanese experienced improving diet, food storage, housing and health care. The main cause of death shifted from infectious diseases to chronic degenerative disease. Today life expectancy in Japan is over eighty-three. This is the highest of any UN member state and, of the territories covered by the UN, higher than any except Hong Kong, and the difference in life expectancy between Japan and Hong Kong is tiny. Japan's life expectancy is not much short of five years ahead of the United States.[36] Japanese women, who are now the longest-living group in the world, have enjoyed a life expectancy extension of three months every year for the past 160 years.[37] Whatever its demographic difficulties (more on this shortly), Japan should be given credit for this extraordinary achievement. It can also boast one of the lowest infant mortality rates in the world at around two per thousand compared to three in France and Germany and six in the USA.[38]

With a flagging birth rate but mortality depressed by ever-longer life expectancy, Japan experienced a long period of population growth. Initially this was a standard case of demographic momentum, with a young population creating many births in absolute terms even if it was not reaching long-term replacement level, while the old are so relatively few that mortality is low. At some point this effect ceased to be the force behind the rise in population growth: instead population growth was fuelled by the fact that a relatively elderly population was succeeding in cheating death for longer and longer. Although additions to the population – births – were fewer and fewer, so were subtractions from it.

The population of Japan kept growing into the twenty-first century despite the low birth rate, but at a decelerating rate. The average annual population growth was over 1% in the post-war period up to and including the late 1970s, halving in the 1980s and halving again in the 1990s; in the first decade of this century it was barely at a tenth of its post-war level, and total population finally peaked in 2012 at a little over 128 million.[39] At this point natural population decline (deaths minus births, i.e. taking no account of migration) was over 200,000 per annum although the actual decline has been slightly slower due to modest net immigration.[40] By the middle of this century Japan's population may fall to 80 million, less than two-thirds of its current level.[41] The mainstream UN forecast is that it will have lost a third of its population by the end of the current century. This population decline, although it has only just begun, has been coming for decades: the government was shocked when data for 1989 showed a fertility rate below that for the freak year 1966 when fertility was significantly depressed by the inauspicious horoscope of the 'fiery horse'.[42]

Japan is unlike other countries in several respects. Whereas the US and Western Europe have to some extent compensated for their impending population declines by importing immigrants from the Third World (and in the case of Western Europe, en masse from eastern Europe), with a corresponding impact on the ethnic composition of the population, this has not been something Japan has seriously contemplated, although there has been modest in-migration in recent years.

If the sharp contrast between Japan and the West relates to immigration, the sharp contrast between Japan and Russia relates to life expectancy. Whereas Russia's population decline has been *precipitated* by stubbornly high mortality compounding low fertility, in Japan's case population decline has been *delayed* by ever-increasing life expectancy offsetting the low birth rate. If the Japanese had not managed to continue increasing life expectancy, their population decline would be faster. So Japan remains more or less ethnically homogeneous but is increasingly old.

Japan is particularly interesting because it shows us a glimpse of a society with low fertility and an ageing population, and in this it is a pioneer. Such has been the speed of its demographic transition that it has overtaken Europe and the UK, despite starting behind them, particularly in the sphere of ageing. As the world's population growth slows and faces possible reversal, so ageing is inevitable: Japan's median age is now over forty-six, and this makes its population the world's oldest along with Italy and Germany, and nearly nine years older than that of the United States.[43] Its population has sometimes been the fastest ageing in recorded history;[44] those aged over sixty-five rose from below one in twenty of the population in 1950 to over one in five in 2005.[45] Between 2005 and 2015 alone, while the Japanese population as a whole levelled off, the number of its centenarians almost trebled.[46]

This has given rise to the same ageing effects experienced in Europe, but more so. Whereas in Bulgaria and Italy it is the villages which are being depopulated, in Japan this has even started happening in some of the suburbs. This gives rise to an impending problem of physical decay. Japan already has 8 million empty homes. 'Tokyo could end up being surrounded by Detroits,' complains one real estate agent.[47] The situation in the countryside is predictably worse, with not only wolves but also bears now roaming where schools once stood. Village children are now so few that they have to be bused over long distances.[48] With historically small family sizes and many having had no children, it is estimated that up to 30,000 elderly Japanese die in their homes alone and, for a time at least, unnoticed. A whole industry has grown up around dealing with the removal and fumigation necessary when a body is found weeks or even months after death.[49]

This dramatic greying of the Japanese population has significant economic consequences. As we saw in the context of the industrial revolution, the link between economics and population is not straightforward and usually works in two directions. Demographic change affects economic development and economic development affects demographic change. In the case of Japan as in that of the West, economic and population expansion arrived more or less simultaneously, and in the case of Japan, as in the case of Western countries, GDP rose as a result of both rising population, rising productivity and rising per capita income. This was true both after 1868 when Japan opened itself to the world and after 1945 when it enjoyed the demographic dividend of a fast-growing population but falling fertility, allowing increased workforce participation. What is striking was the way the country's economic dynamism seemed to dry up at precisely the point when the share of its workforce-age population peaked.[50]

Japan now faces unprecedented pressures on its pensions system, which was significantly reformed in 2004. The older population will also put pressure on elderly care (particularly in the absence of immigrant care workers) and health care expenditure. It seems likely that there is a relationship between the fact that Japan is the world's oldest and most rapidly ageing country and that in 2015 it had by far the highest government debt–GDP ratio in the OECD at 248%, well ahead even of Greece and Italy at around 150% each.[51]

Meanwhile, it is not just economics but also politics which is affected by ageing. We have seen the link between population growth and aggressive imperialism leading to Japan's involvement in the Second World War. After its defeat in 1945, Japan pursued a more or less pacifist policy, sheltering under the wing of the United States from a defence perspective and, like Germany, avoiding both defence expenditure and projection of itself overseas. In 2005 it spent barely 1% of its GDP on defence, while the US spent 4% and the UK and France around 2.5%. However, perceptions of Japanese pacifism, at least from the Western perspective, have been linked to economic rather than military actions, with a rich literature up to the early 1990s suggesting that Japan's economy and finance would be all-conquering. Much less has been heard on this topic since then, as the Japanese economy has gone from outperforming to underperforming by comparison with the economies of the West. In the 1970s and early 1980s, when fear of Japan's impending global economic domination was at its peak, Japan's population was just above half that of the United States. By 2015, when the Japanese menace seemed to have disappeared from popular discourse, it was around 40% and falling.[52] Despite limited recent changes in military policy, it continues to rely essentially on the US for its defence, initially in the cold war context but now principally against a perceived threat from China. For Japan, demography and destiny seemingly cannot be untangled. With the expansionist years long behind it, the question will be how Japan copes with an increasingly old and, from now on, shrinking population. In this, being a trailblazer, it may have lessons for the rest of us.

China: Towards the First Billion and Beyond

China has undertaken some of the greatest engineering works in history to tame its rivers, bringing water and electricity to millions and displacing millions in the process. That China has also engaged in history's most epic – and ultimately futile – effort to tame its human tide should come as no surprise.

China long ago surpassed any other country for population size – although it is about to be eclipsed in this respect by India. By some measures it has already overtaken the United States in economic size – although clearly not on a per capita basis. This global population giant, so long said to be asleep, has in the past few decades become wide awake as its modernisation in scale, scope and speed has eclipsed anything the world has ever seen. China's gargantuan population of around 1.5 billion makes it what it is today, and has played a central role in how it arrived at this point.

China's antiquity as a continuous state and people marks it out from Europe, whose states and nations post-date the first Chinese state by at least a millennium. China was the first country to pass the 1 billion population mark, a status it attained in the early 1980s. By dint of the scale of its population, it can only *fail* to be a major global political and economic entity in eras when it is in a particularly dire condition. China may have chosen not to project itself overseas after the fifteenth century, but it could not be dominated by any other power thanks to both its scale and relative technical advancement. Dynasties came and went, but even when they came from outside – such as the Manchu Qing – they were essentially co-opted into the system and the culture of China.

By the nineteenth century, however, while still a demographic giant, China had failed to move forward with the dynamic momentum of Europe, either in demographic or industrial terms, and it paid a price that included the Opium Wars (1839–42 and 1856–60) and the putting down of the Boxer Rebellion (1899–1900). Why this was so is an intriguing question that has spawned a literature all of its own. Even a relative minnow, Japan, was able to replace Chinese dominance of Korea and rule of Taiwan from 1894 and to conquer and control large areas of China in the 1930s by dint not of absolute demographic advantage, but of a mixture of demographic and economic dynamism.

Yet once China was able to combine size with industrial progress, it came to stand once again at the threshold of global power and with at least the potential to challenge the hegemony of the demographically smaller powers. In China's case, its demographic forward movement (up to the 1970s) was achieved before its industrial progress (from the 1980s). Taken together, demographic and industrial momentum put it back at the centre of the international stage. The historical status and role of China owes much to the remarkable path of its demography.

For Japan, 1945 makes sense as a 'zero hour'. This was the year of its defeat at the hands of the Allies following nuclear strikes on Hiroshima and Nagasaki, the year from which, like Germany, it needed to start reconstructing itself from the rubble within a new international framework of US hegemony. For China, 1949 makes more sense as a starting point, the year of the ending of the civil war and the founding of the People's Republic. (It is also the point at which the demographic data becomes more or less reliable.) However, it is not possible to get any kind of grasp of China's demography and the role this played in its story without going back to an earlier age.

An understanding of China's demography in earlier periods is hampered, as elsewhere, by a paucity of definitive data. As a continuous state, albeit with the interruptions of dynastic changes, China does have official population data going back to the mid eighteenth century, and there are estimates of population based on official records at least as far back as the start of the Ming period in the second half of the fourteenth century.[53] The reliability of much of this data is, however, questionable. Comparing these to estimates further back, it appears that China's population did not grow between the start of the Common Era and the middle of the seventeenth century, with a population of around 60 million both in the year AD 2 and the middle of the seventeenth century.[54] Malthusians have identified five cycles of famine, epidemic and war operating during this period, cutting back the population, followed by regrowth up to what can be considered some kind of natural frontier.

China, then, was remarkably different to Western Europe in that although suffering the same ups and downs over the long term, it experienced more than a millennium and a half without moving forward. This should not be seen as a sign of 'backwardness', however, since for most of this time China was technologically the most advanced part of the world; and for this reason the pattern should be seen in the reverse, as China having arrived at or somewhere near its own Malthusian frontier much earlier than the West, mastering the arts of irrigation and rice cultivation and the population density that this agricultural system can support. Indeed, Malthus recognised China as the archetype of a society which, lacking constraints, lived at the frontier of the highest population it could support and therefore at the frontier of misery and hunger.

Exactly when and why Chinese population growth took off is unclear, but it seems to have gathered momentum between the mid seventeenth and mid nineteenth centuries, at precisely the time Japan's population was stagnating, with China's population reaching around 430 million in 1850.[55] This represents a growth rate of more than 1% over two centuries. It appears to have been achieved by means of an intensification of agriculture involving capital investment, irrigation and greater use of fertiliser, raising agricultural output and thus the population it could support, albeit at a very low standard of living.[56] Estimates of the country's population at various times, despite the existence of some records, are still uncertain, and some estimates of population growth set it at not much more than 0.5% for 1650–1929. Unlike the progress of Britain during the course of the nineteenth century, it was a growth rate achieved without rather than despite mass emigration. There was some Chinese emigration, particularly within Asia, but in 1940, even counting the Chinese in Manchuria as 'overseas', the total Chinese population outside China amounted to barely 20 million. This may have represented a significant presence relative to some of the places where the Chinese lived, such as Malaya, but was less than 5% of the domestic population in that era.[57] Population growth seems to have slowed from the middle of the nineteenth century, perhaps to 0.25% between 1850 and 1947,[58] at least in part the result of the bloody Taiping rebellion, responsible for the deaths of 20 million people.

The data on the fertility and mortality underpinning this 200-year expansion followed by a century's slowdown is obscure, but it is certain that throughout the period, at least by modern standards, both fertility and mortality rates were high. It was until recently generally believed that China was closer than Japan to the pre-modern norm assumed by Malthusians and by proponents of the demographic transition theory.[59] However, even this has now been challenged, with some historians suggesting that the Chinese, like the Japanese, may have been managing, by means of a number of techniques including widespread infanticide, to keep their population below the maximal frontier and thus living standards above the Malthusian minimum.[60]

The story of Chinese demographic change in the quarter-century or so of Mao's era is one of the most dramatic extremes presided over by a regime with a highly inconsistent population policy. Marxist ideology argued that the size of a population was artificially constrained by the social system: once the people were freed from feudal or capitalistic bonds, the plenty of socialism would arrive and this would result in the population flourishing both in terms of the living standards of individuals and absolute numbers. In line with traditional Marxist anti-Malthusianism, Mao stated in 1949 that it was good for China to have a large population, that it would find ways to feed it and that 'of all the things in the world, people are the most precious'.[61]

Whether this triggered or merely accompanied a booming population, the fertility rate remained high, at close to six children per woman, while mortality fell and the population expanded rapidly. In 1950 the population grew at nearly 3%, a step change up from the annual population growth rates reviewed up to this point and testimony to the rising intensity of the human tide as it progressed beyond Europe and North America.[62] In some circles this gave rise to alarm, particularly when the results of the 1952 census became available, showing more than 600 million people in China as compared with just 470 million in 1947.[63] The numbers were almost certainly inaccurate, suggesting an implausible 5% annual increase in population, but nevertheless they radically changed the terms of the debate. The pro-natalist rhetoric was toned down, contraceptives became more available and a more 'liberal' view gave way to increasing birth control propaganda from 1957. In that year abortion was legalised.

Policy changed again in 1958 when Mao insisted that 'it is still good to have more people' and population control came to be regarded as 'rightist'.[64] This was part of the lead up to the Great Leap Forward, which demographically as well as economically was precisely the opposite of what its name implied – it was a series of madcap schemes for rapid modernisation which set the country back. Whilst the population had indeed been leaping forward until that point, at least in terms of numbers, it probably went into reverse as grain production dropped by around 30% and famine ensued.[65] Mao's ruthlessness and lack of concern for human life was clear in his preparedness to fight a nuclear war if it would mean the triumph of the Communist camp. He wrote:

> Let us imagine how many people would die if war breaks out. There are 2.7 billion people in the world, and a third could be lost . . . I say that if the worst came to the worst and one half [of the world's population] dies, there will still be one half left, but imperialism would be erased and the whole world would become socialist. After a few years, there would be 2.7 billion people again.[66]

Within China agricultural policies were applied in the 1950s which in many ways resembled those that Stalin had imposed, specifically collectivisation and forced delivery of grain 'surpluses'. Unsurprisingly, the results were the same. There was a clash between the vast forces of demographic momentum which had been driving up the size of the population and the mass starvation brought on by the Great Leap Forward. The fertility rate appears to have fallen from nearly six in 1958 to not much more than three just three years later, a symptom of and a response to the brutal conditions of the time rather than to a government population policy that was turning back to pro-natalism.[67]

Once this period of economic mayhem was over, the fertility rate shot up again to five or six, and once again the authorities worried about population growth, which in the late 1960s was again approaching the 3% per annum mark. China's buoyant underlying demography was a key to its rapid recovery from Mao's ravages, but this was of little comfort to the millions who had starved as a result of them. A once lively countryside conveyed the depths of the disaster following the devastation: 'an eerie, unnatural silence descended upon the countryside. The few pigs that had not been confiscated had died of hunger and disease. Chickens and ducks had long since been slaughtered.' Even the wildlife was affected; there were

> no birds left in the trees, which had been stripped of their leaves and bark, their bare and bony spines standing stark against an empty sky. People were famished beyond speech. In this world plundered of every layer that might offer sustenance, down to bark and mud, corpses often ended up in shallow graves or simply by the roadside. A few people ate human flesh.[68]

Horrendous though the Great Leap Forward and the later Cultural Revolution were, the loss of life they entailed could not and did not hold back the human tide. Just as with Stalin's Russia two or three decades earlier, underlying demographic momentum was so great that the population kept growing. A little over half a billion in 1950, it rose to three-quarters of a billion by 1967. This was thanks to a fertility rate which stayed above six children per woman well into the 1960s and a life expectancy (i.e. a falling mortality rate) which was extended from under forty-five to over sixty in the two decades from 1950.[69]

From 1970, however, things began to change. Life expectancy continued to lengthen but fertility rates fell to below three within in a decade.[70] Indeed, the 1970s in China was a most extraordinary period, once again showing how the later the tide, the stronger both its flow and ebb. The halving from around six to around three children per woman had taken five times as long in pioneering Britain, and at least twice as long in Russia. It was achieved by a combination of social change – specifically an increase in urbanisation and female education – and political direction. In 1981, for example, the urban fertility rate was less than half that of rural areas, so an increasingly urban China was bound to have a falling fertility rate.[71] Mao had engaged with and then toned down his pro-natalist rhetoric, and after his death contraceptives became more available after the chaotic years of the Cultural Revolution. Indeed, for anyone seeking to guess which direction China would take next, the modernisation of its family size and structure in the 1970s was a clue to the fact that something extraordinary was about to happen, namely the entry of China into the world economy, its massive and rapid industrialisation and what can best be seen as the greatest act of modernisation that has ever occurred in human history and – given China's size – is ever likely to.

After Mao: One Child China

A few years after Mao's death in 1976, China aligned itself to an unambiguous policy of 'modernisation' of which population control was a key element. This was signalled by senior Communist Hu Yaobang, late party chairman and general secretary, who declared in 1978 that 'the population problem is the most important problem'.[72] Having ditched the Marxian view that socialism would create plenty and so obviate the need for restraint of numbers, the Communist Party now revived a view first put forward much earlier, that the planning of population should be seen as part of a rational planned economy. Vice Premier Chen Muhua insisted that it should be possible 'to regulate the production of human beings so that the population growth corresponds to an increase in material things'.[73] The slogan regarding family size changed from 'Two Just Right' to 'One is Best'.[74]

From 1979 to 2015 an explicit 'One Child Policy' was pursued, involving exhortation, monetary inducements and sanctions including potentially loss of home and job. The policy was codified in 1980 and implemented between 1980 and 1984.[75] In some cases it involved direct coercion. Exceptions were made, for example for national minorities, and there have been periodic relaxations, such as the recent exemption where both parents are single children. Initially the policy was strongly resisted in the rural areas where, following the return of land to the peasants, it ran counter to people's interests. The fertility rate in China today is somewhere between 1.2 and 1.5; in the capital Beijing it is barely 0.75.[76]

Yet the great irony of the One Child Policy was that it was almost certainly not necessary. This can be demonstrated in two ways: first by reference to historical trends within China, and second by contrast to other countries. In 1981, as the One Child Policy was being implemented, China's population passed 1 billion, a truly staggering number which both astonished and frightened many outside China and was clearly terrifying China's own leadership. Yet at this point, fertility rates had tumbled already – from six to three children per woman in a decade. The trends were sharp and clear from 1970, so the implementation of the One Child Policy cannot be held responsible. Unsurprisingly, China's population growth was slowing too. At 1.4% per annum it was still high, but half the nearly 3% that it had reached little more than a decade earlier. So it is clear that by its own dynamics, Chinese society was addressing the issue without the coercive intervention of the state.

The second way of demonstrating that the One Child Policy was not necessary is by international comparisons. The actual trajectory of fertility in China was not so different to that of other countries in east and south-east Asia whose governments did not apply such draconian, top-down methods. In Taiwan, the rebel island province controlled by nationalist opponents of Mao, fertility had fallen to around three in the mid 1970s, a little ahead of the mainland (and not surprisingly; spared Mao's excesses, Taiwan simply progressed towards modernity more quickly): by the late 1990s it had fallen to between one and a half and two, the same level as in the People's Republic, again without any draconian top-down policies. In South Korea, where likewise a total fertility rate of three children per woman had been reached by the late 1970s, the fertility rate was one and a half by the late 1990s.[77] Thus both Korea and Taiwan – and other Asian countries too – with around the same starting point as the People's Republic at the point of the implementation of the One Child Policy – achieved similar or even greater falls in fertility rates without resorting to the levels of coercion the Chinese Communist Party felt were necessary. (Another valid comparator, the ethnic Chinese population of Malaysia, has a fertility rate of around one and a half children per woman, close to that of China's, again achieved without draconian measures.[78])

If ever there was a lesson that the human tide is best managed by ordinary human beings themselves and not by their self-appointed engineers, it is here. Given education, some level of opportunity and access to contraceptives, most men and women, but particularly women, are capable of making decisions in their own interests which also match the requirements of society, at least in terms of reducing fertility. Adam Smith's hidden hand works in demography as well as in economics: individuals left to their own devices, if informed and enabled to make their own decisions, will tend to make decisions in their own interests which are in the interests of society, at least when it comes to the need for falling fertility rates. But it is unsurprising that Smith's Marxist ideological enemies, who were running China, did not recognise it. The policy can be thought of as a 'great leap' in population control, the demographic corollary of the earlier disastrous policies in agriculture and industry: 'The approach was guided by the Leninist notion that if the party exerted enough effort, every problem could be solved.'[79]

As ever when such top-down policies are implemented, it is important not to lose sight of the individual tragedies within the bigger statistical picture. Professionals have lost their jobs because of their insistence on having a second child.[80] In a country which performs well over 20 million abortions every year, not all of them are voluntary. One Chinese woman who wanted a second child decided to go ahead, despite the serious ramifications for her family and the rights of the newborn to an education:

[I]n March of 2014, a group of six to seven people from the Family Planning Committee forced their way into my home. They set two people to watch my house. Four others dragged me into a car that had been waiting at my door. My helpless mother followed me in another car to the hospital. In the hospital, on that same afternoon, the doctor injected the abortion drug oxytocin into my abdomen . . . Afterward, the doctor gave me another shot, saying that it was to stop the pain. But the pain did not stop. When they performed the operation to clean my womb, it was so unbelievably painful. Lying on that bed, I felt my body was cut open and broken. I kept crying. My baby didn't have a chance to come into this world and call me 'Mom'. My baby didn't have a chance to make a single sound. My baby was deprived of life by the government . . .[81]

The Chinese Rollercoaster

With its huge size, rapid growth and then plummeting fertility, China's population has been on an extraordinary journey since the foundation of the People's Republic. Whatever the cruelties and inconsistencies of its policies, China has gone through the classic demographic sequence of falling mortality, rising population, then falling fertility and stabilising population. Life expectancy since 1950 has extended from under forty-five to over seventy-five, an increase of nearly six months every year, an achievement not much less impressive than and clearly related to the rapid growth of the Chinese economy and rise in living standards. It is difficult at this stage to take stock and understand what these changes mean for the future, but some themes can be observed: first ageing and its implications for the Chinese economy, second the structure of Chinese families, and third the point at which China will reach 'peak population'. Beforehand, however, it bears stating the obvious: that China's prominence in world affairs, including economic matters, is dependent on its gargantuan population size. Other countries have undergone economic growth as rapid, or almost as rapid, as China's, either in the past or concurrently with China, but it is only because of China's billion plus people that when the country moves, the world notices.

China is ageing quickly, as would be expected from its falling fertility rates and lengthening life expectancy. The median Chinese citizen remained in his/her twenties throughout the first forty years or so of the People's Republic, but in the first fifteen years of the twenty-first century the median age has risen by seven years.[82] This is nearly three times the speed of ageing experienced in the UK and the US, and the trend will continue. Between 1975 and 2050 the number of Chinese over the age of sixty is forecast to rise sevenfold while the number of those under fourteen years will more or less halve. Those aged over sixty as a share of the population will pass the share in the United States in around 2030.[83]

China's working-age population has already started to decline in absolute terms, not just as a percentage of the population. The Chinese population will continue to be extremely large at least for the rest of the twenty-first century, but we are already at the stage where one of the motors of Chinese economic growth – population growth feeding into a growing workforce – is close to shutting down. Future economic growth will need to come from greater workforce productivity, and it is questionable whether this alone can deliver the kind of growth rates that have come to be expected from the Chinese economy. It is unclear how China will cope with the pension challenges. The lack of state old-age provision is generally seen as the driver of the high Chinese household savings rate. This was one of the great motors of financial instability leading to the 2007/2008 crash as vast quantities of Chinese savings found their way direct, or through banks, into the hands of over-borrowed Western governments and consumers.

Chinese families have not only aged and become more urban: they have also become more male. The One Child Policy coupled with increased availability of sex tests for foetuses and selective abortions has resulted in a sex imbalance of 120 boys to 100 girls.[84] Often selective abortions occur because of family pressure in what is still a fairly patriarchal society, especially in the countryside. As one woman put it: 'I can't really blame [my in-laws]; their view was a common one. We have a saying, "The better sons you have, the better life we can have," because men have more strength and can carry out more work.'[85] Such preference for males has a number of effects. First, it creates a marriage problem for a later period which, given the overall size of China's population, cannot be fully resolved by importing brides other than on a massive scale. Secondly, it increases the replacement level of fertility: if women are less than half the population, then each woman must on average have a higher number of children for the population as a whole to reproduce itself. Thus a total fertility rate of around one and a half for China (according to the UN; China's own figures suggest 1.2) is further below replacement level than it would be for countries without a sex imbalance. Beyond the issue of the male to female ratio, China is also a country where siblings are increasingly rare and cousins too have become rarer, resulting in a single child being indulged by one set of parents and often by two sets of grandparents. This is not the place to consider the psychological implications and their social ramifications, but in this respect China is hardly unique, with plenty of other countries in east Asia and south and east Europe experiencing similar or even higher levels of single children. Given the additional factor of the sex imbalance, or perhaps for specifically historic reasons, it is perhaps no surprise that the term 'Little Emperor' is of Chinese provenance.

Increasingly old and disproportionately male though it may be, China's population continues to grow, albeit at a markedly slower rate than was the case for much of the twentieth century. It also continues to be the world's largest – but not for long. In the early 1970s China's population was almost half as large again as India's; in 2015 it was less than 7% larger. India too has been subject to draconian population policies from above, but these have been applied less systematically and for a shorter period than in China. Furthermore, India has been behind China in terms of industrialisation and urbanisation, with around one-third of Indians now living in cities as opposed to one-half of Chinese. The recent relaxation of the One Child Policy appears to have had little impact on birth rates.[86] This is not surprising: there is no reason why Chinese attitudes and practices should significantly diverge from other east Asian countries that are more or less uniformly experiencing sub-replacement fertility.

The result has been that, although India's fertility rate has fallen, the average Indian woman now has almost a whole child more than the average Chinese woman.[87] According to the median fertility projection of the United Nations, the population of India is set to exceed that of China sometime in the mid 2020s. The UN expects that by 2030 China's population will peak and start declining, some way short of the 1.5 billion mark. Demography is hardly an international competitive sport – although it can get competitive in situations of ethnic conflict[88] – nevertheless, whatever the future has in store for China, it is likely in considerable degree to be shaped by the peculiarities of the shape, size and characteristics of its population. China will lose its position as having the world's largest population while it is already a fast-ageing and at best a middle-income country.

The Human Tide Across Asia

While Japan and China have each acted as protagonists on the modern world stage and pioneered demographic developments, their changing demographic advances have proven surpassable. Since the mid 1960s it has been Indonesia, not Japan, which has had east and south-east Asia's second highest population, now exceeding a quarter of a billion. Five other countries (which, together with Indonesia, will be referred to as the Asian Six) in east and south-east Asia have populations of 50 million or more: the Republic of Korea (South Korea), Vietnam, Myanmar, the Philippines and Thailand. Collectively they have a population of nearly 800 million, well over twice that of the United States.

Looking simply at the population size of the Asian Six in the twentieth century, two things are very striking. The first is that their populations have grown astonishingly since the middle of the twentieth century: in 1950 they constituted collectively fewer than 200 million people, but by 2015 their numbers had more or less quadrupled, a collective average rise of more than 2% a year for sixty-five years. Population growth in the Asian Six peaked in the early 1960s at nearly 3% per annum but is now down to less than half of that and falling. The second thing to note is how that growth has slowed. First, mortality rates plunged, particularly infant mortality. Life expectancy, for example, in South Korea extended from under fifty to around seventy in the three decades following the end of the Korean War. Since 1950 Korean babies not making it to their first birthday have fallen from 138 per thousand to three. Over the same period, the average Korean woman has gone from having six children to less than one and a quarter.[89] This is giving rise to the same sort of demographic problems for Korea that Japan is experiencing: the number of children in Korean schools has almost halved since 1980.[90]

The other countries in the group, although less prosperous than Korea, have followed a similar population pattern. Thais, for example, now live for only four fewer years than Americans and have fewer children. (In the early 1950s, their lifespan was nearly twenty years less than Americans and they had nearly twice as many offspring.)

Childlessness in Thailand is becoming common, particularly in urban areas, and seems to be driven by the same spirit of female emancipation as found elsewhere in Asia. The *Bangkok Post* reports a conversation in a coffee shop between fifty-four-year-old Varaporn and her twenty-nine-year-old niece, May. The aunt declares: 'I have a house, a car and a high academic status. What else do I need? My life is complete.' The niece, with a partner but no children, takes a similar line: 'Having a kid is just too expensive . . . If I can't offer my kids the best care, I'd rather not have any.'[91]

Already the median age in Korea has doubled from twenty to forty since 1950 and the UN expects it to reach fifty by 2040. Thailand, a much poorer country, is not far behind. Despite economic progress in recent decades, its demographic progress has been faster, so that it is one of a host of countries which threaten to become old before they become rich.

After running at full flow across Asia during most of the twentieth century, the human tide has ebbed dramatically in this region in recent decades. Just as neither the Anglo-Saxons nor Europeans more generally had a monopoly on the early, expansive stages of demographic transition, so they have had no monopoly on the later stages, with smaller family sizes leading to older and eventually shrinking societies across many other parts of the world.

At least for now, east Asia enjoys the benefits of peace and in most countries a high degree of social harmony associated with diminishing populations. It is a dubious trade-off − of current stability for future prospects − and one which nations less advanced in the demographic process, in the Middle East and North Africa for example, are yet to experience.

9

The Middle East and North Africa

The Demography of Instability

On 17 December 2010 Mohamed Bouazizi, a twenty-six-year-old Tunisian street fruit vendor, set himself on fire in protest at the corrupt and bureaucratic system he encountered while trying to earn a living. His anger and frustration reverberated around a region in which millions of others faced the same frustrations, setting off what came to be known as the Arab Spring, a chain of hopeful revolts against hopeless regimes. While this action succeeded in toppling the governments of Tunisia, Libya, Egypt and Yemen, and seriously challenging the Syrian and Bahraini regimes, it was followed not by the hoped-for democratisation or liberalisation of these countries but rather by a messy mixture of reaction, chaos and civil war.

The Arab Spring may be over, yet the instability to which it gave rise continues to ricochet around the region. It is clear, however, that the developments triggered by Bouazizi's protest marked a sharp discontinuity: namely, that the Middle East and North Africa had been paralysed by ageing and unchanging rulers, with men like Muammar Gaddafi in Libya and Hosni Mubarak in Egypt, never mind royal houses from Morocco to Qatar, having ruled their respective nations for multiple decades with no democracy or accountability. Demography surely played an important role in events. For while regimes from the Atlantic to the Gulf were sitting static atop their subjects, run year in, year out by the same ageing monarchs or presidents, the societies beneath were changing fast and a key characteristic of that social change was demographic.

No country in the region illustrates this point more vividly than Yemen. When Ali Abdullah Saleh came to power in 1978, the total population of this country (including south Yemen, over which, at that point, he did not preside) was 7.5 million. In 2012, at the time he was ousted, it was 25.5 million. In some years during the 1990s, the population of Yemen was growing at a mind-boggling 5% per annum, a rate at which a population will grow more than *one hundredfold* in the space of a century. (If Germany were to grow at this rate for a century, for example, then there would be more Germans than there are people in the world today.) This was being achieved purely through natural causes, through an excess of births over deaths. Yemen had not become a destination of migration. (Far from it. It was and remains so economically and socially underdeveloped that it has not even been capable until recently of generating significant emigration, so poor and immobile have been its people; cross-border and par-ticularly intercontinental migration begins significantly only when a certain level of prosperity and modernity occurs as we have seen in the case of people from southern and eastern Europe flocking to the US in the late nineteenth century.) Yemen's level of population growth puts Britain's mere near quadrupling of its population during the nineteenth century in the shade. In 1990, the median Yemeni was aged just fourteen.

Although Yemen has been an extreme example of this hyper-charged demographic trend, it was nevertheless representative of what was going on in the region as a whole. In 1950 Egypt's population was less than a third of Germany's; today it has surpassed it. Most of the countries in the region have populations with a median age below thirty and in some, such as Sudan and Iraq, it is below twenty, although in most cases the median age is rising fast.[1] Precisely *how* such striking demographic change worked its way into the region's political scene is complex; *that* it did seems beyond question, for it is hard to envis-age such youth and dynamism at the level of the population not somehow making its mark on the course of events. A country cannot experience a multiplication of its population and remain the same; it cannot have a young population without this somehow influencing just around everything around it. At least in the modern world, an autocracy cannot sit immobile and stagnant forever atop a young and dynamic population that is growing apace.

Population Shock

As everywhere else, wars and famines in the Middle East had set populations back and good times allowed them to grow. However, it was only as a process of modernisation began that here, as elsewhere, demography started to follow a recognisable journey rather than a more or less random path. Although much of the Middle East contin-ued to be ruled by the Ottoman Turks up to the end of the First World War, European empires were making their inroads, with the British, French and Italians occupying Egypt and North Africa and the Germans increasingly influencing the Ottoman Empire itself; with European occupation and influence often came the start of demographic transition.

In this region as elsewhere the data may be imperfect, but it is notable that Ottoman censuses began in 1831, not so long after those of the UK and the USA. Many of the Ottoman records have their limitations. Often this is because the objective of gathering the data was to estimate the forces which could be raised for the army and so focused on male Muslims, who alone would be recruited. The data was often compiled with little clear instruction from the centre, giving rise to issues of consistency. Nevertheless, early Ottoman censuses provide at the very least a useful foundation on which to base estimates of population.[2]

Understanding the demography of the Ottoman Empire in the nineteenth century is made more difficult by the fact that its borders were changing and, for the most part, contracting. The Turks were under attack from the emerging Balkan Christian nations, such as Serbs and Bulgarians, who were wishing to liberate themselves from Muslim rule; from an ever-pressing Russia in the Caucasus; from the British and French expanding their empires, and eventually from Italians wishing to found theirs. Yet taking data based on the censuses of 1884 and 1906, more or less for consistent territory, it can be seen that the overall population grew between these dates from 17 to 21 million, an annual average growth rate of only slightly less than 1%.[3]

In contrast to Britain, which attained this rate throughout the nine-teenth century despite a significant population outflow to the US and the Dominions, the Ottoman Empire achieved its population growth with the assistance of what appears to have been significant immigration, particularly from the Caucasus and Balkans from which as many as 5 million Muslims had fled by the early part of the twentieth century.[4] These refugee populations were escaping the territorial advance of Christian powers including Russia and the emerging Balkan nations, who were adopting what today would be called policies or at least practices of ethnic or religious cleansing, and retreating with the Ottoman armies back into the Muslim Empire's shrinking territory, and thus helping the population of the Ottoman Empire to grow. The extraordinary brutality with which both Russians and Serbs cleansed their Muslim populations as they advanced into Islamic areas is today mostly forgotten. It is estimated that 90% of the Muslim population of the Caucasus was massacred or exiled as Russia extended its rule to the area.[5] Populations known as Circassians continue to exist across the Middle East and beyond, the descendants of those who fled.

On the other hand Turkey's treatment of its own Christian population was often little better, and in some cases worse. The Armenian genocide of the First World War involved the extermination of more than a million Christian Armenians in eastern Anatolia and was but the largest and most brutal of the massacres inflicted on this unfortunate people by their Muslim overlords.[6] Much of the dirty work was undertaken by local Kurds, albeit under the auspices and guiding hand of the rulers in Istanbul.[7] The killing was often accompanied by rape and the enslavement of women. It was followed by a process of forced assimilation and conversion for those who remained.[8] A similar process of massacre, expulsion and forced assimilation was soon afterwards applied by the newly emergent Turkish state to the Greeks of western Anatolia, a response to a disastrous Greek invasion in the wake of the collapse of the Ottoman Empire.[9]

While Muslims were pouring into the Ottoman Empire from the Balkans and the Caucasus, immigration of a different kind was experienced in North Africa, namely the arrival of Europeans, first in Algeria in the wake of the French conquest (starting in 1830) and later in Tunisia, again following its incorporation into the French Empire. By 1900 there were over half a million Europeans in Algeria, 40% of them not French but drawn from other south European countries, and by 1911 over 200,000 Europeans in Tunisia, predominantly of Italian extraction.[10] As in the United States and parts of the British Empire, it might have seemed at the time that such overspilling of expanding European populations would make for an inevitable and irreversible transformation of the ethno-demography of the region. However, as in South Africa, this was not to be; demographically, the European arrival was numerically too feeble and too late, encountering the first stirrings of the demographic whirlwind among the indigenous populations and thus their own numeric expansion. In 1941 there were a million Europeans in Algeria, a number similar to the total indigenous population at the time of the French invasion just over a century earlier. Yet by this time the Muslims had expanded in number to 6.5 million.[11]

The impact of imperialism on the region is today still widely resented, and with justification, just as is the far longer-lasting impact of the Ottoman Empire on the Balkans. But the demographic effect of European colonialism was to stimulate a population explosion among the local people which was ultimately to prove the grave-digger of colonialism, creating demographic circumstances that made continuing European domination impossible. In the twenty-first century there are barely any Europeans left in Algeria while France has a significant North African population. This is not the demographic outcome which would have been expected at the time of France's occupation, when Europeans still seemed all-conquering. Naturally, many factors were at work in freeing Algeria from French rule, but it is hard to imagine a settler population in Algeria continuing to rule in the face of burgeoning population growth from the indigenous population; and this fact is as true for Algeria as it is for South Africa or Zimbabwe. General de Gaulle considered the nine to one ratio of indigenous Algerians to Europeans as decisive in necessitating French withdrawal.[12]

It is difficult to prove a direct link between Europe's loss of imperial will, the growth of confidence on the part of colonial populations and the shift in population, but the circumstantial evidence is strong. The fact that European powers were awarded not colonies but League of Nations 'mandates' in the Middle East and elsewhere after the First World War has perhaps more to do with Woodrow Wilson's ideology than it does with demographic factors, yet a close reading of Europe after the war suggests a change of mood regarding empire. At this stage the societies of the Middle East and North Africa were only starting their transitions. Both fertility and mortality rates remained high – albeit that a fall in the latter was fuelling population growth – and population advances could still be checked by the traditional Malthusian horsemen. Three hundred thousand died in the famine of 1866–8 in North Africa and periodic outbreaks of disease in the interwar years could raise the annual mortality rate in Algeria from less than twenty per thousand to over thirty-five.[13] Albert Camus' novel *La Peste* (*The Plague*) was set in Algeria soon after the war, although it probably relates to a much earlier cholera outbreak. Still, plague should not be thought of as entirely a thing of the past; as recently as 2003, at least ten cases of bubonic plague occurred in Oran, Algeria, the very town where Camus' novel was set.[14]

Egypt, the most populous country in the region after the fall of the Ottoman Empire, provides a good illustration of how the demographic dynamics in the region at this time were still pre-modern. Egypt's population in 1800 was probably no higher than it had been in 1300 or even at the start of the Common Era, at about 3–4 million.[15] During the nineteenth century, however, it more than doubled. People married early, with nearly a third of sixteen- to nineteen-year-old women married in the 1930s (over five times the rate in Western Europe in that decade), and there was a birth rate persistently over forty per thousand.[16] Mortality fluctuated and could still be periodically impacted by outbreaks of cholera, but the effect of these events was diminishing. The standard of health remained low with the population experiencing poor diet, housing and sanitary facilities. Yet even the limited and rudimentary impact of modernisation had been sufficient to trigger significant population growth. The population of Egypt, experiencing neither material immigration nor emigration, doubled in the first half of the twentieth century, representing an annual population growth of 1% per annum, similar to that experienced by Britain in the first half of the nineteenth century.[17]

From the middle of the twentieth century, piecemeal and patchy modernisation in the region started to become more consistent, uniform and powerful. The human tide was gathering force. Material conditions for ordinary people remained meagre at best but a gradual growth of transportation, education and health care facilities was making its mark here as elsewhere. The result was a repeat of the pattern first seen in Britain more than a century earlier and subsequently replicated or being replicated across the globe, albeit at a far greater pace.

As ever, infant mortality is a good indicator of what was happening. In North Africa as a whole, it fell from 20% to under 3% between 1950 and 2017. In Yemen, the poorest country in the Middle East and North Africa, it fell from over one in four to under one in twenty over the same period. Life expectancies lengthened significantly (for example, Libyans have gone from living to their mid thirties to surviving into their early seventies since the middle of the twentieth century). Meanwhile, typical of countries in demographic transition, fertility rates at first held up: Iraqi and Saudi women were typical in continuing to have six children each well into the 1980s.

The result has been, in line with patterns observed elsewhere, the ballooning of population sizes and the extreme youth of societies. Egypt's 20 million in 1950 is fast approaching 100 million while Algeria's 9 million has passed 40 million during the same period, despite large-scale emigration to France; in short, populations are multiplying four- or fivefold in not much more than half a century.[18] It is this phenomenon that lies at the heart of the demographic whirlwind: namely, later demographic transitions have tended to be significantly more intense and result in greater population growth, with countries in the post-war developing world, including in the Middle East and North Africa, quadrupling their populations in half the time it took England to do so. This is, in a sense, a 'last mover advantage', and it will mean that European first-movers in the demographic transition will eventually be outnumbered by their later followers.

However, here as elsewhere, the power of the human tide has started to ebb. As Middle Eastern societies become more urban and literate, so their fertility rates have plunged. Egyptian women today are having three children, not six as was the case as recently as the 1970s. Libyan women, who were bearing more than seven and a half children each in the 1970s, are today having fewer than two and a half. Even Yemeni women have halved their fertility rate since the late 1980s. The medal for falling fertility, however, belongs to Iran, where the rate of childbearing was brought down from well over six in the early years of the Islamic revolution to under two just twenty years later. Sustained but then collapsing fertility, the extension of life expectancy and the booming population have both fed and been fed by the wider developments shaking the Middle East and North Africa.

Islam, Oil and Policy: The Makings of Middle Eastern and North African Demography

With rudimentary improvements in the quality of life having a big impact on infant mortality and life expectancy, the persistence at first of high fertility rates and their eventual fall as people became more urbanised and women more educated, one might expect the transi-tion of the Middle East to resemble that of the West and Asia. However, fundamental differences and characteristics make the Middle Eastern story unique.

The role of Islam must be considered crucial. Very often, where Muslim populations have lived in close proximity to non-Muslims or as minorities in a predominantly non-Muslim state, they have expe-rienced a relatively high fertility rate.[19] This has been true of the Soviet Union in its later years and at times in the Balkans, Israel and south-east Asia. It is also to some extent true in India, where Muslims have had a persistently higher birth rate than Hindus, and in south Asia as a whole, where the birth rate of Pakistan has outstripped that of India. It is true as well of those countries in Western Europe which have received significant Muslim populations. As a consequence, the impression has often been given that there is something inherently pro-natalist about Islamic societies and therefore about Islam. This is rather reminiscent of those in France who in the first decade of the twentieth century feared that the Germans were inherently fertile and likely to generate an endlessly burgeoning population. It is rem-iniscent too of Germans taking exactly the same view of Russians in particular and Slavs in general at around the same time. Today, the Germans and Russians have among the lowest fertility rates of any of the major nations: neither, it turns out, was perennially fertile. Thus, while there is clearly a tendency to think of the fertility rate and population growth currently characteristic of a nation or ethnic group as perennial, demography often pulls surprises – races are not perennially fertile or unfertile, and neither are cultures, at least unchangingly. When circumstances change, the demography changes too.

With Islam, therefore, as with other religious cultures, there is nothing inherently high about its fertility. There are pro-natalist statements in the Quran and particularly in the Hadith, just as there are in the Bible: 'Marry the one who is loving and fertile for I will be proud of your great numbers before the nation.'[20] The Quran is clearly against infanticide, which perhaps was common in pre-Islamic societies: 'Kill not your children on a plea of want. We provide sustenance for you and them. Come not near shameful deeds, whether open or secret. Take not life which Allah has made sacred.'[21] However, according to most interpretations, this does not forbid the use of contraceptives.[22] Abortion in the first few months of pregnancy is generally seen as permissible. One Hadith of the Prophet says:

> All of us have been kept as a drop of seed . . . for forty days. Then for another forty days, it remains in the form of a clot of blood. Then another forty days it remains as a lump of flesh. Then an angel is sent to the foetus who blows spirit [life] into it.[23]

There have been occasions when the Islamic authorities have opposed birth control, such as Deobandi hardliners in Pakistan in the 1960s, but this is the exception rather than the rule.[24] There has been no blanket ban on birth control by significant religious authorities in the Muslim world as there has been in the Roman Catholic Church (however much these may in fact be ignored by Catholic practitioners). Indeed, reflecting early concerns about rising population, a fatwa permitting contraception was issued by Egypt's Grand Mufti as early as 1937.[25]

Yet there are certain characteristics of some Islamic societies which can predispose them to higher fertility. A reluctance to educate

232

women and the correspondingly low levels of female literacy in parts of the Islamic world are associated with a high fertility rate. In a society where birth outside marriage is very rare, the existence of women living outside marriage guarantees a certain rate of childlessness; however, the probability of a woman remaining unmarried and therefore almost by definition childless is reduced where polygamy is practised, as in much but by no means all of the Islamic world. The early marriage of women also tends to a higher fertility rate, and across the Arab world the average age for a woman at first marriage is still low. Meanwhile, in Morocco and Tunisia female participation in the workforce remains at less than half the world average, and at less than a third in Egypt. This is another correlate of high fertility.[26]

Pro-natalism, therefore, is perhaps more associated with Islamic cultures than with Islam as such, and this may explain the slow and sluggish efforts in many places on the part of regimes to propagate family planning. In Egypt, for example, a study in the early 1970s found that barely one in ten married women had attended a family planning clinic, at that stage still overwhelmingly the most common way in which contraception was obtained.[27] Once policies were adopted, however, they could be very effective. The speed with which fertility rates fell in Iran has already been noted, and although this may have happened anyway, it was certainly prompted by the Islamic Republic.

Indeed, Iran makes an interesting case study, which in some ways resembles China. The Khomeini regime which took power in 1979 was at first pro-natalist, as was Mao's – again like Mao's basing this stance on its ideology. The Shah's family planning programmes were partly discontinued and, with the outbreak of war with Iraq in 1980, the permitted age of marriage was lowered. There was a modest rise in what was already a high fertility rate and by the end of the decade the Mullahs were starting to get alarmed at the burgeoning population growth. Fatwas were produced confirming the acceptability of birth control while programmes of family planning were reintroduced and expanded; the first state-supported condom manufacturing facility in the Middle East was established. The results were dramatic, with fertility rates falling to two and below by the early years of the twenty first century. Now the Iranian government, like the Chinese, is starting to have second thoughts, with Supreme Leader Ali Khamenei saying that he is 'shaking with fear' over the ageing of the population and its low fertility rate; he is introducing a fourteen-point programme to encourage the birth rate, including free maternity wards, longer maternity leave and a move not only to end free vasectomies but to make them illegal.

However, with high levels of female literacy, and higher levels of education and urbanisation, it is debatable whether even a complete about-face by the regime will materially impact the choices made by Iranian women. The latest UN data shows Iranian fertility rates not much higher than those in Russia, at sub-replacement level and falling. Stories of young urban Iranians avoiding parenthood suggest both economic and political motives. 'If I were to give up my job to have kids, how would we manage to rent a house for ourselves?' complains one middle-class woman in Teheran. 'I don't want to bring children into this hell,' complains one recent college graduate disaffected with the regime, while another admits to having had two illegal abortions, saying: 'We are really serious about not having kids.'[28] Yet there also seems to be a cultural aspect, beyond economic or political concerns, making young Iranians sound rather like their Japanese peers in associating early marriage and childbearing with conservatism, religiosity and lifestyle limitations. Even Islamic societies, it seems, are not immune to the second demographic transition, in which fertility choices are more a reflection of personal values and preferences than of purely material conditions, and many eschew parenthood altogether to prioritise other projects.

Although generally fertility rates have held above two and have even risen in recent years (in Egypt and Algeria, for example), it is striking how low fertility rates have fallen not only in Iran but also in Lebanon, where at under 1.75 children per woman, fertility is even lower than in Iran. Here too there may be a religious element in the overall picture. Throughout the Middle East, Christians tend to have lower fertility rates than Muslims, and Lebanon still has by far the highest share of Christians of any population in the region. The sharp falls in fertility rates here in more recent years have been associated with somewhat rising marriage ages and an increase in the use of contraceptives;[29] they have also been associated with rising levels of female education, even if, relative to other areas, the region still lags in this respect. Urbanisation too has played its parts. There is nothing special about the fall in fertility in the region; what has required some explanation has been its delay.

Beyond religious ideology and government policy, there is also the abundance and influence of oil in the shape of the oil-rich Gulf. While the benefits of the oil bonanza were not evenly spread across the region, they did provide employment and remittance benefits even for populations outside the oil states, and this may have supported high fertility rates across the region into the 1970s and 1980s.[30] The oil states themselves have unusual and skewed population patterns. They tend to have high but falling fertility rates (from over seven to under three since the early 1980s in Saudi Arabia, for example) and long life expectancy supported by relatively high-quality health care (up from below forty-five to over seventy-five in the UAE since 1950, for example), but the most astonishing thing in terms of population has been the influx of immigrants, most of them offering low-skilled cheap labour. Qatar, for example, has seen its population grow from 25,000 to 2.5 million since the post-war years, a figure achieved not through impossibly high natural growth but rather by immigration of labourers – less than 20% of Qataris are indigenous.[31]

While the basic forces contributing to population growth – falling mortality and particularly infant mortality rates and persistently high fertility – are not unusual, they have been achieved here differently from elsewhere. It might be argued that in this region they have been more 'exogenous' than in other societies, and have often been achieved in large part either through aid programmes from the West or by intra-regional transfers funded ultimately by the oil boom. Today, Egypt in part manages to feed its population thanks to aid from the US and Saudi Arabia: without these funds, and without health care and other welfare programmes provided from outside, it is hard to see how Egyptians would have managed to stretch longevity into the early seventies. This creates a vulnerability in populations quite unlike those from Britain to China, which have effectively pulled themselves up numerically and in every other way by their own boot straps. It means that if the oil price plummets sufficiently for Saudi Arabia to cut its support, or if Cairo and Washington fall out, Egypt's population would be at risk. Migration, which has so far occurred over the Mediterranean, might eventually be seen as but a foretaste of what is to come. A hundred million hungry, desperate Egyptians poised on the Mediterranean shores would knock into the shade any migration crisis Europe has seen to date.

Population Pressure and Implosion

Cause and effect are the currency of history and the social sciences. No matter how national policies are pursued, demography is not an external factor, injected into a society from outside and simply having a one-way impact; rather, it emerges from society itself, and is as much caused by its environment as it is shaped by it. Nevertheless causal links can be traced from demographic patterns to the way the world works and the way in which events unfold. And while the human tide does not determine the course of history, it moulds it, and it seems clear in most cases that a different demography would have led to a different outcome. Demography cannot be extricated from the socio-economic failings of the Middle East and North Africa, and in many places has fomented the political collapse. Failed states and civil war are more likely where there are young, fast-growing populations, particularly where these are not successfully integrated into the economy and where opportunities for making a productive contribution to society are closed off.

The Middle East and North Africa have many problems which are particularly associated with political instability, the lack of democracy and human rights and a failure in socio-economic development. The oil-rich states are able to provide their populations with a high stand-ard of living and social and health services, but even here educational attainment and human productivity are poor. The region's shortcom-ings and failures need to be addressed head-on, but before doing so and arousing sensitivities, three points need to be made. First, the region's shortcomings can be attributed in some part to demography, although this is not to say that there are simplistic solutions – the plugging in of Western-style political and economic institutions has clearly failed where it has been tried. Second, while it is easy to be dismissive of the conspiracy theories which are rife in the region, it cannot be denied that outside intervention, whether well intentioned or not, has been frequent and usually unhelpful. Finally, it would be wrong to blame the region's failings entirely on its religious culture – there have been periods in history when Islam has underpinned the most innovative and flourishing societies.

There is a huge variation in income levels across this region: in per capita terms, some of the countries under consideration are among the richest in the world, and this is entirely due to the presence of hydrocarbons for export. Qatar has one of the highest per capita incomes of any country in the world thanks to the scale of its exports of gas and its relatively small population. Yet the successes or failures of the area as a whole cannot be simply assessed on the basis of income. Moreover, even in purely economic terms, the Arab world has little to boast of: in 1999, before the oil price spiked upward, the collective economies of the Arab countries were smaller than that of Spain.[32] Turkey has had more economic success in recent years but remains at best a middle-income country. And Iran's economic progress has been hindered by its confrontation with the international community and the resulting sanctions, only lightened relatively recently.

One way of analysing socio-economic development which takes into account such chance effects as income coming from large-scale oil and gas production is to compare the human development of a country relative to that of other countries with a similar income. A study in 2002 found that the overwhelming majority of Arab countries, whether impoverished or super wealthy, were underachieving on levels of human development versus other countries of similar income.[33] The Human Development Index used for such exercises, which weights education, health and income, may have imperfections, but looking at individual measures, the same picture emerges. For a start, participation in the workforce is low, whether due to general unemployment or specifically to low female employment. The employment to population ratio stands at 46%, making the Arab countries worse than any other region in the world on this index.[34] Water consumption per capita is 20% of the world average and 2% in Yemen, a sign of low standards of living.[35] It might be objected that this is a dry region and so low water consumption is to be expected, but the problem of water shortages in dry climates has been tackled successfully, for example (if not very sustainably) in the US south-west and (more sustainably) in Israel, through conservation, recycling and desalination. If water insecurity is a problem, so is food insecurity. Cereal imports in the region as a whole represent more than one-half of supply versus 15% for the world as a whole.[36] That makes the Middle East and North Africa one of the parts of the world least able to feed itself. As has often been pointed out, Egypt was once the breadbasket of the Roman Empire but is now heavily dependent on imports to feed its large and growing population. Egypt's inability to feed itself is a product not only of a large and growing population but also of poor agricultural productivity.

Educationally, too, the Arab world has made only modest progress, particularly in relation to women. While great gains have been made in literacy, female literacy rates in Arab countries in the early twenty-first century are still well below those of areas such as east Asia and Latin America.[37] This is reflected in the ratio between female and male workforce activity, which is lower in the Middle East than anywhere else in the world.[38] In higher education, few Arab institutions make the academic grade. According to the Academic Ranking of World Universities, four Israeli institutions make it into the top 200 while only one Arab institution does so.[39] Data from 1987 suggested that the production of 'frequently cited' academic papers in Egypt was two-thousandths of the level in Israel and even in Kuwait, with its oil wealth, frequently cited papers were at less than one-seventieth of the Israeli level.[40]

As ever, the cause of the region's ills are not demographic alone. Oil has turned out to be a curse in many places where democratic institutions are not already fully embedded, cultivating a rent-seeking rather than an entrepreneurial culture. Where the state controls a great source of relatively easily accessed wealth such as oil, the most lucrative way of enriching oneself is to get a position as close to the trough as possible rather than setting up a business or offering a service of real value. A culture of corruption tends, then, to seep downward into society. The Middle East and North Africa has often come to be caught in the crossfire of great power rivalry, not least during the cold war, with outside forces supporting repressive regimes prepared to do their bidding. Looking internally for explanations, it cannot be denied that a strong streak of misogyny in many cultures of the Middle East has stunted their development. Where women are not allowed to thrive, societies will rarely thrive. Where women are not allowed even to leave the home without male approval, let alone to drive, as until recently was the case in Saudi Arabia, it is hard to see how women can thrive. Yet this too is bound up with demography. At the heart of demographic and human progress has been women taking control of their own bodies and fertility. A culture which resists this is likely to be stymied.

Although the populations of the region are particularly young and population growth has been exceptionally rapid, other countries with similar demographic profiles have experienced rapid economic growth and social progress, for example in the case of China, whose population was still growing fast during its period of economic take-off. Indeed, under the right circumstances, a booming population can be an economic advantage. Nevertheless, some of the woes cited above can be clearly attributed, at least in part, to population pressures. It is true that other countries have solved their water problem, but with a smaller population the pressure on existing water sources in the Middle East would be less acute. Similarly, it is undoubtedly the case that agricultural productivity could be much higher, but at its current level relative to the space available, there would be more food per mouth if there were fewer mouths. Educational failings have many sources, but difficulties meeting the needs of a fast-burgeoning population of school and university age are among them.

Likewise, while population growth can create its own demand, where other systems such as markets, trade and education are failing, it is more difficult to cope with employment when the workforce is growing so rapidly. It is also difficult to absorb ever-growing populations into the workforce in a productive manner when educational attainment is low and there is a lack of capital investment. A 2002 UN report estimated that 10 million children in the Arab world between the ages of six and fifteen were not in school; now that all of those affected are adults it is difficult to see how they are likely to fit into an increasingly global economy.[41] Given the disruption in much of the

Arab world since then, particularly in Syria, where millions of children are unable to go to school, the picture in the future may be worse. Nor has economic performance been assisted by the fact that the countries under consideration have had an exceptionally high dependency ratio: that is, the ratio of those outside the age of the workforce to those within the workforce. Whereas the developed world is used to high dependency ratios due to the rising number of elderly, in the case of these countries it has been due to the high number of the young requiring the investment of care and education.

Sharply falling fertility rates in the Middle East should in principle provide their populations with an opportunity to make economic progress as the dependency ratio falls from over ninety in 1980 to an (estimated) under sixty by 2020.[42] This so-called 'demographic dividend' is often seen to apply where the number of children relative to the workforce reduces; this may in part be responsible for the economic rise of Turkey, and it has been claimed as a factor in countries such as Japan and Indonesia. Again, it is difficult to unpick causally because it is often precisely those countries where economic and social progress is being made that are those witnessing falling fertility rates, and cause cannot always be separated from effect. Nevertheless, as fertility rates fall, women are freed up for the labour force and more funds become available for capital investment. However, these factors work only if the economy is able to absorb female workers, if society can accept their employment, and if the structures of law and governance and political stability are in place to absorb capital into the economy.

When it comes to the Arab world, this is hardly the case. The 'youth bulge' has been accompanied by high unemployment, a recipe for social disruption and violence. In the case of the Middle East, it has been accompanied by a rise in religious fundamentalism.[43] Indeed, this fundamentalism itself has direct demographic roots: there is evidence of a link between fertility and religious intensity found in Islam, just as there is in other religions, and provided more devout groups manage to retain their offspring, this suggests that demographic as well as other factors will drive the continued growth of Islamic conservatism and even Jihadism.[44] Thus while demography has not been the sole cause of the social and economic woes of the region, it has compounded them.

In part, the problematic demography of the region has itself been caused by failures of family planning policy. Although fertility rates have fallen, fertility remains high in much of the Middle East and North Africa, and in some places has started to reverse, rising in the last decade or so. Access to contraception is far from universal: whereas two-thirds of married Moroccan women of childbearing age use contraception, barely half do in Iraq and less than a tenth in Sudan.[45]

If the Arab Middle East has experienced a failure of material development, it has also suffered a failure of political development. This can be seen both in terms of the oppressive regimes which have ruled in the area, depriving its populations for the most part of democratic and human rights, and the more recent disintegration of some of those regimes and the descent of their societies into chaos and civil war. With 6% of the world's population, the region was reckoned to contain a fifth of its armed conflicts even before the current wave of instability was fully under way.[46] This statement is not about the allocation of blame, enough of which is already in circulation, nor an attempt to provide a comprehensive explanation, but rather to illustrate the extent to which human conflict stems at least in part from demographic causes.

The political failures of the region, compared with most if not all other regions of the world, are fairly self-evident. Within the region as a whole, according to Freedom House's 2014 Index, all the states except Israel were either categorised as 'not free' or only 'partially free'.[47] Much of the region stands between the oppression of autocratic regimes and breakdown into chaos and civil war. As I write, there is no single governmental authority effective throughout the national territory in Yemen, Libya, Lebanon, Syria and Iraq, and high levels of recent instability have affected Egypt and Bahrain.

There is an almost total lack of democracy in the region, although Turkey can be seen as partly democratic (or could until recently). Tyrannical rule and anarchical breakdown may seem like opposite ends of a spectrum, but the former can be thought of as a prelude to the latter, with progress towards stability and democracy as a third stage.[48] According to this model, it is unlikely or difficult for a country long under the iron grip of dictatorial or authoritarian rule to move directly to stability and democracy. To get there, a period of civic strife and violence is likely, but this can be seen as a transition to a desirable end point rather than just a descent into chaos. This would be an optimistic interpretation of the Arab Spring. At this point, however, few Arab countries can be seen as seriously making their way to the third stage, out of chaos and towards a liberal, democratic order. Indeed, the most populous country in the region, Egypt, appears to have stared over the abyss and returned to the status quo ante. (Tunisia may be such a case, although it is too early to say that it is an exception and, if it is an exception, it is a rare one.)

Demography has perhaps inevitably made its contribution to this desultory political picture just as it has to the failings of economic and social development. There is a good deal of evidence to suggest the link between instability and conflict on the one hand and demographic trends on the other, the general consensus being that 'youth bulges' are associated with increased risk of political violence.[49] Where there is a large share of men in the population aged in their teens and early to mid twenties, the chances of civil strife are higher, and it is no coincidence that some of the oldest societies in the world, such as Japan and Germany, are among the most orderly, while some of the youngest, such as Yemen and the Democratic Republic of Congo, are among the most strife-riven. On this basis, it is hardly surprising that the Arab Middle East has been at the centre of so much violence and strife in recent years, and that prior to that, the outbreak of such strife appeared only to be avoided by the imposition of exceptionally harsh regimes. Emigration to some extent takes the pressure off internal systems, but it can often result in the exporting of the problem. Finally, other regions of the world have managed to undergo demographic change without nihilistic terror along the lines of al-Qaida or ISIS.

Thus while population numbers cannot be a sufficient explanation for failure, they are inevitably bound up with it. Without its youth and expanding population, it is almost unimaginable that the Middle East and North Africa would be as violent as it is. Just as the First World War as it came to be fought – as mass industrial slaughter –

cannot be envisaged without the huge population expansions that took place across Europe in the preceding half-century, so the New York bombings of 9/11 and those in Madrid and London, as well as the violence from Yemen to Syria, may be seen at least in part as the product of the Islamic Middle East's explosive demography in the decades which preceded them. Between 1980 and 2010 population growth in this most volatile of regions was nearly a full percentage point per annum higher than for the world as a whole. In 1980 the fifteen- to twenty-four-year-old population of the Arab Middle East, as a share of the total population, was the same as for the world as a whole; thirty years later it was one-fifth higher.[50]

The Syrian civil war, in particular, is arguably as much a demographic conflict as it is a political or religious one. At the time of its independence from France in 1947, Syria had barely 3 million people. Sixty years later, on the eve of civil war, it had more than 20 million. The causes of this population explosion will be familiar – tumbling mortality rates and stubbornly high fertility. The consequences are less easy to trace. Nevertheless, when Syria was struck by drought in the early years of the current century, hundreds of thousands left the countryside and headed for the towns and cities, especially to Damascus, where they often found basic accommodation on the outskirts, held at bay by a suspicious government. This was particularly so since most of the migrants came from the majority Sunni sect, changing the demography of cities such as Damascus which had previously been disproportionately peopled by minorities (such as Christians, Alawites and Druze) who tended to back the Ba'athist regime. Thus the conditions were put in place for a rebellion at its most intense in a ring of poor, neglected and majority-Sunni suburbs which surrounded the capital. And while many seek to attribute the ensuing conflict to global warming,[51] indeed while climatic conditions were undoubtedly part of the picture, none of this would have been possible had the size of the Syrian population not exploded so dramatically in the preceding decades.

As ever, the causality is working both ways. Just as demography has played a role in shaping the Syrian civil war, so the war is shaping the demography. Roughly one-quarter of the population has fled the country and another quarter is internally displaced. There are accusations that the government is consciously trying to change the ethno-demographic balance of certain areas, reducing the Sunni element. Meanwhile, although the losses of life have been shocking, they themselves (unlike the emigration) have not had a significant statistical impact on the demography of Syria. Half a million deaths, an approximate estimate as this book goes to print, represents a single year of Syria's population growth in recent times. None of this takes away from the suffering of individuals but it does show how, just as was the case in Europe at the time of the First World War or Russia during the height of Stalinism, when the human tide is in full flow, even the most horrific carnage can slow but not stop it.

A rapidly growing youth, often poorly educated, politically marginalised and unable to participate in the global economy, is a recipe for instability. As one woman working on youth programmes in Jordan put it: 'Young people are facing increasing barriers to education and economic opportunities with minimal chance to engage in social and civic life. They are being pushed further into the shadows, feeling disempowered and frustrated.'[52] Where economies are not developing, it can be particularly difficult for university graduates to find work; in 2014, 34% of recent graduates were unemployed compared with only 2% of those with a primary school education.[53] Unemployed graduates, usually urban-based and in a position to become activists, are more likely to prove politically disruptive than under-employed farmhands. and while social conservatism is in some part shared by the young generation, many are pushing against it, particularly women, whose sense of frustration is made worse where they are given educational opportunities and then heavily discriminated against in both society and the workplace. In Saudi Arabia there has recently been some opening up of jobs. Educated women still feel highly restricted by the need to seek permission from fathers or husbands: 'He won't allow me to work even though I need the money . . . He doesn't allow me to travel with my mother.'[54] While the middle-aged and old may have accommodated themselves to such circumstances, the young are more likely to push against them, and this matters more when the young are more numerous.

While the region's growing youth have been turning their frustrations inwards – as the political instability since 2010 testifies – they have also turned outwards, and this has resulted in a huge wave of migration towards Europe. This has not only been from the Arab world but from countries such as Afghanistan, which are facing similar problems of political instability, fast-rising would-be entrants into the jobs market and a lack of opportunities. In 2015 there were more than 350,000 Syrian asylum seekers to the EU and more than 150,000 from Afghanistan. Nearly half a million people sought asylum in Germany in the final quarter of that year alone.[55] This trend, which has deep demographic roots, will have profound consequences for the demography of Europe. Our television screens in recent years have been hit by streams of people trying to make their way to Germany through the Balkans, or those trying to make it across the Mediterranean to Italy; these migrants are almost always coming from young, high-fertility countries and almost always heading towards old, low-fertility countries. Migration has many causes and has taken many directions over the past centuries, but it is invariably the case that most migrants are young and often they are leaving young societies where opportunities are not opening up or where there is too much competition among too large a cohort.

What happens in the Muslim Middle East matters increasingly to the world as a whole. In 1970 Muslims constituted 15% of the world's population; by 2010 this figure had risen to around 23%, and by the middle of the century it is forecast to grow to not much less than 30%.[56] If realised, this would make Islam very close to Christianity as the world's largest religion.

The Arabs and Israel: The Demography of Conflict

Until the start of the revolts across the region from the end of 2010, the Middle East and its conflicts were often seen through the prism of the conflict between Israel and its Arab neighbours, especially the Palestinians. In 2009, for example, Bishop Desmond Tutu of South Africa suggested that unless there was a solution to Israel–Palestine,

you can give up on all other problems. You can give up on nuclear disarmament, you can give up on ever winning a war against terror,

you can give it up. You can give up any hope of our faiths ever working really amicably and in a friendly way together. This, this, this is the
problem, and it is in our hands.

This suggestion, highly questionable at the time, came to look even
more difficult to justify in the following year when strife swept
through the wider Middle East.[57]

There are several reasons for the disproportionate focus this conflict
receives, at least in the West. One is that the story of the Zionist enterprise is intimately bound up with European history, given that the
Zionist movement was at first a movement of European Jews respond-
ing to anti-Semitism in Europe. A second is that, for so long, the
regimes across the region seemed to have their societies within their
grip and in many countries very little seemed to be happening politically, throwing the focus on the question of Israel and Palestine. Third,
the conflict is often seen as one between people of profoundly different
cultures and origins, which is always easier for Western consumers of
the news media to grasp – or to think they grasp – than conflicts, say,
between Sunnis and Shias or Druze and Maronites. Finally, on a more
cynical but perhaps realistic note, it was pleasanter to report on a scuffle
on the West Bank from the comfort of the American Colony Hotel in
Jerusalem, or to take a short trip from there down to the border in
Gaza, than to make the effort of reporting the civil war in Yemen in the
early 1960s or to send back news from the bloody and dangerous front
line between Iran and Iraq in the 1980s – the media have been able to
operate more freely here than in other parts of the region.

The conflict, first between Israel and its neighbours, then increasingly between Israelis and Palestinians, was always modest in terms of
casualties when compared to others. Nevertheless, it had the tendency
to capture front pages in the West in a way that far bloodier conflicts
in the region never could. The best estimate is that around 50,000
have died in conflicts related to Israel since 1950, roughly in a ratio of
two Arabs to one Israeli; deaths of Muslims in the Israel–Palestine
conflict represent, at 1%, a small fraction of total Muslim deaths in
conflict since the middle of the twentieth century even before the
current outbreak of bloodshed in Syria, Libya and Yemen.[58] Nevertheless, for many this has been *the* Middle East conflict.

With the revolutions and strife in Egypt, civil breakdown in Libya and civil wars and the rise of ISIS in Syria and Iraq, the Israel–Palestine conflict has been somewhat overshadowed. Nevertheless, it is worthwhile for our purposes to understand that conflict because, as has been argued extensively elsewhere, it is one which, more than most, has had demography at its heart.[59] This can be seen from three angles, namely the great influx of Jews into Mandate Palestine and then Israel, the birth rates of Jews and Palestinians, and the fate of the territories captured by Israel in the Six Day War of 1967.

The state of Israel would not exist without the Jewish immigration which has been attracted, in ever larger waves, first to Ottoman Palestine, then to Palestine under the British Mandate, and, since 1948, to the state of Israel itself. There has been both a 'push' and a 'pull' aspect to this population movement – both the attraction of Zionism and the land of Israel as a homeland and the impulsion of anti-Semitism and persecution in the lands from which Jews have emigrated. Before the First World War there were around 60,000 Jews in Palestine, some recent Zionist immigrants, some the descendants of small waves of religious Jewish migration over the centuries. Many were displaced by the war but, under the umbrella of the Balfour Declaration, the Treaty of Lausanne and the British Mandate, the Yishuv or Jewish community in Palestine reconstituted itself. Between the wars it experienced waves of immigration first from communities in eastern Europe and then, after 1933, from Jews escaping Nazi persecution in Germany. In 1925 there were over 30,000 Jewish immigrants, in 1935 there were over 60,000, these representing the two peak years of the interwar waves.[60]

At this point a word must be said about the Holocaust, the Jewish tragedy which, from a demographic angle, is an exception to the rule that wars and disasters cannot in the modern era fundamentally reverse the human tide. We have seen how the European population kept growing through the decade of the First World War, albeit more moderately than previously, and how despite the man-made famines and persecutions of Stalin and Mao, Russian and Chinese numbers kept growing. By contrast, where a relatively small population is singled out for annihilation by an efficient executioner, the demographic impact can be devastating. In 1939 there were 9.5 million

Jews in Europe; by 1945 there were 3.8 million.[61] Globally, Jewish numbers are still below those of the pre-Holocaust era, and as a share of world population, Jews have fallen from around 1 in 150 people to around 1 in 750.

Despite a shift in British policy and efforts to restrict Jewish immigration in the face of increasing Jewish desperation but growing Arab opposition, the Jewish population in British Mandate Palestine had by 1948 grown tenfold from its post-First World War level. Even in the face of a war for its survival, newly born Israel prioritised immigration and within its first five years of existence it had more than doubled its Jewish population.[62] The initial wave came from the displaced persons camps of Europe, then from the Arab lands where Jews suffered discrimination, persecution and in some cases expulsion. Today in Morocco the number of Jews who remain is perhaps 1% of its peak level in the 1940s. In many Arab countries which once had tens or hundreds of thousands of Jews whose communities dated back well before Islam, not a single Jew remains. More recently, Jewish immigration to Israel has come from Russia and the lands of the former Soviet Union. In 1990 nearly 200,000 Jews came from the Soviet Union and between 1968 and 1992 as a whole, over three-quarters of a million.[63] Having grown from 60,000 to 600,000 between the end of the First World War and its independence in 1948, Israel's Jewish population has again grown tenfold to over 6 million in the years since 1948. Thus while globally Jewish numbers have sunk in absolute and relative terms, in Israel they have grown exponentially.

The numbers alone make it evident that immigration has been Israel's lifeblood and that without it, the country could not have come into existence, never mind survived and prospered. For this reason, *Aliyah*, or Jewish immigration to Israel, has always been a driving imperative of Zionism. The state has required a solid population base, particularly in the face of Palestinians' exceptionally high birth rate. The imperative for the Jews to be a majority was always explicit; as Israeli prime minister, Levi Eshkol, stated: 'In some place, in this place, we have to stop being a minority.'[64] Israel's founding prime minister, David Ben-Gurion, was obsessed by numbers: 'The State cannot be firmly based, its mission will not be fulfilled and the vision of redemption will not be realised except through immigration.'[65]

There is lively historical debate over whether the exodus of Palestinian Arabs during the 1948–9 Israeli war of independence was in some way preplanned or preordained by the Zionists, but whatever the reality of this highly controversial issue, the fact remains that it would have been difficult to build the state had its Arab population not largely moved – or been moved – to neighbouring countries or to those parts of Palestine not initially under Israeli control. Similarly, without the great wave of hundreds of thousands of Jews from Iraq, Morocco, Yemen and other Arab lands, the survival of the state would have been difficult, particularly after the destruction of European Jewry for whose salvation its creation had been originally designed. It has been estimated that, without immigration in the wake of the Balfour Declaration, the Jews of Israel would today constitute a population at most of a quarter of a million, as opposed to over 6 million.[66] Under such a scenario, it is unthinkable that the state of Israel could have come into existence, or, had it done so, could have survived.

Another aspect of the Arab–Israeli conflict which is striking from a demographic perspective is fertility rates. It is never easy to prove why a group as a whole has a fertility rate at a particular level – generally, the best way is to compare its fertility rate to those of other comparable groups, look at the statements of its leaders, and examine any studies of its population which have tried to get to grips with the reasoning behind fertility choices. In the cases of Palestine and Israel, a strong case can thus be made that both have exceptionally high fertility rates which have been driven to a considerable extent by the conflict and by what can be termed 'competitive breeding'. The increase in the Palestinian population has been rapid both within Israel and in the West Bank and Gaza Strip. In the early 1960s Israeli Arab women were bearing no fewer than nine children each.[67] The Arab population of Israel rose from a little over 150,000 after the 1948–9 war to over 800,000 forty years later, a compound annual growth rate of over 4%.[68] In the early part of the twenty-first century, the fertility rates in Gaza and the West Bank were still around five – almost double the rate in Morocco, for example – despite the fact that female literacy in the former was almost universal whereas in the latter it was probably below 50%.[69] At least part of this very high fertility rate can be attributed to the conflict with Israel and an attempt to compete with a fast-growing Jewish population: Yasser Arafat is supposed to have spurred Palestinians into a demographic race with Israel, while Hamas has described Palestinians as engaged 'in a demographic war that does not know mercy'.[70] One Israeli demographer recounts a visiting Arab school headmaster, who while making a gesture indicating the reproductive organs, commented: '[T]his is our only weapon.'[71]

The other factor that has bolstered Palestinian numbers in the above area has been the dramatic increase in life expectancy and fall in infant mortality rates. In the occupied territories, infant mortality at the time of the Six Day War was around one hundred per thousand. Since then, whatever else might be attributed to the Israeli occupation, infant mortality has seen this fall to twenty per thousand, below the average for the region as a whole. Life expectancy over the same period has extended from the mid fifties to the mid seventies[72] – a figure comparable to some of the more deprived parts of the UK, such as Glasgow, or the poorer states of the USA. This is in line with the sort of modernisation seen elsewhere: for example, before 1967, there had never been a university in Gaza or the West Bank, but today there are half a dozen such institutions.

The Palestinian fertility rate has come down sharply in recent years: today, it is around three children per woman both among Arabs in Israel and those in the West Bank, although somewhat higher in Gaza. The pattern it is following is more or less normal, albeit one in which falls have been delayed by the conflict, which has motivated large families. Israeli Jewish fertility is more extraordinary. Early Zionist immigrants to Palestine were predominantly from east European Jewish families who had already undergone a demographic transition, and when Jews from the Middle East joined them in Israel after 1948, their birth rate too fell rapidly to what would be considered 'normal' for a modern society. Jewish Israeli fertility reached two and a half by the mid 1990s but then went into reverse. Today it is at a level of three children per woman and nearly three and a half for Israeli-born women.[73] This is at least a child more, or 50% higher, than that of any other country in the developed world.

While this is to some extent the product of exceptionally high fertility rates among Israel's ultra-Orthodox, it is also a secular phenomenon. Again it cannot be definitively proven that it is a response to the conflict, but it is notable that Jewish birth rates in the United States, where the only other multi-million Jewish population lives, are among the lowest in that country. It is likely that high Israeli Jewish fertility has more to do with the specific situation in which Israeli Jews find themselves than with anything to do with Judaism or Jewishness as such, reflecting a more communitarian and less individualist society than most countries of comparable modernity and maybe also a fear of losing children in a war. It is true that ultra-Orthodox or Haredi Jews do have an exceptionally high fertility rate wherever they live, and they make a meaningful contribution to rising Jewish fertility in Israel. For Haredim, large families is a matter of prestige. But both the ultra-Orthodox *and* secular in Israel have a higher fertility rate than Jews of similar religiosity (or lack thereof) outside Israel. It may be that the greatest demographically related challenge Israel faces today is not maintaining its Jewish majority – at least within its 1967 lines – but preserving its economic success as the number of Haredim rises, given their resistance to modern education and, in the case of many men, their preference for a lifetime of study rather than employment.

Feminists in Israel and women who do not particularly want to have large families or families at all have certainly pointed to a pro-natalist culture that runs deep, going well beyond government policies like generous child benefit and the world's highest spend, per capita, on helping couples with fertility treatments. As sociologist Larissa Remennick comments: 'Making and raising children is a national Israeli sport . . . The wish to mother is expected by default from all women, regardless of their education, careers and other achievements.' One woman who runs a Facebook page for women who do not want to have children complains that it is 'really hard to be the one who doesn't want to be a mother in a country where there is a straight path from kindergarten to high school to the army to marriage to children'.[74]

Without the vast immigration of Jews and the resurgence of Jewish fertility, the state of Israel would have had profound difficulties in sustaining itself. Nevertheless, the countervailing high fertility of Palestinians, even if now less pronounced than recently, has put Israel in a quandary regarding the fate of Gaza and the West Bank following their capture during the Six Day War. Many Israelis would like to annexe them, for either ideological or security reasons, but so far this has not happened with the exception of Jerusalem (which is of exceptional ideological importance) and the Golan Heights (which has only a light population of Syrian Druze). To incorporate the territories and their people into Israel proper would result in a population more or less evenly balanced between Arabs and Jews, and with the loss or impending loss of a prized Jewish majority which has always been core to Zionist aspirations. Priding itself on its democracy, Israel has not been prepared to annexe the areas without offering citizenship to their peoples, and so the West Bank has retained its 'occupied' status while Israel has completely withdrawn from Gaza although it still controls its air space and most of its borders.

Demography has played only a part in the fate of Gaza and the West Bank – ideological, economic and security concerns are prominent too – but the part it has played is an important and often unappreciated one. After the 1967 victory Yigal Allon, at one point Israel's acting prime minister, proposed the annexation of the sparsely populated Jordan valley, abandoning the more populated western part of the West Bank to Jordan, thus ensuring much additional territory with few additional Arabs. While this has never been adopted as official Israeli policy, it did guide the location of early Jewish settlements, which tended to be predominantly in the Jordan valley. When Israel reached the Oslo Accord with the Palestinians, the border between the areas which the Palestinians were to control and the area over which Israeli control would continue was broadly in line with the Allon Plan, with allowance made for Israeli settlements in more populated Arab areas which had been established since Allon's day. The fence erected by Ariel Sharon has never been formally proposed as a border, but it has been claimed that Sharon saw it as much in terms of the demands of demography as the requirements of security.[75]

So far as the Gaza Strip is concerned, its demography too has shaped its fate. Initially Ariel Sharon was a proponent of Jewish settlement here, but it was pointed out to him that a few months of Palestinian population growth was the equivalent to the entire Jewish population: demographically, it could not be absorbed. By pulling out of the Gaza Strip, Sharon could surrender an area representing around 1% of the total area under Israeli control while extricating himself from the difficulties involved in the direct occupation of over a million Palestinians. It is likely that this was a major consideration in his 2005 withdrawal. In the area Israel continues to control – that is, pre-1967 Israel plus the West Bank and the Golan Heights – it is unlikely that there will ever be a Palestinian majority, particularly given the lower and falling fertility rate on the West Bank. Nevertheless, the precise numbers and percentages as well as the population prospects are matters generating much debate, which seem to lie at the heart of this demographically charged conflict.[76] In any case, it is clear that there will continue to be a large Palestinian Arab population within the area Israel currently controls whether or not it has the potential to become a majority.

Again, while demography is not all of destiny, it acts as an unseen hand. At the point of the Palestinian intifada of 1987, the median age of Palestinians in Gaza and on the West Bank was barely fifteen. It was not much higher when the second intifada broke out in the early years of the current century. Today the median age in the Palestinian Territories has passed twenty and by mid-century it will be heading for thirty. This is not to argue that further intifadas are impossible, but it is notable that each time one seems to be getting started, it fizzles out. Twenty is still a young median age, and there are plenty of disenfranchised and angry young Palestinians who might spark an uprising any day, but the likelihood of one diminishes as the society ages. Whatever else they may rely on to advance their cause, it seems less likely that Palestinians will be able to depend on the raw street anger and violence associated with young, unattached men with nothing to lose. Over the next twenty-five years, short of any surprises, including population movements in or out of the area, the populations of the contending sides are likely to be more or less even, contributing to an ongoing stalemate.

For the region as a whole, there are demographic grounds to be pessimistic, with a large youth wave passing through populations, bearing the potential for much instability ahead. Yet if this vast human wave can be channelled productively, it need not be destructive.

Sharply falling fertility from Morocco to Iran suggests changing norms and expectations. Europe was a violent and war-torn continent when its age profile was similar to today's Middle East. There is reason to hope that when the Middle East's demography comes to resemble that of Europe – a prospect which seems remarkably closer now than it did a few decades ago – it might be as peaceful as Europe is today.

10

Nothing New Under the Sun?

Final Frontiers and Future Vistas

The truly extraordinary thing about the human tide is that it is global. At first it looked as if it might be just a phenomenon of the peoples of the British Isles and their offspring in North America and Australasia; then it seemed to be a purely European phenomenon. But the second half of the twentieth century proved that it tells us something about people the world over, almost regardless of their race, ethnicity, religion or continent, albeit local variations of timing have made a great difference. This is clear when we look at two vast, complex and utterly different regions – Latin America and south Asia. Each has a unique and distinct history, but shares a recent demographic pattern that is now thoroughly familiar.

Meanwhile in sub-Saharan Africa, we are presented with a final frontier in terms of demography: a last, vast region on the globe still in the middle of its demographic transition. The pace at which Africa continues through this transition will have huge implications for the future of the whole planet. It can be predicted with near certainty *that* this transition will occur, but its precise timing is unclear at this stage.

Nothing New Under the Sun: Latin America

Latin America can be divided into three very unequal subregions (unequal at least in terms of population size), namely South America, Central America and the Caribbean. Because each is culturally as well as geographically distinct, it is worth considering them separately, although we should not lose sight of their relative weights: in 2015,

South America had more than 400 million people, Central America a little over 170 million and the Caribbean barely more than 40 million.

Moving irrepressibly from high tide to low tide, the pattern of fertility in the region is striking. In the post-war period all three sub-regions had the kind of fertility rates you would expect, of between five and seven children per woman. By 2017, all three had fertility rates of between two and two and a half. When the musical *West Side Story* received its premiere in 1957, featuring the line 'Puerto Rica – you lovely island . . . always the hurricanes blowing, always the population growing', the women of this US dependency in the Caribbean were bearing nearly five children each; today they are having one and a half. (In fact, even in the late 1950s the population was not growing, despite the high fertility rate, thanks to mass migration to the US mainland.)

The rise in life expectancy and fall of infant mortality are objectives which all societies will achieve if they can. It is a biological imperative and part of human nature to want to preserve one's own life, to put off the moment of death and to do what one can to preserve the lives of one's nearest and dearest, particularly one's children. In this, if in not much more, humans are pretty uniform. Only species with these inbuilt drives can survive and thrive. Nature has, however, mediated the urge to procreate. People do not necessarily want children (although many do), but they do overwhelmingly want sex. Once humans have learnt to dissociate sex from childbearing, to enjoy the former without necessarily incurring the latter, fertility becomes a matter of choice. Yet although it may not be biologically driven, it is nevertheless the case that in most societies, once people have the ability to limit their number of children, they normally do, especially if they are assured high survival rates from those children they do have. In this, Latin America and the Caribbean are no exception. In the region as a whole, 128 children in a thousand did not reach their first birthdays in 1950: the latest data suggests that this has fallen steadily to below twenty per thousand, a figure that is still high – five or six times the best achieved in the most developed countries – but clearly an extraordinary transformation to be celebrated rather than taken for granted. Life expectancies across the region have risen from a mid-twentieth-century fifty to around seventy-five today.[1]

It would of course be a gross simplification to view the region as one which has simply moved from 'backwardness' to 'modernity' in the sixty years since the Second World War, although for many countries when looking at literacy rates or per capita incomes, for example, this would be true. Argentina was in many ways an advanced and modern country in the mid twentieth century, the product to a large extent of a sizeable wave of European emigration and investment over the preceding seventy years. The countries which in 1950 were most advanced have made the least progress, and those that were least advanced have made the most. Argentina's life expectancy has only increased by around ten years since 1950, testimony to its high level then as well as to the political and economic challenges the country has faced since. (Still, at seventy-five, it is not bad, being just four years short of the United States.) Countries like Honduras and Guatemala, by contrast, with a low starting point, have made more dramatic progress, with life expectancy over the same period growing by around thirty years.[2]

Data is more readily available and uniform at the national level than at the local, and failing to dig beneath the former means some useful insights can be lost. Brazil is a noteworthy case, deserving of special comment, because it is by far the largest among the countries of the region, both geographically and in population terms, being home to around a third of the total population of Latin America and half the population of South America. It is also worth closer examination because it incorporates regions which are economically advanced and largely peopled by Europeans, and others, particularly the north-east, where the population is much more African in origin and where levels of development are much lower, yet it has a fertility rate that has been universally declining. Whereas in the early 1960s women in the north-east had a child and a half more than the national average (nearly seven and a half as against six), by the early 1990s they were having only one child more (three and a half versus two and a half).[3] Thus the gap has narrowed within countries as well as between them.

Brazil's steady urbanisation, like that of the rest of the region, has also been closely associated with falling fertility rates. As early as 1950 it was noted that urban areas such as Rio had a fertility rate one-quarter below the national average.[4] As the country became more urban, so urban (i.e. lower) fertility rates became more common, as in other parts of the world: this trend was as true of Germany under the Kaisers as it was of China under Mao. By the start of the twenty-first century, Brazil was already three-quarters urban,[5] a pattern that is typical not only of the region (it is almost inevitable, of course, given its regional preponderance) but also of countries around the world. Its demographic transition has occurred along with economic development, and while fertility fell sharply so life expectancy lengthened well before the arrival of high levels of prosperity.

The immediate cause of the fall in fertility in Brazil appears to be the usual mix of increased use of contraceptives and abortion (and perhaps increasingly disrupted marital patterns), although one much discussed social factor has been increased access to mass media and in particular to the soap opera, presenting and popularising a vision of modernity which features smaller families.[6] Television lowers fertility rates not because 'people have something else to do in the evenings' – a decline in sexual activity, even if it is occurring, need not meaningfully reduce the fertility rate; very little sex, if well timed, is required for a woman to fall pregnant six or seven times in her life – but because television in the right circumstances can offer a vision of a different sort of life, and this plays a role in shaping aspirations as effectively as does education. The impact of television on fertility has less to do with sex than with aspiration, and the link is not just the result of anecdote; research in Brazil has shown that, particularly among lower socio-economic groups, access to TV soap operas has a significant impact on fertility rates.[7] In the past, significant material and educational progress had to be made before fertility rates were reduced. More recently it has become easier and cheaper to achieve. Of course, it is far better to educate a girl and give excellent work opportunities to a woman, and this will inevitably lower her fertility rate at least at the aggregate level (allowing for the fact that there are always exceptions). If, however, the objective is simply to lower fertility, it appears this can be done much more cheaply by providing contraceptives and access to TV shows portraying smaller families in a positive light. Educated women are unlikely to want six or more children, but the same is true of women looking to buy cars and fridges even if they do not have an education. As a result, countries from Thailand to Brazil, which are still relatively poor, are seeing their fertility rates falling below replacement level. This whirlwind has been picking up speed, overtaking the wave of economic development, with the result that some relatively poor or middle-income countries are coming to have fertility rates more usually associated with the wealthy developed world.

Faster into and out of the whirlwind was Cuba. Because of its early adoption of low fertility, Cuban women were having fewer than four children before the revolution, and although with the arrival of the Castro government in 1959 there was a surge, perhaps related to a clamping down by the socialist regime on abortion, this was later reversed. By the late 1970s the fertility rate had reached replacement level, and today it is a little above one and a half children per woman, almost as low as some of the lowest in Europe and east Asia. The low starting point can be attributed to the island's higher level of economic development compared with many nearby countries, and to a population more largely of European extraction than many other countries in the region. (The European ethnic composition of the populations of Argentina and Uruguay is also an important consideration in these countries too, as they also had relatively low fertility in the middle of the twentieth century.) The Castro regime not only reversed its abortion policies but, from the mid 1970s, made contraception increasingly available.[8] The regime's fairly inconsistent approach to abortion in particular is reminiscent of both the USSR and China, where an initial socialist cornucopian outlook – proclaiming in line with Marx that only capitalism consigned expanding populations to economic misery – later gave way to a more accepting attitude. This may be driven by rising belief in a woman's right to choose or concern for rising population and a preference for a cheap form of contraception. That women in Cuba and Germany should have almost the same fertility rate currently is astonishing, underlining the fact that people in poor countries no longer necessarily have large families.

Given rising longevity and high but then falling fertility rates, it was to be expected that the region would undergo a population explosion which is now diminishing, and this is exactly what has happened. Overall since 1950, Latin America and the Caribbean have seen their populations nearly quadruple from over 150 million to about 600 million. Annual growth rates have fallen from almost 3% in the 1960s to barely 1% today. That is approximately the difference between doubling every twenty-five years and doubling every seventy years. Some Latin American countries have seen faster growth than others, predictably those where fertility came down more slowly and life expectancy grew more strongly. Guatemala is a case in point: since 1950, its population has grown more than fivefold. Yet here too the slowing trends are clear: its fertility rate has fallen from seven to three children per woman (still high by the standards of the region) and its annual population growth rate has fallen from 3% to 2% over the past half-century.[9] The median age of the region has moved from the teens to nearly thirty.

Mexico has in many ways been typical of the region, but its proximity to the United States has meant that the impact of its demography has been more noticed and commented on than most, as we saw earlier in Chapter 6. Mexican women were bearing nearly seven children each in the early 1970s, when the impression of the 'perennially fertile' Hispanic was born. (This was a long way from the position 120 years earlier when the Americans had annexed half of Mexico with almost no people in it and in which some had thought the Mexicans would evaporate before the Yankee hordes, just as the native Americans had done.[10]) Instead of being a people to be disregarded with an arrogant wave of the hand, Mexicans had grown to become a people to fear, above all because of their burgeoning numbers. It was of course not the case that Mexican women were having more children than before, but that more of them were surviving and life expectancies were rising, and as a result their numbers were increasing dramatically just as had those of the Americans before them.

The mass arrival of Mexicans into the US was typical of what happens when one neighbour is poor and young and the other is rich and relatively old. The young go in search of economic opportunity and to some extent are drawn in by the old needing additional hands in factories or farms, gardens or care homes for the elderly. Yet the great age of Mexican immigration to the US may have come to an end. Since around 2012 more Mexicans have been leaving the US

NOTHING NEW UNDER THE SUN?

than arriving,[11] and this has to do with improving prospects in Mexico. As one returnee puts it:

> Mexico is up and coming and I see a better future for my daughter in Mexico. She wants to study medicine and being able to go to school in Mexico might be beneficial cost-wise. If . . . she decides she wants to live in Mexico, it will be her choice.[12]

The improving standard of living in Mexico is linked to its altered demography. Mexico is enjoying the demographic dividend which often comes when a fertility rate drops. Regardless of the economy, the number of young Mexicans has stopped growing, and so the need for Donald Trump's wall, at least insofar as it is designed to prevent Mexicans coming to the United States, is highly questionable.

Demography in South Asia

South Asia – the Indian subcontinent (for our purposes including not only India, Pakistan and Bangladesh but also Afghanistan) – is home to 1.75 billion people, close to a quarter of all humanity and nearly three times the population of South America, Central America and the Caribbean combined. Its population as well as its geography is dominated far more by one country, India, than the Latin region is dominated by Brazil. India's population is around 1.33 billion and is projected to overtake China's as the world's largest at some time in the 2020s. Some say that it already has.[13] (It should not come as a surprise that there is some uncertainty in counting such large numbers of people in countries which have until recently been poor. The consensus view, however, is that India will not overtake China as the most populous country on earth until 2027.[14])

The tremendous if now slowing rise in the populations of the countries of South Asia since independence began later than in many other parts of the world. From 1891 to 1921 the population of British India grew at barely a fifth of 1% per annum.[15] In the second decade of the twentieth century its population fell.[16] Famines were still demographically significant up to the end of British rule; by the end of this period, however, population growth was established, since when it has nearly quadrupled.

A significant distinction between the south Asia region and Latin America is its religious diversity, which is relevant in terms of demography. Whereas Latin America as a whole is overwhelmingly Roman Catholic – or at least has a strong Roman Catholic heritage even if evangelical Protestants are today making major inroads into countries like Brazil and Guatemala – south Asia has more religious variety. India, around 80% Hindu, has a large and growing Muslim population and other minorities such as Sikhs. Afghanistan, Pakistan and Bangladesh are overwhelmingly Muslim, while Sri Lanka is predominantly Buddhist. This matters where religion and fertility tend to be linked.[17]

Religious differences explain much of the region's demographic change. Immediately after independence in 1947 (1948 in the case of Sri Lanka), the fertility rate of Muslim Afghanistan was one and a half children higher than India's, and Pakistan was half a child higher. Since then, India has experienced a steady fall in fertility, from nearly six to barely two and a half children per woman. Sri Lanka, considered in late imperial times to be a 'model colony' and more economically advanced than the rest of the subcontinent, experienced an earlier fertility drop and has been at below two and a half for most of the last quarter of a century. It is worth noting that while Sri Lanka was one of the first developing countries to experience the demographic transition, its fertility rate has stabilised at around replacement level, unlike many countries in the developed world, which have had fertility rates that undershot replacement and then continued to fall. Countries like Sri Lanka prove that once replacement level is reached, it need not then be undershot, even if it often is. This could become an important precedent, because if the world is not ultimately to fall into large-scale population decline, other countries will need to follow the example of reaching and then hovering at replacement fertility levels rather than plunging below them. For all its other problems, Sri Lanka has become a model of demography if the ideal is a steady-state; its fertility rate has been hovering a little over two for the best part of thirty years, making it in demographic terms the equivalent to the economists' 'Goldilocks' scenario: not too hot and not too cold, not too fast and not too slow.

Each of the three Muslim countries in south Asia has experienced a different fate. Bangladesh, with much heralded woman-centric policies, has brought its fertility rate down since independence from Pakistan in the early 1970s from nearly seven children per woman to fewer than two and a half. It can therefore be held out as a strikingly successful example of a Muslim country which has brought down its fertility rate. This has been achieved not by accident but by the provision of family planning clinics and often family planning counsellors – invariably women – who travel from village to village. Along with the reduction in fertility, Bangladesh has managed to pull itself up from the direst level of poverty and to bring infant mortality down from over 10% to around 3% in just thirty years. In the long run, its population will stabilise, but not before it reaches 200 million in the middle of the current century.

Pakistan, from which Bangladesh broke away, has been less successful and slower in reducing fertility, but nevertheless the rate has come down very substantially from six and two-thirds to three and two-thirds since the mid 1970s. This is a significant fall, although high by the standards of the developing world outside Africa. A large part of the explanation probably lies in the resistance of many Pakistani religious leaders to the use of birth control, a phenomenon which is not typical of the Muslim world as a whole.

Afghanistan had the highest fertility rate in the region in the post-war period and maintained it to the turn of the century, through the Soviet invasion and withdrawal and the arrival of the mujahideen and Taleban. Only since the start of the present century, possibly related to the NATO occupation and social programmes launched since then, has it started to fall; and although this has been very rapid, it has so far taken place only over a short period. Afghanistan still has (excepting tiny Timor Leste) the highest fertility rate outside Africa at over five children per woman, almost a child more than Yemen, the country in the Middle East with the highest fertility rate. Such anyway is the latest available UN data; more recently available information suggests that Afghanistan's fertility rate is now falling so fast that it may have come down below five. As we have already seen, Islam as such is not necessarily a pro-natalist religion, but traditional Islamic societies seem to be exceptionally late in experiencing falling fertility – although, like everyone else, they get there eventually.

The fertility rate in India has notable regional variations. It is highest in the poorer states of the northern Hindi belt, lowest in the states of the south such as Kerala, where female education has been stressed. In Kerala and Tamil Nadu it is already below replacement level. There are also religious differences. Just as Pakistan and Afghanistan have a higher fertility rate than India, so Muslims in India have more children than the Hindu majority. The data for 1999 suggested that Muslim fertility in India was more than two and a half children higher than that of Hindus, although this seems improbable.[18] The gap now appears to be much smaller, but still material. Although Muslim population growth in India is slowing, it is still half as high again as in the population as a whole, and so the Muslim share of the population continues to rise, from 13.4% to 14.2% of the total between 2001 and 2011.[19] At independence and following the huge, chaotic and violent population exchange between India and Pakistan, it was less than 10%. Higher Muslim fertility and growing Muslim population share are controversial subjects in India and have at times been used to fuel intercommunal tension. In 2015, prime minister Modi's government released a religious census, controversially, into the public domain, showing that the Muslim population had grown faster than that of the country as a whole since 2001. Modi's enemies have accused him of stirring up demographic worries on the part of the Hindu majority in order to strengthen his political position.

While the general fall in fertility in India can be attributed to the normal causes – economic development, rising female literacy and urbanisation – government (both the Indian government and that of the US), has played a notable role in encouraging a hard line on population control.[20] India was one of the first countries to make family planning an integral part of public policy. Policies have included raising the legal age of marriage and fixing constituency representation regardless of population rises to prevent local politicians encouraging the boosting of numbers to strengthen their clout at national level.[21] In the 1970s, under prime minister Indira Gandhi and her son Sanjay, a campaign to encourage voluntary sterilisation got out of hand and became one of the most notorious excesses of the Emergency. More than 6 million men were sterilised in a single year and 2,000 died from botched operations.[22] A total of 11 million men and women were sterilised from mid 1975 to mid 1977: in some areas water was with-held from farmers who refused, in another teachers' salaries were withheld if they did not submit. One reporter recounts what happened in a village in Haryana in northern India:

> The villagers of Uttawar were shaken from their sleep by loudspeakers ordering the menfolk – all above 15 – to assemble at the bus-stop on the main Nuh-Hodol road. When they emerged, they found the whole village surrounded by the police. With the menfolk on the road, the police went into the village to see if anyone was hiding . . . as the villagers tell it, the men on the road were sorted into eligible cases . . . and they were taken from there to clinics to be sterilized.[23]

The discrediting of the campaign was a major setback to family planning policies.

These excesses were widespread but not long-lasting. In 1977 the Emergency was lifted and Indira Gandhi's Congress Party was swept out of power in part thanks to the forced sterilisation scandal. Yet India's fertility rate kept on falling steadily before, during and after the excesses, just as China's had before and during the One Child Policy (as suggested in Chapter 8 above, it may not reverse itself). From China to India and Bangladesh, the lesson is everywhere the same: even without the desirable fruits of female education and economic development, people will generally choose to have fewer children when given the opportunity to choose for themselves. Coercion is not only cruel and even deadly; it is not necessary.

Life expectancy in south Asia has also followed a familiar pattern. Since independence, Indians have gone from expecting to live to their mid thirties to expecting to live into their late sixties. Indian life expectancy, although still lower than the global average, has taken dramatic strides, reflecting improved if still rudimentary public and personal health care and improving diets. Pakistani life expectancy, a little ahead of India's at independence, is now a little behind, but still huge material progress has been made. Even Afghans, who in the early 1950s could not expect to live to thirty, can now expect to live to over sixty. It is once again a testimony to the power of the human tide that moderate improvements in material conditions, even when accompanied by all the violence and bloodshed in a country like Afghanistan over the past four decades, can still deliver transformative improvements in life expectancy.

These overwhelming numbers are driving world history and power just as surely as they were when Britain escaped the Malthusian trap. A country the size of India, like China, can only be of little international account when stricken with poverty and immobility. With the first stirrings of sustainable economic progress, India is fast on the road to becoming an economic superpower. A still poor but rapidly rising population is making the world increasingly reliant on India for its contribution to global economic growth. With the decline in its fertility rate, India is set to enjoy a demographic dividend as China's fades. Both India and China undertook cruel and unnecessary coercive steps to curb population as well as sensible ones allowing women to make their own choices. In part because of its slower economic development, in part because of its culture, India has the prospect of a long demographic dividend to enjoy, while China faces imminent challenges of a declining workforce and an ageing population.

Sub-Saharan Africa: The Final Frontier

The human tide takes some surprising turns. Nevertheless, in some ways its course is fairly predictable. The great surprise, taking the historic long view, was breaking out of the Malthusian trap, something that now seems almost universal, and the rich world has taken on global responsibility for aiding even the poorest to achieve this. Once out of the trap – with fast-falling mortality rates and fast-growing population – there is then a fairly standard process through which eventually fertility rates fall towards replacement level. After that, the bets are off; it is far from clear, for example, that the second demographic transition of personal choice, individualism and sub-replacement fertility will become truly universal. Perhaps we are simply too close to events to be able to see the new emerging pattern, as was Malthus in the early nineteenth century or those in the UK before the First World War, who lamented the fall of the national birth rate without realising that it would become universal. One of the most important factors in history at any one time is where in this transition different societies and cultures are.

To put it another way, demographic development is like a film playing at different times at different cinemas; although the screening has yet to finish at a number of venues, we know how it ends. That, at least, is the theory which, throughout most of the world, seems to hold. UK fertility fell between the 1870s and the period before the First World War from around six to around three children per woman. The same happened in India over a period of similar length, between the middle and the end of the twentieth century, slowly compared with many other countries undergoing a late-twentieth-century transition. In general, later falls in fertility have been faster but, as the case of India shows, not always. Rises in life expectancy, meanwhile, have occurred much faster as countries have rapidly and relatively cheaply been able to adopt the techniques, technologies and policies which reduce mortality.

Africa south of the Sahara is the final frontier of the demographic transition. This can be seen simply from the data produced by the UN in 2017. Of the forty-eight states and territories with fertility rates of four or above, all but seven are in sub-Saharan Africa. Nine out of the ten countries with the highest fertility rates are in Africa. Every one of the thirty countries with lowest life expectancy is in sub-Saharan Africa; so are all but two of the thirty with highest infant mortality rates and the lowest median age. The population of sub-Saharan Africa is growing more than twice as fast as the world as a whole.[24] These are not random data but, as those who have followed the argument in this book so far will realise, part of a very clear pattern. Africa south of the Sahara as a whole is in the early stage of the demographic transition, with persistently high fertility, life expectancy still low but lengthening fast, meaning more births, fewer deaths and a ballooning population. And so it is here that the demographic whirlwind is now at its most intense.

We have been careful so far to speak of 'sub-Saharan Africa' because, as already seen, the picture on the Mediterranean littoral, the countries of North Africa, is very different. That said, the picture across sub-Saharan Africa itself is far from uniform. For a start, South Africa is in a category of its own. For all the problems it is encountering, it has a combination of physical infrastructure and political institutions which still make it the envy of the continent. Whether cause or effect, its demography is in line with its development status. Its fertility rate is around two and a half children per woman, half that of the continent as a whole; infant mortality, still high at just below forty per thousand, is notably better than the continental norm of closer to sixty per thousand; and median age is around twenty-six, more than five years older than the regional average. Other countries in southern Africa are not that far behind, with Botswana enjoying a fertility rate of below three and Lesotho and Swaziland not far above three. The South African government continues to prioritise birth control with a stress on free provision and choice. This is a model for the continent, and has meant that for all the other problems it faces, South Africa will not have to cope with an unmanageable surge of young people putting pressure on economic resources.

Yet in one way, South Africa has been disappointed. Its life expectancy, at just short of sixty, is barely better than that of sub-Saharan Africa as a whole. Given its superior achievement in bringing down the infant mortality rate, this is surprising; the reason is Aids. Although much of Africa has been stricken, South Africa has been a particularly bad case. Life expectancy in South Africa was higher in the late 1980s than it is today (although it has been lower since and is now rebounding). One report has shown that in 2013 nearly 30% of South African schoolgirls were HIV positive. Drugs for treating HIV and preventing full-blown Aids are now much more affordable than in the past, but until recent times it was not only cost that was preventing their use. South Africa's previous President, Thabo Mbeki, took an unorthodox approach to Aids, questioning its link to HIV. Following Mbeki's departure, the use of anti-viral drugs for those infected by HIV has more than doubled, and the effects are now being seen in a slowly improving life expectancy rate.[25] This was one of the happier legacies of Jacob Zuma, but while it has helped, there is still much to do; it is estimated that 7 million of South Africa's 55 million population are HIV positive,[26] and thousands are becoming infected every week.

The impact of Aids on neighbouring Botswana has been even more devastating relative to the size of the country; here, life expectancy fell from over sixty to under fifty between the late 1980s and the start of the new century, and today nearly one in four adults is infected. Supported financially by global aid, particularly from the United States under the administration of George W. Bush, the government aggressively and successfully tackled the problem. In one small village where there were funerals every week, one villager reported: 'Most of the people who were very, very down, now they're starting to pick up and being able to assist themselves. Some who couldn't even walk, now they're even walking around the village.'[27] In the past, the human tide often persisted by its own momentum in the face of genocidal forces; today, it is helped along by the intervention of the international community.

The development in terms of fertility is not so encouraging elsewhere in Africa. Overall, contraceptive use, although much higher than forty years ago, is still the lowest in the world.[28] Some countries are making great strides in bringing down their fertility rates, however. Women in Ethiopia are having nearly three children fewer than they were in the 1980s – but still well over four each. Kenya has halved its fertility rate since the late 1960s when it was, astonishingly, more than eight children per woman. Today, however, it is still just above four. As ever, urbanisation and a rise in personal aspirations are motivating the use of contraceptives where they are available. As one resident of a Kenyan suburb says:

> I feel that the cost of living has gone up and the number of children that I have are the ones I am able to take care of. If I give birth to more children, I don't have that kind of job which I can say will make me meet the needs of more children and that's why I decided to use family planning, so that I can take care of my children.[29]

These are precisely the sentiments which drove down fertility rates in Britain a hundred years earlier and in Puerto Rico fifty years earlier.

Kenya is rapidly proving that African women are no more perennially fertile than any other group. Where the usual benefits of modernisation, even in moderation, are introduced and women are given access to birth control, patterns of family size change. UNICEF reports that over 80% of Kenyan women in the eighteen to twenty-four age bracket are literate. Literate women are not only likely not to want extremely large families but are also more able to prevent them.

By contrast, progress in reducing fertility rates has been slow in other parts of Africa. Nigeria matters because it has by far the largest population in the region. Its fertility rate, although falling slowly, is still not much below six children per woman. The same is true of Uganda. Meanwhile, the Democratic Republic of Congo – insofar as any data coming out of this vast and chaotic country can be trusted – still has a fertility rate of over six.[30]

The better news, and usually a precursor to further falls in fertility rates, is that infant mortality rates and life expectancy are improving almost everywhere. An infant mortality rate of around sixty per thousand sounds scandalous in the second decade of the twenty-first century but it is one-third of the level of 1950 and falling fast. It is worst in Sierra Leone and the Central African Republic, with ninety-four in a thousand children not reaching their first birthday. This is not a place to counsel complacency, and every effort should be made to save life, but it is worth noting that the infant mortality rate in even the worst performers is better than, say, in the Russia of 1950. Life expectancy, although still short of sixty, is again around where it was in Russia in the middle of the twentieth century and more than two decades longer than it was in sub-Saharan Africa at the time.[31]

Unsurprisingly, given high fertility rates and falling infant mortality, this is a young continent. The median age in sub-Saharan Africa is around eighteen and it has barely changed for sixty years. That might come as a surprise, given the lengthening life expectancy, but recent population growth means that there are relatively few older people while there are more young people thanks to gains in child survival. The median African is less than half the age of the median European. This can be a blessing or a curse. A large number of young people in a population can make for political instability and violence, as in the Middle East, but it can also make for dynamism and economic growth, as in many countries from Britain and Germany through Russia to China. With its large number of countries and rich diversity of cultures, Africa will probably experience both effects, and others besides. Already the young populations of the continent are driving some of the most rapidly growing economies, from Rwanda to Côte d'Ivoire. At the same time, Africa is experiencing the most devastating (and under-reported) wars in the world. Numbers are uncertain, but it is likely that 5 or 6 million people died in the recent civil war in the Democratic Republic of Congo, and although the conflict appears to have died down, the situation is far from settled as this book goes to print.

In any case, Africa's population explosion is remarkable even within the story of the human tide. If the biggest global news story of the last forty years has been China's economic growth, the biggest news story of the next forty years will be Africa's population growth. It arises out of the very same factors as elsewhere, and yet what may be the great-est variable in the history of demography since 1800 is how fast fertil-ity rates fall in Africa. For most of the planet, we can be pretty sure from here onwards, short of any real shocks, how things will turn out: lifespans will gradually lengthen, particularly where they are already short (they are in fact below sixty almost nowhere else outside sub-Saharan Africa) and fertility rates will be either below or converging towards replacement level. The detail will matter, particularly locally: fertility rates of Israelis and Palestinians may well determine the outcome of their struggle; the convergence of Latino with majority US fertility rates will help to determine how large the Latino minor-ity grows. From a global perspective, then, the future is largely in the bag. This is not so for Africa, where huge and (short of calamity) inevitable demographic momentum means that even if fertility rates fall fast, there will still be very many young women bearing children and relatively few old people dying of natural causes, meaning big population growth regardless. Moreover, the pace at which fertility falls will have huge implications for the peak population of the planet.

Sub-Saharan Africa has more than quintupled its population since the 1950s, from around 180 million to close on a billion. There is powerful evidence that at the earlier date Africa was under-populated, the victim not only of a difficult geography but of centuries of Arab slave-trading and a shorter but more intense period of European and American slaving, which left it denuded. The Atlantic slave trade alone is estimated to have taken 12 million people.[32] The Islamic slave trade may have taken as many as 14 million, although some estimates are much lower.[33] It is certainly striking to realise that in the continent as a whole in 1950 there were far less than half as many people as there were in Europe, a fact all the more striking when you realise that Africa is three times the size of Europe. Today, Africa's population is around a third larger than Europe's, and by 2100 it is likely to have quadrupled again, while Europe's will have shrunk. That, at least, is the mainstream prediction of the United Nations; much will depend on the pace of falling African birth rates and on inflows of immigration.

One particular source of this incredible growth is Nigeria. Today, Nigeria has around 180 million people – sub-Saharan Africa's entire population in the middle of the twentieth century. At the time of its independence from Britain in 1960, Nigeria had a population of around 45 million, a figure which was lower than that of its colonial master: now its population is nearly three times the size of the United Kingdom's. The UN medium fertility projection has Nigeria's population at around 800 million by the end of the current century. If that turns out to be the case, Nigeria would have gone in the space of a century and a half from being 1.5% of the world's population to 7%.

Meanwhile, Nigeria has urbanised rapidly. Lagos has seen a rise in population from 1.5 million in 1970 to over 20 million forty-five years on. Life in this mega-city, as in other African mega-cities, is not attractive from the perspective of someone from a developed country. As one correspondent describes it:

A thick layer of acrid, blue smoke hovers just above the waterfront slums that skirt Lagos lagoon, filtering out sunrise and sunset. This man-made mist that clings to the rusted shack rooftops comes from the countless fish-smoking cabins that drive the slum economy. There's an uninterrupted view of the city's dramatic sprawl of poverty from the road bridges that carry daily commuters between the islands and the mainland.[34]

Yet the rural poor keep coming, escaping the more grinding prospect of rural poverty in an ever-more crowded countryside. Few would have guessed that one-time colonial outposts would by the dawn of the twenty-first century dwarf the capital of the imperial metropolis. Lagos is foremost of the mega-cities which are now dotted not only across Africa but throughout the developing world and which could only have come into existence with the recent vast population growth, which the countryside was unable to absorb.

As with India and China, countries growing on this demographic scale can only fail to be important players on the world stage if they lag behind. Nigeria has many challenges, but its economy has certainly started to stir. It is an oil power, and this has helped to get it started, although in some ways oil has been a curse, cultivating a rentier mentality and corruption at every level in society and the economy. There is some confusion about whether the South African economy or the Nigerian is the largest in Africa – it depends on the assessment method used and prevailing exchange rates as well as the precise timing of the calculation. Nevertheless, it is clear that Nigeria has the potential to emerge as at least a regional superpower. As ever, demography is not all of destiny, and much will depend on whether Nigerian energy and creativity can be channelled into economic progress or whether corruption will stymie developments. Nigeria already has a large military budget, much of which is currently required to counter the domestic Islamist threat, although the country is also a major contributor to UN peacekeeping missions. It faces internal security challenges and always the prospect of fragmentation, as nearly happened with the Biafran war in the 1960s. That Nigeria's population will grow enormously is almost guaranteed; that this provides it with the potential to play a large regional and global role is certain. Whether it can realise this potential will have vast ramifications for the region.

Seen with hindsight, demographic change looks like a whirlwind hitting one region after another, along with and then sometimes ahead of general social and economic development. From this perspective, many are confident that Africa's fate will resemble that of every other region, and in the north and south of the continent this is already happening. History however is never reliable as a guide to the future. Even so, in terms of the demographic pattern the first and second phases are already in evidence across most of the region and the third has begun in most places. African parents are just as keen as any others to ensure that their children survive and that they themselves extend their lives as long as possible, and given the right material resources are as likely to devote these to those goals as all other peoples have been. It seems likely that, as they become more urbanised and educated and have access to family planning, African women will want to stop having families of six or seven, as has been true of women from Chile to China and Vietnam to Venezuela. Yet even if this process accelerates, there is still huge demographic momentum in Africa, and this means that population growth will for decades accompany falling fertility rates. Large cohorts of young women, the product of earlier high fertility rates, will collectively produce many children even if individually they produce fewer than their mothers. There will be relatively few deaths as the old are a small group relative to the population as a whole and more people are living longer. As a result, with births far outstripping deaths, populations will continue to boom even as fertility rates fall.

Whatever Next? Colours of the Future

Much about demography is 'baked into the future' and is certain to happen. And this demographic future can be summarised in three colours: more grey, more green and less white.

Starting with 'more grey', society after society is becoming older through a combination of fewer births and longer life expectancy. Ageing of populations is a phenomenon which has been observed in region after region, as fertility rates have fallen and life expectancy has risen. The median age of the world's population has already risen by around seven years since 1960. In the developed world, it has risen by more than a decade in the same period, while in east Asia as a whole it has risen by sixteen years and in South Korea, an astonishing twenty-two years. Meanwhile, outside sub-Saharan Africa there is barely a country or territory where the median age has not risen in the past sixty years. Yet the process is only just beginning. According to the middle-range UN forecasts, by the end of the present century median man or woman will be over forty, a dozen years older than today. This means that between 1960 and 2100 the median person will have doubled in age from barely twenty to more than forty. Among the record-breakers for greater age will be Ethiopians (today on average eighteen, by 2100 aged forty-three), and Syrians (today aged barely twenty, in 2100 likely to be aged nearly forty-seven). Many countries, from Poland to Sri Lanka and Japan, will have a median age of over fifty. By the end of this century, Libya's median age is projected to be roughly where Japan's is now. Such aged societies have never been seen in history. Retuning to Leonard Bernstein's *West Side Story*, when it was first produced in 1957 the median age among Puerto Ricans (in Puerto Rica rather than in New York, it is true) was around eighteen; by 2100 it will be little short of fifty-five.[35] It is only a slight exaggeration to say that, to be age representative, a latter-day Bernstein would need to set his musical in an old people's home rather than among street gangs.

How this marked ageing will affect the world cannot be predicted with any certainty, but it is surely the case that a world in which the median age is around twenty (1960) is profoundly different from one in which it is over forty (2100), not only because of all the political, economic and technological changes that are likely to have happened, but also by sheer dint of its ageing population. The changes effected by ageing are likely to be both positive and negative. Viewed optimistically, the world is more likely to be a peaceful and law-abiding place. As we have seen, there is a strong correlation between the youth of a society and the violence and crime within it. Not all young societies are embroiled in crime and war, but almost all old societies are at peace. Not only are older people less likely to take up arms or become criminals; young people, where they are few and far between, are more valued and more heavily invested in. Mothers who have only one son are less likely than mothers with many sons to goad them to take up arms against enemies real or perceived. On the other hand, older societies are less likely to be dynamic, innovative and risk-taking. An older population is more likely to want to hold the safest sort of investment, high-quality bonds rather than equities, for example, and this will affect markets and in turn the real economy. Real estate demand will also change as more and more accommodation is required by elderly singles and less and less by growing families – these effects are already at work in much of the developed world, and are set to go global.

While median age captures the age of a society as a whole, it is the rise in the number of elderly which tends to receive the greatest attention, not least because of the pressure this is likely to put on the welfare states of developed countries where state provision for older people is advanced. This is often expressed as a 'support ratio' – the number of people of working age (however defined) to each older person – and as early as 2050 in Japan this figure will be approaching one to one. In Western Europe, although lower than Japan, it will be twice as high in 2050 as it was in 2005.[36] Pensions in the developed world as a whole are set to double as a share of GDP without significant reform by 2050, and the greater demands of older people on health services will also be a fiscal challenge for a developed world where budgets are already under strain and debt to GDP ratios are seen by many as perilously high.[37]

There will also be a sharp rise in the 'older old' – in the UK there are 1.4 million people aged over eighty-five today, and this figure will double in twenty years and treble in thirty years as the baby boomers move from the frontiers of ageing into its more advanced stage.[38] Some would argue that the welfare state as we have known it since the Second World War has the characteristics of a Ponzi scheme: it works only if each new generation of workers is larger than the last. Where old-age pensions are funded from current taxation, there is certainly something in this, and it seems unlikely that welfare states will be able to carry on in anything like their current form as societies age. Yet, at the same time, with more and more people having no children to care for them, reliance on the state will grow. The UK's 2017 general election was in large measure fought on the issue of 'social care', namely who will pay for the daily assistance the elderly need – such an issue would never have gained such prominence at a time when the elderly made up only a small share of the total population. It is, however, but a foretaste of things to come.

In the developed world, with state welfare provision, this may still be an issue, but in the developing world the question will be more critical. Countries will have to cope with growing old before they grow rich. In the developed world, however financed, young workers from countries like Thailand and the Philippines can be drawn in to help with elderly care, at least if allowed to do so by local immigration legislation. For developing countries with an ageing population this will not be a luxury they can afford. The median Thai will hit fifty by mid-century and it is unlikely that in the few decades until then Thailand will have reached the level of development which will allow for comprehensive services for elderly care. In the past, the lucky few who survived to old age were usually cared for by multiple offspring. When there are no longer offspring and the state cannot fill the gap we face a global epidemic of elderly people going to their deaths uncared for and neglected. The only hope in this respect is technology, and here, unsurprisingly, the leader in the field is Japan (today the world's oldest society), which has been developing robots to deliver basic elderly care, provide company and even to act as pets.[39]

Accepting that almost come what may, the world is set to become more grey, there is also every chance that it could become more green. This flies in the face of conventional wisdom, which suggests that humanity is still in the midst of a population explosion which is wrecking the planet. There is no doubt that the great increase in human population on the one hand and the vast increase in living standards on the other has done much environmental damage. Humankind has taken over more and more of the planet for living space and farming, and modern lifestyles certainly churn out a great deal of environmentally damaging substances. Carbon emissions are not just a function of the living standard of the global population but of its sheer size, prompting some environmental campaigners to counsel smaller families, particularly in the developed world.[40] On the other hand, human ingenuity and technology has played a role, and could play a still greater role, in limiting or even reversing these effects. The declining growth in human population – globally from around 2% per annum to around 1% in the last forty years or so – gives rise to a great opportunity to create a greener planet. Although the population of the world will continue to grow, perhaps slowing to close to zero growth by the end of this century, the rate of human innovation need not. And although the average human being will be older, there will also be more human beings and in all likelihood they will be ever better educated, better networked and with greater access to information. That means, for example, that with the appropriate resource allocation and investment, crop yields per hectare should be able to outpace human population growth more easily than when the latter was faster. That could mean, even if people are to be better fed than they are today, that land can be returned to nature and it will be possible to live in a greener planet.

The same is true of other resources. If efficiency grows faster than population then sustainability can be enhanced, whether it is more fuel-efficient cars or better storage and transport of food. Where human population starts to decline, from Japan to Bulgaria, nature moves fast into the void. Because of slower than once expected decline in African fertility rates, the UN now expects the global population to exceed 11 billion and not to have stopped growing by the end of the current century; however, by then it should just about have stabilised, with growth at a tenth of that experienced today and a twentieth of that experienced in the late 1960s and early 1970s.[41] To use an analogy from earlier in this book, demography is a car that first trundles along slowly, then reaches tremendous speed and most recently has decelerated so significantly that in the course of this century it is very likely to have ground to a halt.

The third colour we can predict with some certainty is 'less white'. With the great population explosion starting among the Anglo-Saxons and then moving on to other Europeans, the white population of the world experienced an extraordinary expansion both in absolute and relative terms from the start of the nineteenth century to the middle of the twentieth century. This has had profound political consequences, and without it, it is hard to imagine that European imperialism could have grown so extensive or had such an impact on the world. However, the Anglo-Saxons had no monopoly on falling mortality and sustained high fertility (and hence high population growth), and neither have people of European extraction. Until recently the lowest fertility, oldest and slowest-growing populations in the world were in Europe, and it was here, too, that population decline in recent times first set in. More recently, however, the peoples of north-east Asia have begun to catch up and in some cases, on some measures, overtake Europeans, and in time no doubt others will follow. Thai women, as noted, already have fewer children than British women, although Thailand still has some 'demographic momentum' to enjoy.

While some non-Europeans may be embracing the small European family, demographic momentum will remain powerful for some time to come. And as we have seen, many civilisations which have experienced the demographic transition later have experienced it more intensely, with higher population growth at some periods in the twentieth century than, say, Britain ever managed in the nineteenth. This means that the global population has grown less white and the trend is set to continue. It amounts to a 'first mover *dis*advantage': those who went through the demographic transition earliest experienced the least growth and are set to decline as a share of global population.

The decline in people of European origin can be seen on two levels: continental within a global context, and country by country. Starting with the first of these, in 1950, as the era of European imperialism was ending, the population of the European continent contained around 22% of humanity. Adding in overwhelmingly white Canada, Australia, New Zealand and the USA, the figure came to 29%. Sixty-five years later, Europe's share was down to 10% and that of the 'wider white world' down to 15%. Taking UN median projections, these two figures will by the end of the current century fall to 6% and 11% respectively.[42] Many countries in Europe are already experiencing population decline, or would be were it not for inward migration. If UN projections are correct, then Bulgaria and Moldova will have lost half their population by the end of the current century and Latvia will not be far behind. Germany will have lost 10% and Italy 20%.

Moreover, those countries are themselves becoming less white. By the middle of this century people of 'white British' origin may be just 60% of the population of the UK, although admittedly many of the immigrants and people of immigrant origin will be of European extraction.[43] The white population of the United States, 85% in 1965 and 67% in 2005, is projected to dip below 50% by mid-century.[44] In both countries it is likely that a 'mixed origin' element will be significant and fast-growing.

Just as the Anglo-Saxon and then the wider European world was the laboratory for rapid and sustained population expansion from the middle of the nineteenth century, so too perhaps these countries will be the test-beds of a much more fluid world in racial, ethnic and national identity terms. There is no absolute reason why someone of Italian descent in the USA should be described as 'white' while someone of Spanish descent should be described as 'non-white – Latino'. It is true that many Hispanics in the US are a mixture of Spanish and indigenous origin, but then Sicilians are themselves likely to be of partly non-European origin. As ever, distinctions are never absolute.

The flipside of white decline in relative numbers has been and will continue to be the rise of Africa. In the middle of the twentieth century, after centuries of being sidelined, colonised and subject to slavery, sub-Saharan Africans accounted for barely one person in ten on the planet; by the end of this century they are likely to account for one person in four. With Africa still poor and young, the pressure of migration to Europe will be strong. To date, most African population growth can be seen arising from people pouring into towns and cities. Once prosperity gets above a certain level, however, the prospect of looking further afield than the nearest mega-city for economic salvation becomes more realistic.

Beyond Imagination

The world has changed at a frantic pace in the last few centuries, and the trend only appears to be accelerating. Much of this has to do with technology but it also has to do with demography, for the two are interdependent. Just as a world of European domination was unimaginable without the expansion of populations of European origin, so their contraction will inevitably have a global impact. For now, much of that impact is felt within countries once 'white' but now increasingly multicoloured. At some point, it is bound to have an impact on the international environment, whether because of the sheer weight of numbers or because of related issues of economic power.

Yet history defies prediction. A Londoner of a hundred years ago would be astonished at the global face of his once more or less exclusively British city and astonished that the British Empire was no more. A Parisian would be similarly surprised to know that the Algerian experiment is over, having left no demographic trace at all in North Africa, while his own city is heavily North African. The demographic trends of the future are to some extent already in process: short of global pandemic or mass movement, we know how many fifty-year-olds there will be in Nigeria or Norway in 2050. However, there may still be surprises in store, and these may be driven by science and technology. It was technology which doubly broke the old Malthusian equation: the earth, it turned out, could provide exponentially for human beings, with the opening up of vast new territories using new ways of moving people and things, and using new ways of growing food; population growth, by contrast, could be cheaply and easily tamed by people's choices without their having to restrain their natural appetites.

The science and technology of the future may also reshape population in ways currently hard to envisage. What would global demography look like if ageing were reversible and people were able to live for centuries? What impact would that have on fertility rates? What if birth and sex were entirely divorced and if clones or designer babies could be ordered 'over the counter'? Beyond technology, there are some more purely demographic developments which, if they continue, could behave unpredictably. Southern Africa's rapid progression to lower fertility has been charted, and this might spread to the rest of sub-Saharan Africa far more quickly than expected, bursting the African demographic bubble. In a number of European countries, there has been a modest rise in fertility rates that may well persist beyond the end of the 'tempo' effect, which had not been envisaged. If Israeli women have three children, there is no reason why British or American women should not. The impact on Britain and America would be profound. On the other hand, in the US and UK we have seen some early signs that life expectancy growth may be faltering, with dementia and the diseases of rich lifestyles such as diabetes seemingly to blame.[45] Life expectancy for men in the UK has fallen by a year and for women by a year and a half since 2011.[46] This could be a glitch or the start of a new trend in which, once again, the Anglo-Saxons are pioneers.

Social trends might also surprise us. Given reasonably good luck and good timing, little sex is required to have a large family, so a general loss of interest in sex need not as such reduce fertility rates. But the recent emergence of the 'herbivore' in Japan – a young person who seems to have no interest in romantic or sexual relations with another person – could be part of a general culture of low fertility. There is some evidence that a trend towards less interest in sex and relationships is becoming common among the young in the West.[47] Data still reports on 'men' and 'women', but the rise of LGBTQ could have a significant impact on demography and certainly on how it is measured.

Whatever the future holds, of one thing we can be sure: that just as in the past, demography and destiny will continue to be entwined. Demography will shape the course of history as long as birth and death, marriage and migration remain the most fundamental events in our lives.

Appendix I

How Life Expectancy is Calculated

Life expectancy is the best measure of how long-lived people are in a society, since it accounts for the fact that some societies are older than others and, all things being equal, would have a higher death rate (deaths over total population). To calculate life expectancy at birth in any given year – a calculation that was first used by the life insurance industry in seventeenth-century England – take the number of those aged 0–1 who died during the year as a share of all those aged 0–1. Add to that the share of those aged 1–2 who died during the year as a share of all of those aged 1–2. Continue this procedure until the cumulative share reaches 50%, at which point life expectancy at birth for that year is reached. In a country with a high infant mortality and child mortality rate, the percentages will rack up quickly and soon reach 50%, which is why high infant mortality means low life expectancy and falling infant mortality significantly extends life expectancy. Where deaths of young or even middle-aged people are uncommon, the 50% mark will not be reached until much later.

This means that life expectancy at birth is not really about what someone expects but rather what he or she *would* expect knowing the incidence of death and therefore the likelihood of dying in a particular age cohort in a particular year.

Normally the data is presented separately for men and women, although it is often aggregated for the whole population too. A gendered approach allows demographers to highlight differences between the sexes. For example, in Russia the differential is particularly wide: normally the life expectancy for men is shorter than it is for women, but in Russia the difference has been and continues to be particularly marked. By looking separately at male and female life expectancy we learn something useful about a society. In the case of

Russia, knowing that men are dying much earlier than women leads to examinations of lifestyle, alcohol consumption and the suicide rate between the sexes so that a deeper understanding of the social causes of low life expectancy can be gained.

The table that follows is an example of a life table. It is for Singapore in 2015, and column A shows the age at the start of the year while column B shows the percentage of those at the given age who died during the year. Less than a quarter of 1% of Singaporeans aged 0–1 (actually 0.214%) on 1 January 2015 died by 31 December 2015, while slightly more than 12% of those aged 90 at the start of the year had died by the end of it. Column C adds up each of these probabilities: if the probability of dying aged 0–1 is 0.214% and the probability of dying aged 1–2 is 0.012% then the probability of dying aged 0–2 is 0.226%. This probability, column C, gets higher and higher as we add in the share of deaths in each age cohort. Adding in all the cohorts to age eighty-one gets us just less than 50%. By adding in another cohort, we get to just over 50%. Therefore, at birth, we can say that a Singaporean could 'expect' to live to eighty-one. In fact a new-born in Singapore is likely to witness an extension in life expectancy during his or her life and so live longer than this; to reiterate, by 'life expectancy' we only mean what could be expected if the experience in future years is the same as the one at which we are looking.

We can also consider life expectancy at later ages. A seventy-year-old in Singapore in 2015 had no chance of dying aged one or two or any other age below seventy, so for him or her the calculation can start again. We can add the column B probabilities but not starting until age seventy. This is shown in column D. For a seventy-year-old in Singapore in 2016, as we can see, life expectancy is eighty-three, or another thirteen years beyond his or her current age.

Table 2: Singapore Life Expectancy: Both Sexes 2015[1]

A	B	C	D
Age	% Deaths	Cumulative from 0	Cumulative from 70
0	0.214	0.214	
1	0.012	0.226	
2	0.012	0.238	

3	0.011	0.249
4	0.009	0.258
5	0.007	0.265
6	0.005	0.27
7	0.005	0.275
8	0.005	0.28
9	0.006	0.286
10	0.007	0.293
11	0.008	0.301
12	0.009	0.31
13	0.011	0.321
14	0.013	0.334
15	0.016	0.35
16	0.018	0.368
17	0.02	0.388
18	0.021	0.409
19	0.022	0.431
20	0.023	0.454
21	0.024	0.478
22	0.024	0.502
23	0.025	0.527
24	0.025	0.552
25	0.026	0.578
26	0.026	0.604
27	0.027	0.631
28	0.029	0.66
29	0.03	0.69
30	0.032	0.722
31	0.034	0.756
32	0.036	0.792
33	0.039	0.831
34	0.041	0.872
35	0.043	0.915
36	0.046	0.961

37	0.051	1.012	
38	0.057	1.069	
39	0.065	1.134	
40	0.073	1.207	
41	0.082	1.289	
42	0.091	1.38	
43	0.101	1.481	
44	0.112	1.593	
45	0.122	1.715	
46	0.134	1.849	
47	0.148	1.997	
48	0.165	2.162	
49	0.184	2.346	
50	0.204	2.55	
51	0.25	2.8	
52	0.249	3.049	
53	0.281	3.33	
54	0.316	3.646	
55	0.353	3.999	
56	0.39	4.389	
57	0.428	4.817	
58	0.468	5.285	
59	0.508	5.793	
60	0.549	6.342	
61	0.593	6.935	
62	0.646	7.581	
63	0.711	8.292	
64	0.783	9.075	
65	0.857	9.932	
66	0.937	10.869	
67	1.037	11.906	
68	1.169	13.075	
69	1.319	14.394	
70	1.474	15.868	1.474

71	1.636	17.504	3.11
72	1.826	19.33	4.936
73	2.057	21.387	6.993
74	2.313	23.7	9.306
75	2.575	26.275	11.881
76	2.847	29.122	14.728
77	3.158	32.28	17.886
78	3.526	35.806	21.412
79	3.926	39.732	25.338
80	4.33	44.062	29.668
81	4.746	48.808	34.414
82	5.222	54.03	39.636
83	5.809		45.445
84	6.504		51.949
85	7.233		
86	8.032		
87	8.907		
88	9.863		
89	10.905		
90	12.039		
91	13.271		
92	14.606		
93	16.048		
94	17.604		
95	19.278		
96	21.073		
97	22.994		
98	25.044		
99	27.226		
100+	100		

Appendix II

How the Total Fertility Rate is Calculated

The birth rate shows the number of births as a share of the population but does not account for the fact that some populations have more fertile women than others and so would be expected to have more children relative to population size. Completed fertility for a cohort – how many children the average woman born in a particular year or decade bore – is historically very revealing, but the data will always tell us what was happening some time ago and not give us a contemporary picture of what is going on now. The best measure to compare contemporary societies to others or to their own immediate past is the total fertility rate (sometimes known as TFR).

The total fertility rate is calculated by looking at the number of births by women in a particular year or period and then calculating how many children a woman would have if her childbearing experience were typical of women in that year or period. Usually, fertile years are considered to be ages fifteen to forty-five or fifty (while there are births outside this range, in most societies they are statistically insignificant). In only the least developed countries do many girls below fifteen years of age have many children. As for older women, fertility technology is changing but to date birthing after this age has been sufficiently rare for demographers to be able to ignore it.

Normally we look at the experience of women in particular age groups as this provides useful data. The table below shows the picture for Egypt in an average year from 1997 to 2000. In such a year there was an incidence of 0.051 in 1, or 5.1%, of a woman aged 15–19 having a child. A hundred such women would collectively have had just over five children on average in a year. Therefore, for any woman going through the ages of fifteen to nineteen with the typical experience of the period, there was a slightly more than one in four chance of her having a child in those years as a whole (i.e. 0.51 x 5, which is 0.255 in 1 or 25.5%). The right-hand column is simply the middle column multiplied by five, since we are looking at an annual incidence over five years.

There was an incidence in an average year of 0.196 in 1 for a woman in her early twenties having a child. This means that, in an average year, there were nearly twenty children born (19.6 to be precise) for every hundred women in their early twenties. With that incidence, a woman going through that annual experience every year for the five years of her early twenties is likely to have had one child in those years, i.e. 0.196 x 5, or 0.98. In the late twenties the incidence was slightly higher at 0.208 in 1 or 20.8%, which means that the average woman going through those years would have another child in her late twenties.

Adding the total incidences in the right-hand column we get to 3.505 or (to simplify and round slightly down) three and a half children. This means that a woman who shares the average experiences for women of different ages in a given period will have three and a half children. Ten such women will have thirty-five children.

Table 3: Egyptian Fertility for an Average Year 1997-2000[1]

Age range	Children born per woman per annum	Children likely to be born in the period
15–19	0.051	0.255
20–24	0.196	0.98
25–29	0.208	1.04
30–34	0.147	0.735
35–39	0.075	0.375
40–45	0.024	0.12
45–49	0.004	0.02
Total fertility rate		**3.505**

Acknowledgements

Nick Lowcock has provided encouragement and thoughtful insight throughout my writing of *The Human Tide*. Professor Eric Kaufmann has been an invaluable source of wisdom and support. I am extremely grateful to Toby Mundy, whose inquisitiveness has driven the writing forward and whose professionalism has helped bring it to its conclusion. I cannot thank David Goodhart enough for all his help. Joe Zigmond and the team at John Murray and Clive Priddle at Public Affairs have been a pleasure to work with. Sir Brian Harrison, an outstanding tutor when I was at Corpus Christi College Oxford over thirty years ago, took on the process of review and comment with extraordinary but characteristic thoroughness and timeliness. A number of people have kindly looked at drafts of chapters or ideas, and I would like to thank them for the time they have taken and for their input. These include Daniel Benedyk, Michael Lind, Claire Morland, Sonia Morland, Ian Price, Jonathan Rynhold and Michael Wegier. I had the privilege of discussing this book in its early stages with my late and lamented friend Professor Anthony D. Smith, who as ever provided inspiration. Mike Callan was kind enough to pass an actuarial eye over the life-expectancy appendix. It goes without saying that any errors are entirely mine.

Finally I must thank my mother, Ingrid Morland, my wife Claire Morland and our own small human tide, Sonia, Juliet and Adam Morland, to whom this book is dedicated.

Notes

Chapter 1: Introduction

1. Hitchcock, p. 70.
2. Sherwood, p. 80; author's translation.
3. Hufton, pp. 62–3.
4. Woolf, pp. 57–8.
5. Zweig, pp. 25–6.

Chapter 2: The Weight of Numbers

1. Potter (ed.), p. 564; Livi-Bacci, *Concise History of World Population*, p. 25.
2. Livi-Bacci, *Population of Europe*, p. 120.
3. English, pp. 38–9.
4. Neillands, p. 212.
5. Harvey, *War of Wars*, p. 885.
6. Keegan, *First World War*, pp. 379, 402.
7. Jackson and Howe, p. 21; Mahdi, pp. 208–9.
8. Bashford and Chaplin, p. 51.
9. Reinhard, pp. 78, 129, author's translations; Jackson and Howe, pp. 22, 81.
10. Urdal.
11. Jackson and Howe, p. 22.
12. Jacques, p. 36.
13. Inevitably we are forced to confront the words 'modern', 'modernity' and 'modernisation'. These words will be unavoidably – and liberally – used throughout this book. Much has been written on the theory of modernisation and there has been considerable debate around these terms and what they mean, if anything. Quite simply, for our purposes,

'modernisation' means movement towards and 'modernity' arrival at three characteristics of societies which are not specifically demographic: first, urbanisation (most people living in towns, however defined); second, literacy and education (most people being able to read and write and ultimately a very high share of the population being educated at tertiary level, i.e. in university or college); and third, industrialisation or post-industrialisation (a large part of the economy consisting of non-agricultural activity and the bulk of the population employed in factories and offices rather than in fields). With this last element comes a high level of energy use per person, usually derived from coal, oil, gas or, more recently, hydro-power, nuclear power or increasingly solar power, rather than human, animal and primitive water and wind power of earlier eras. The demographic features generally associated with these features of a 'modern' society thus defined are: a fall in and then a low level of infant mortality (say, from one in five or more babies not making it to their first birthday to as few as three in a thousand); an extension of life expectancy – itself in part the result of falling infant mortality rates (from around thirty years at birth to sixty, seventy or more); and a fall in fertility rates (from six or more children per woman to three or fewer). Societies have not moved in the direction of 'modernity' thus defined in a consistent or uniform pattern, and certainly not at the same time. In some cases, urbanisation might have run ahead of industrialisation or industrialisation ahead of education; in other cases all three non-demographic changes might lead or lag behind the demographic change. Nevertheless, this is clearly the direction of travel for country after country, society after society, since the United Kingdom commenced its journey along this path around the year 1800. To date, in most cases, that direction of travel has been in one direction and reversals minor or temporary.

14. UN Social Indicators, UN Population Division 2017 Revisions.
15. *The Economist*, 15–21 April 2017, pp. 25–6.
16. Marshall and Gurr, p. 1.
17. Morland, *Democratic Engineering*, pp. 1–26.
18. For a full treatment of why demography has become increasingly important as industrialisation, modernisation and democratisation have spread, see ibid., pp. 9–21.
19. Ibid.
20. Ibid.; Bookman, p. 61.
21. Fearon and Laitin.

22. Note that the data for England and Wales is different from the data for the whole of the UK, the former including around 90% of the population of the latter.

23. For a discussion of the problems of determining the size of the population of England in the Middle Ages, which gives a good general sense of the issues involved, see Goldberg, pp. 71–83.

Chapter 3: The Triumph of the Anglo-Saxons

1. Wilson, p. 787.
2. Wrigley, pp. 348–9.
3. Malthus, p. 51. Malthus's thought developed with each version of his essay and he came increasingly to the view that, with restraint and later marriage, as observed in Western Europe, a society could avoid extreme misery. For an account of the development of Malthus's thought and a discussion of whether Malthus was a Malthusian, see Wrigley, pp. 216–24.
4. The concept and timing of the industrial revolution is itself controversial and complex. Wrigley, pp. 64–5 describes the decisive discontinuity as essentially a move from using the organic product of recent photosynthesis for the basic needs of food, fuel, shelter and clothing (e.g. eating the current year's crops, burning wood at most a few hundred years old) to being able to tap into millions of years of accumulated power from photosynthesis, initially through mass production and the use of coal. He therefore distinguishes sharply between what happened in Britain at the end of the eighteenth and early nineteenth centuries from earlier developments in e.g. the Netherlands.
5. Carey, pp. 46, 120, 12.
6. Macfarlane, pp. 144–53, 303–4.
7. Tranter, p. 53.
8. Morland, *Demographic Engineering*, p. 7.
9. Wrigley et al., pp. 134, 355.
10. For the extent to which fertility in early years of potential marriage outstrip those of later years, see ibid., p. 411.
11. This is not uncontroversial; some have suggested that England's early nineteenth-century population growth was fuelled more by falling mortality than rising fertility rates. See ibid., pp. 431–8.
12. Wrigley et al., p. 295.
13. Macfarlane, pp. 110, 184, 192–3.

14. Pomeranz, p. 276.
15. But see 11 above.
16. United Nations Population Division, 2017 Revisions.
17. Woods et al., p. 35; however, note distinction between endogenous and exogenous infant mortality in Wrigley, pp. 321–4.
18. Wrigley.
19. Ibid., pp. 431–2.
20. Maddison, pp. 160, 169–70, 180.
21. Connell, p. 25.
22. Charlwood, p. 58.
23. Townsend, p. 271.
24. Brett, pp. 67, 120.
25. Maddison, pp. 160, 169–70, 180.
26. Braudel, p. 437.
27. Charlwood, pp. 66–7.
28. Snyder, p. 158.
29. Canadian Encyclopedia, vol. 1, p. 595, vol. 3, p. 1453; UN Committee of International Coordination of National Research in Demography, World Population Year 1974, p. 59; Kalbach and McVey, p. 195; Livi-Bacci, *Concise History of World Population*, p. 61.
30. Wilkinson, p. 244.
31. Ibid., pp. 220, 224, 242, 247; Borrie, p. 55.
32. UN World Population Year 1974, pp. 9, 13, 51, 53.
33. Thompson, p. 53.
34. Beinart, p. 353.
35. Osterhammel, p. 448.
36. Merk, p. 189; Osterhammel, p. 331.
37. De Tocqueville, p. 371.
38. Genovese, p. 45.
39. Wilkinson, p. 150; Klein, p. 131; Thompson and Whelpton, p. 294.
40. Seeley, p. 12.
41. Thomas, p. 114.

Chapter 4: The German and Russian Challenges

1. Andrillon, pp. 70–8, author's translation.
2. Paddock, pp. 66, 74, 87.
3. Lieven, p. 60.

4. McLaren, p. 11.
5. Iliffe, p. 21.
6. Wood and Suitters, p. 91.
7. McLaren, p. 96.
8. Ibid., p. 128.
9. Ibid., p. 119.
10. Mullen and Munson, p. 79.
11. Armstrong, p. 195.
12. Lipman, p. 45; author's private conversation with the late Professor David Cesarani.
13. Anderson, 'Population Change', p. 211; Maddison, pp. 182–3.
14. Ibid.
15. Luce, loc. 1848.
16. Livi-Bacci, *A Concise History*, pp. 136, 132–3, 135; Woycke, p. 3.
17. Woycke, pp. 2–3.
18. Gaidar, p. 259.
19. Livi-Bacci, *A Concise History*, p. 132; Maddison, pp. 182–3.
20. Livi-Bacci, *A Concise History*, p. 132.
21. Figes, p. 160.
22. Foner, p. 31.
23. Tooze, loc. 4483–8.
24. McLaren, p. 11.
25. Ibid., p. 149.
26. Garrett et al., p. 5.
27. Wood and Suitters, pp. 157–8.
28. Soloway, pp. 22–4; National Birth-Rate Commission, pp. 36–8.
29. *The Lancet*, 10 November 1906, pp. 1290–1.
30. Soloway, p. 5.
31. Reich, pp. 120–2.
32. Quinlan, p. 11.
33. Andrillon, pp. 70–8, author's translation.
34. Okie, p. 15.
35. Paddock, p. 66.
36. Woycke, p. 133.
37. Ibid., p. 134.
38. Paddock, pp. 66, 74, 87; Lieven, p. 60.
39. Stolper, p. 24.
40. Osterhammel, p. 364.
41. Schierbrand, p. 95; Gatrell, *Government, Industry*, pp. 175, 255.

42. Figes, p. 298.
43. Winter, p. 249; Livi-Bacci, *Population of Europe*, p. 132.
44. Urdal.

Chapter 5: The Passing of the 'Great Race'

1. Hitler, pp. 28, 38, 74, 93, 207, 261.
2. Winter, p. 259.
3. Johnson, pp. 174–5.
4. Davies, p. 113.
5. Livi-Bacci, *Population of Europe*, p. 165.
6. Using Livi-Bacci, *Population of Europe*, pp. 132–3, we see that for the period 1800–1913, Britain's population never grew faster than an average of 1.33% per annum. For Germany's peak period, it was slightly higher, at 1.38%. For Russia it was 1.47%. Britain's birth rate did not exceed 40 per thousand while Germany's did, and Russia's exceeded 50. Again using Livi-Bacci (pp. 168, 166), we find that between the early 1920s and late 1940s England's fertility fell by a fifth of a child, Germany's fell by over half a child, and Russia's fell by around three children. In 1920–50 life expectancy rose by twelve years in the UK, fourteen years in Germany, and nearly twenty-five years in the Soviet Union.
7. Mouton, pp. 109–10.
8. Livi-Bacci, *Population of Europe*, pp. 136, 168; Kirk, pp. 14, 48.
9. Kirk, pp. 48–9.
10. Ehrman, p. 42.
11. Livi-Bacci, *Population of Europe*, pp. 135, 166.
12. Gerstle; Gratton.
13. Kirk, pp. 75–6.
14. Ibid., pp. 279–80.
15. Ibid., pp. 282–3.
16. Ehrman, pp. 33–4.
17. McCleary, *Menace of British Depopulation*, p. 18.
18. Kirk, p. 42.
19. Maddison, pp. 182–4.
20. Morland, *Demographic Engineering*, pp. 143–4.
21. Gerstle, pp. 105–6.
22. Grant, p. 263.

23. Ibid., p. 167.

24. Ibid., p. 220.

25. *Guardian*, 1 May 2014, https://www.theguardian.com/books/2014/may/01/f-scott-fitzgerald-stories-uncensored-sexual-innuendo-drug.

26. East, p. 113.

27. Ibid., p. 115.

28. Ibid., pp. 116, 271.

29. Ibid., p. 128.

30. Ibid., p. 145.

31. Cox, p. 77.

32. Offer, p. 172.

33. McCleary, *Menace of British Depopulation*, p. 63.

34. Dennery, p. 229.

35. Wilson, pp. 174, 228.

36. 'Sydney'.

37. Haggard, pp. 170–2.

38. McCleary, *Menace of British Depopulation*, p. 59.

39. Haggard, pp. 170, 185.

40. Ibid., p. 185.

41. McCleary, *Menace of British Depopulation*, pp. 49, 52.

42. Money, pp. 83, 159.

43. Bertillon; Boverat, p. 16.

44. Leroy-Beaulieu.

45. Kirk, pp. 282–3; Camisciole.

46. Morland, *Demographic Engineering*.

47. Cossart, pp. 57–77.

48. Camisciole, p. 27.

49. Reggiani.

50. Goldman, p. 7.

51. Ibid., p. 254.

52. Ibid., pp. 254–5.

53. Ibid., pp. 7, 256, 258, 289.

54. Ibid., p. 333.

55. Livi-Bacci, *Population of Europe*, p. 175.

56. Ibid., pp. 132–4, 165, 166, 168; Kirk, p. 279.

57. Sigmund, p. 25 (author's translation).

58. Kirk, pp. 102, 111; Mouton, pp. 170–1, 224.

59. Mouton, pp. 15, 17.

60. Stone, p. 145.

61. Maddison, pp. 182–5; Livi-Bacci, *Population of Europe*, p. 132.
62. De Tocqueville, pp. 399, 433.

Chapter 6: The West since 1945

1. *The Times*, 11 March 1964, p. 12.
2. Easterlin.
3. Macunovich, p. 64.
4. Easterlin, pp. 10–12.
5. Macunovich, pp. 1–2.
6. Croker, p. 2.
7. Derived from Maddison 1982, p. 185.
8. Croker, p. 2.
9. Easterlin, pp. 27–30.
10. E.g. Willetts.
11. Djerassi, p. 11.
12. UN Population Division, 2015 Revisions; Macunovich, p. 118.
13. French, p. 47.
14. Westoff, p. 1.
15. Ibid., p. 25.
16. Ibid.
17. Kaufmann, *Shall the Religious Inherit the Earth?*, pp. 94–5.
18. UN Population Division, 2015 Revisions.
19. *Guardian*, 13 February 2015, https://www.theguardian.com/world/2015/feb/13/italy-is-a-dying-country-says-minister-as-birth-rate-plummets (impression: 13 November 2017).
20. Morland, *Demographic Engineering*, pp. 17–20.
21. Ibid., p. 36.
22. Gaidar, p. 242.
23. *The Local*, 23 September 2016, https://www.thelocal.it/20160923/the-real-reasons-young-italians-arent-having-kids (impression: 14 February 2018)
24. UK Office for National Statistics, 2015.
25. UN Population Division, 2015 Revisions.
26. *Washington Post*, 8 December 2016, https://www.washingtonpost.com/national/health-science/us-life-expectancy-declines-for-the-first-time-since-1993/2016/12/07/7dcdc7b4-bc93-11e6-91ee-1adddfe36cbe_story.html?utm_term=.25ef71e054e3 (impression: 13 November 2016).

27. Jackson and Howe, p. 67.
28. Navarro, p. 38.
29. Ibid., p. 92.
30. Ibid., pp. 92–3, 97.
31. Gaquin and Dunn, p. 26.
32. Navarro, p. 93.
33. Passell et al.
34. Smith and Edmonston, p. 35.
35. Waters and Ueda, p. 18.
36. Meacham and Graybeal, p. 6.
37. *Independent*, 7 November 2016, http://www.independent.co.uk/voices/
    donald-trump-us-elections-hillary-clinton-race-hispanic-black-vote-
    white-americans-fear-minority-a7402296.html (impression: 13 Novem-
    ber 2017).
38. Pew Research, 19 November 2015, http://www.pewhispanic.org/2015/
    11/19/more-mexicans-leaving-than-coming-to-the-u-s/ (impression:
    14 February 2018).
39. Goodhart, p. xxviii.
40. Byron, p. 78; Düvell, p. 347
41. Goodhart, p. xxix.
42. UK Office for National Statistics, 2012.
43. Sunak and Rajeswaran, pp. 7, 25.
44. Coleman, pp. 456, 462.
45. Brouard and Tiberj, pp. 1–2.
46. Cyrus and Vogel, p. 131.
47. Australian Bureau of Statistics, 2012–13.
48. Jackson and Howe, p. 190.
49. Haas.

Chapter 7: Russia and the Eastern Bloc from 1945

1. Gorbachev, p. 155.
2. Ibid., p. 171.
3. Ibid., pp. 10, 155.
4. Jones and Grupp, p. 75.
5. Weber and Goodman, p. 289.
6. Lutz, Scherbov and Volkov, p. 143.
7. Gray, p. 19.

8. Ibid., p. 24.
9. Lewis et al., p. 271.
10. Gaidar, p. 253; UN Population Division, 2017 Revisions: Life Expectancy.
11. Lewis et al., p. 285.
12. UN Population Division, 2017 Revisions: Infant Mortality.
13. Haynes and Husan, p. 117.
14. UN Population Division, 2017 Revisions: Fertility.
15. Coale et al., pp. 112–13.
16. Lewis et al., p. 278.
17. Ibid.
18. Szporluk, p. 29.
19. Lewis et al., p. 149.
20. Anderson and Silver, pp. 164–5.
21. Szayna, p. 10.
22. Besmeres, p. 71.
23. Szayna, p. vi.
24. Ibid., pp. 279–5.
25. Brezhnev and Tikhonov, pp. 373–4.
26. Zakharov, p. 921.
27. Botev, p. 700.
28. UN Population Division, 2017 Revisions.
29. See for example Kanaaneh, pp. 83, 108.
30. Zakharov, p. 936.
31. Ibid., pp. 918–19; Perelli-Harris and Isupova, p. 151.
32. Perelli-Harris and Isupova, p. 146.
33. Ibid., p. 931.
34. Ibid., p. 936.
35. UN Population Division, 2017 Revisions.
36. Haynes and Husan, p. 152.
37. Pearce, p. 125.
38. Haynes and Husan, p. 163.
39. Ibid., p. 166.
40. *New York Review of Books*, 2 September 2014, http://www.nybooks.com/daily/2014/09/02/dying-russians/ (impression: 13 September 2017).
41. Eberstadt, *Russia's Demographic Disaster*.
42. UN Population Division, 2017 Revisions.
43. Ibid.

44. Eberstadt, 'Dying Bear'.
45. UN Population Division, 2017 Revisions.
46. Rozanova, p. 36.
47. *Al Jazeera*, 14 February 2017, http://www.aljazeera.com/indepth/features/2017/02/death-throes-russia-iconic-countryside-170207084912286.html (impression: 13 September 2017).
48. Putin, p. 385.
49. Szporluk, p. 34.
50. CIA World Fact Book, https://www.cia.gov/library/publications/the-world-factbook/fields/2075.html (impression: 14 September 2017).
51. Ibid.
52. Morland, *Demographic Engineering*, p. 24.
53. BBC, 2012.
54. Rozanova, p. 44.
55. *International Business Times*, 23 July 2017, http://www.ibtimes.com/moscow-largest-muslim-city-europe-faithful-face-discrimination-public-authorities-2020858 (impression: 13 September 2017).
56. Bhrolgháin and Dyson, p. 15.
57. Ceterchi et al., pp. 54–5.
58. Ibid., p. 54.
59. Bhrolgháin and Dyson, p. 10.
60. King.
61. Judah, pp. 152, 155.
62. Morland, *Demographic Engineering*, p. 25.
63. Slack and Doyon, p. 158.
64. *New Internationalist*, 24 June 2015, https://newint.org/features/web-exclusive/2015/06/24/ghostly-bulgaria (impression: 13 September 2017).
65. UN Population Division, 2017 Revisions.

Chapter 8: Japan, China and East Asia

1. Novikoff-Priboy, pp. 214, 242.
2. Knight and Traphagan, p. 6.
3. Macfarlane, pp. 31–2.
4. Reinhard, p. 557; Cole, p. 399.
5. Nakamura and Miyamoto, p. 233.
6. Reinhard, p. 558.

7. Drixler, pp.18–19, 33, 124.
8. Cornell, p. 211.
9. Obuchi, p. 331.
10. Ishii, p. 24.
11. Tauber, p. 41.
12. Ishii, p. 60.
13. Chamberlain, p. 432.
14. Ibid., p. 433.
15. Ransome, pp. 206, 226, 227.
16. Tauber, pp. 233, 286.
17. Cole, p. 397.
18. Ibid., p. 405.
19. Reinhard, p. 566.
20. Cole, p. 413.
21. Ishii, p. 163.
22. Saito, p. 129; Tolischus, p. 75.
23. Reinhard, pp. 567–8.
24. Tolischus, p. 75.
25. Marshall, pp. 95–6.
26. Diamond, *Lesser Breeds*, p. 12.
27. Tauber, pp. 233–5.
28. Coulmas, p. 5.
29. UN Population Division, 2017 Revisions.
30. *Japan Times*, 6 June 2013.
31. MacKellar et al., p. 50.
32. *Business Insider UK*, 22 February 2016, http://uk.businessinsider.com/how-japan-government-solving-sex-problem-2016-2?r=US&IR=T (impression: 26 July 2017).
33. *Guardian*, 20 October 2013, https://www.theguardian.com/world/2013/oct/20/young-people-japan-stopped-having-sex (impression: 26 July 2017).
34. Ibid.
35. Cornell, p. 30; UN Population Division, 2017 Revisions.
36. UN Population Division, 2017 Revisions.
37. Pearson, p. 117.
38. UN Population Division, 2017 Revisions.
39. Ibid.
40. *Japan Times*, 6 June 2013.
41. Knight and Traphagan, p. 10.

42. Coulmas, p. 47.
43. UN Population Division, 2015 Revisions.
44. MacKellar et al., p. 39.
45. Ogawa et al., p. 136.
46. UN Population Division, 2015 Revisions.
47. *New York Times*, 23 August 2015, https://www.nytimes.com/2015/08/24/world/a-sprawl-of-abandoned-homes-in-tokyo-suburbs.html (impression: 26 July 2017).
48. *LA Times*, 10 July 2016, http://www.latimes.com/world/asia/la-fg-japan-population-snap-story.html (impression: 26 July 2017).
49. *Slate*, 26 June 2015, http://www.slate.com/articles/news_and_politics/roads/2015/06/kodokushi_in_aging_japan_thousands_die_alone_and_unnoticed_every_year_their.html (impression: 26 July 2017).
50. Coulmas, p. 14.
51. Trading Economics.
52. UN Population Division, 2015 Revisions.
53. Ho, p. 4.
54. Geping and Jinchang, p. 14.
55. Ho, p. 282.
56. Fairbank and Goldman, p. 169.
57. Reinhard, p. 553.
58. Ho, p. 282; Geping and Jinchang, p. 15.
59. Nakamura and Miyamoto.
60. Osterhammel, p. 122.
61. Tien, p. 81.
62. Ibid., p. 16.
63. Ho, p. 42.
64. Ibid., p. 45.
65. White, p. 49.
66. Dikötter, p. 13.
67. White, pp. 44–5.
68. Dikötter, p. 320.
69. UN Population Division, 2017 Revisions.
70. White, pp. 44–5.
71. Ibid., p. 73.
72. Cho, p. 62.
73. Ming, p. 10.
74. Cho, p. 63.
75. Greenhalgh, p. 31.

76. *The Economist*, 23 September 2017, p. 61.
77. UN Population Division, 2017 Revisions.
78. Rashid et al., p. 699.
79. Greenhalgh.
80. *The Economist*, 19 August 2010, http://www.economist.com/node/16846390 (impression: 27 July 2017).
81. LifeSite, March 2017, https://www.lifesitenews.com/news/she-was-dragged-from-her-home-and-forced-to-abort.-shes-now-shaming-the-chi (impression: 27 July 2017).
82. UN Population Division, 2017 Revisions.
83. Jackson et al., pp. 2, 10.
84. Greenhalgh, p. 1.
85. *Guardian*, 2 November 2011, https://www.theguardian.com/world/2011/nov/02/chinas-great-gender-crisis (impression: 27 July 2010).
86. *The Economist*, 10 February 2018, p. 55.
87. UN Population Division, 2017 Revisions.
88. See Morland, *Demographic Engineering*.
89. UN Population Division, 2017 Revisions.
90. *Globe and Mail*, 22 October 2014, https://www.theglobeandmail.com/news/world/a-bleak-future-and-population-crisis-for-south-korea/article21249599/ (impression: 28 July 2017).
91. *Bangkok Post*, 23 May 2013, http://www.bangkokpost.com/learning/learning-news/372232/single-no-children-thailand-future (impression: 28 July 2013).

Chapter 9: The Middle East and North Africa

1. UN Population Division, 2017 Revisions.
2. Shaw, p. 325.
3. Ibid., p. 334.
4. Karpat, p. 55.
5. *New York Times*, 20 May 2011, http://www.nytimes.com/2011/05/21/world/europe/21georgia.html (impression: 14 August 2017).
6. Kévorkian, p. 535.
7. Suny, p. 283.
8. Ibid., p. 285.
9. Pelham, p. 37.
10. Reinhard, p. 449.

11. Ibid., p. 461.
12. Fenby, p. 352.
13. Reinhard, p. 461.
14. BBC News, 10 July 2003, http://news.bbc.co.uk/1/hi/world/africa/3056921.stm (impression: 14 August 2017).
15. Iliffe, p. 161.
16. Baer, p. 14.
17. Ibid., p. 25.
18. UN Population Division, 2017 Revisions.
19. Jones and Karim, p. 3.
20. Abu Dawood, Hadith 2050.
21. Quran 6:151.
22. Jones and Karim, pp. 3–4.
23. Kaufmann, *Shall the Religious Inherit the Earth?*, pp. 121–2.
24. Riddell, p. 82.
25. Fargues, 'Demography, Migration', p. 19.
26. Ibid., p. 23.
27. Cairo Demographic Centre, p. 7.
28. *New York Times*, 7 June 2014, https://www.nytimes.com/2014/06/08/world/middleeast/iran-tehran-offers-incentives-to-middle-class-families-to-have-more-children-as-population-declines.html (impression: 14 August 2017).
29. UN Economic and Social Commission for Western Asia, pp. 59–60.
30. Fargues, 'Demography, Migration', p. 22.
31. Winckler; UN Population Division, 2017 Revisions.
32. UN Development Programme 2002, p. 85.
33. UN Development Programme 2011, p. 18.
34. Ibid., p. 40.
35. Ibid., p. 53.
36. Ibid., p. 56.
37. UN Development Programme 2006, p. 74.
38. Ibid., p. 85.
39. Academic Ranking of World Universities, 2017.
40. UN Development Programme 2002, p. 67.
41. Ibid., p. 3.
42. UN Economic and Social Commission for Western Asia, p. 66.
43. Urdal.
44. Kaufmann, *Shall the Religious Inherit the Earth?*, pp. 130–1.
45. UN Development Programme 2016.

46. Bishara, p. 225.

47. Freedom House.

48. Bremmer.

49. Urdal, p. 9.

50. Mirkin, pp. 12, 14, https://www.yumpu.com/en/document/view/48347156/arab-spring-demographics-in-a-region-in-transition-arab-human- (impression: 26 June 2017).

51. *New York Times*, 2 March 2015, https://www.nytimes.com/2015/03/03/science/earth/study-links-syria-conflict-to-drought-caused-by-climate-change.html (impression: 15 August 2017).

52. Al Fanar Media, 25 April 2016, https://www.al-fanarmedia.org/2016/04/study-explores-the-deep-frustrations-of-arab-youth/ (impression: 15 August 2017).

53. *The Economist*, 16 August 2016, https://www.al-fanarmedia.org/2016/04/study-explores-the-deep-frustrations-of-arab-youth/ (impression: 15 August 2017).

54. *New York Times*, 28 October 2016, https://www.nytimes.com/2016/10/29/world/middleeast/saudi-arabia-women.html (impression: 15 August 2017).

55. BBC, 4 March 2016, https://www.bbc.co.uk/news/world-europe-35999015 (impression: 15 August 2017).

56. Kaufmann, *Shall the Religious Inherit the Earth?*, p. 120; Pew Research Center 2015.

57. *Guardian*, 28 May 2009, https://www.theguardian.com/books/2009/may/28/hay-festival-tutu-israel-palestine-solution (impression: 4 May 2018).

58. Daniel Pipes Middle East Forum, http://www.danielpipes.org/4990/arab-israeli-fatalities-rank-49th (impression: 16 August 2017).

59. Morland, *Demographic Engineering*, pp. 113–40.

60. Tessler, p. 170.

61. Pew Research, http://www.pewresearch.org/fact-tank/2015/02/09/europes-jewish-population/ (impression: 16 December 2017).

62. Hacohen, p. 267.

63. Jones, p. 221.

64. Eshkol cited in Bird, p. 219.

65. Ben-Gurion cited in Pearlman, p. 240.

66. Fargues, 'Protracted National Conflict', p. 452.

67. Peritz and Baras, pp. 113–14.

68. Derived from Goldschneider, pp. 113–14.

69. UN Population Division, 2017 Revisions; UN Social Indicators: Literacy.

70. Pedersen et al., p. 16.
71. Morland, *Demographic Engineering*, p. 129.
72. UN Population Division, 2017 Revisions.
73. Morland, 'Defusing the Demographic Scare', https://www.haaretz.com/ 1.5049876 (impression 26 June 2018); Morland, 'Israel's Fast Evolving Demography', https://www.jpost.com/Opinion/Op-Ed-Contributors /Israels-fast-evolving-demography-320574 (impression 26 June 2018); Morland, 'Israeli Women Do It By Numbers', https://www.thejc.com /israeli-women-do-it-by-the-numbers-1.53785 (impression: 26 June 2018); Morland, *Demographic Engineering*.
74. *Tablet*, 11 July 2017, http://www.tabletmag.com/jewish-life-and-religion/239961/saying-no-to-kids (impression: 16 August 2017).
75. Morland, *Demographic Engineering*, p. 122.
76. See for example Lustick.

Chapter 10: Nothing New Under the Sun?

1. UN Population Division, 2017 Revisions.
2. Ibid.
3. Martin, p. 169.
4. Committee on Population and Development, p. 101.
5. Martin, p. 196.
6. Ibid., p. 195.
7. La Ferrara et al.
8. Hollerbach and Diaz-Briquets, pp. 4, 6, 9.
9. UN Population Division, 2017 Revisions.
10. Morland, *Demographic Engineering*, pp. 143–9.
11. *Washington Post*, 27 January 2017, https://www.washingtonpost.com/ news/worldviews/wp/2017/01/27/even-before-trump-more-mexicans-were-leaving-the-us-than-arriving/?utm_term= .70340b7aed5e (impression: 17 August 2017).
12. *Texas Standard*, 28 February 2017, http://www.texasstandard.org/stories /why-are-mexicans-leaving-the-us-in-droves/ (impression: 17 August 2017).
13. *Guardian*, 24 May 2017, https://www.theguardian.com/world/2017/ may/24/india-is-worlds-most-populous-nation-with-132bn-people-academic-claims (impression: 18 August 2017).
14. UN Population Division, 2017 Revisions.

15. Morland, *Demographic Engineering*, p. 59.
16. Desai, p. 3.
17. Morland, *Demographic Engineering*, pp. 17–21.
18. Iyer, pp. 3, 10.
19. *Times of India*, 22 January 2015, https://timesofindia.indiatimes.com/india/Muslim-population-grows-24-slower-than-previous-decade/articleshow/45972687.cms (impression: 20 November 2017).
20. Zubrin, pp. 172–3.
21. Sen, pp. 42, 77–9.
22. BBC News, 14 November 2014, http://www.bbc.com/news/world-asia-india-30040790 (impression: 18 August 2017).
23. Population Research Institute, 24 June 2014, https://www.pop.org/a-once-and-future-tragedy-indias-sterilization-campaign-39-years-later/ (impression: 18 August 2017).
24. UN Population Division, 2017 Revisions.
25. BBC News, 14 March 2013, http://www.bbc.com/news/world-africa-21783076; UN Population Division, 2017 Revisions.
26. Stats SA, 25 August 2016, http://www.statssa.gov.za/?p=8176 (impression: 18 August 2017).
27. NPR, 9 July 2012, http://www.npr.org/2012/07/09/156375781/botswanas-stunning-achievement-against-aids (impression: 18 August 2017).
28. *Guardian*, 8 March 2016, https://www.theguardian.com/global-development/datablog/2016/mar/08/contraception-and-family-planning-around-the-world-interactive (impression: 14 August 2017).
29. VOA, 30 December 2014, https://www.voanews.com/a/in-kenya-family-planning-is-an-economic-safeguard/2579394.html (impression: 15 September 2014).
30. UN Population Division, 2017 Revisions.
31. Ibid.
32. Iliffe, p. 131.
33. Segal, pp. 56–7.
34. BBC News, 21 August 2017, http://www.bbc.co.uk/news/resources/idt-sh/lagos (impression: 21 August 2017).
35. Ibid.
36. Jackson and Howe, p. 54.
37. Ibid., p. 65.
38. FCA, *Consumer Vulnerability: Occasional Paper 8*, London, 2015, p. 9.

39. *Business Insider*, 20 November 2015, http://www.businessinsider.fr/us/japan-developing-carebots-for-elderly-care-2015-11/ (impression: 20 August 2017).

40. *Guardian*, 13 February 2010, https://www.theguardian.com/environment/2010/feb/13/climate-change-family-size-babies (impression: 21 August 2017).

41. UN Population Division, 2017 Revisions.

42. Ibid.

43. Coleman.

44. Passell et al.

45. *Daily Telegraph*, 18 July 2017, http://www.telegraph.co.uk/science/2017/07/17/life-expectancy-stalls-britain-first-time-100-years-dementia/ (impression: 20 August 2017); *Atlantic*, 13 December 2016, https://www.theatlantic.com/health/archive/2016/12/why-are-so-many-americans-dying-young/510455/ (impression: 20 August 2017).

46. *Professional Pensions*, 1 March 2018, https://www.professionalpensions.com/professional-pensions/news-analysis/3027631/latest-cmi-model-reveals-clear-trend-in-life-expectancy (impression: 1 May 2018).

47. *Politicos*, 8 February 2018, https://www.politico.com/magazine/story/2018/02/08/why-young-americans-having-less-sex-216953 (impression: 16 February 2018).

Appendix I: How Life Expectancy is Calculated

1. http://www.singstat.gov.sg/docs/default-source/default-document-library/publications/publications_and_papers/births_and_deaths/life-table15-16.pdf (impression: 15 November 2017).

Appendix II: How the Total Fertility Rate is Calculated

1. https://www.measureevaluation.org/prh/rh_indicators/family-planning/fertility/total-fertility-rate (impression: 20 November 2017).

Bibliography

Note: The websites referenced in this section
have all been accessed during the period 2012–18.

Academic Ranking of World Universities, 2013, http://www.shanghairanking. com/ARWU2013.html

Anderson, Barbara A., and Silver, Brian D., 'Growth and Diversity of the Population of the Soviet Union', *Annals of the American Academy of Political and Social Sciences*, 510, 1990, pp. 155–7

Anderson, Charles H., *White Protestant Americans: From National Origins to Religious Group*, Englewood Cliffs, NJ, Prentice-Hall, 1970

Anderson, Michael, 'Population Change in North Western Europe 1750–1850', in Anderson (ed.), *British Population History*, pp. 191–280

Anderson, Michael (ed.), *British Population History: From the Black Death to the Present Day*, Cambridge University Press, 1996

Andrillon, Henri, *L'Expansion de L'Allemagne: ses causes, ses formes et ses conséquences*, Paris, Librairie Marcel Rivière, 1914

Armstrong, Alan, *Farmworkers in England and Wales: A Social and Economic History 1770–1980*, Ames, Iowa State University Press, 1988

Australian Bureau of Statistics, *Cultural Diversity in Australia – Reflecting a Nation: Stories from the 2011 Census*, 2012–13, http://www.abs.gov.au/ ausstats/abs@.nsf/Lookup/2071.0main+features902012-2013

Baer, Gabriel (trans. Szoke, Hanna), *Population and Society in the Arab East*, London, Routledge, Kegan & Paul, 1964

Baines, Dudley, and Woods, Robert, *Population and Regional Development*, Cambridge University Press, 2004

Bashford, Alison, and Chaplin, Joyce E., *The New Worlds of Thomas Malthus: Rereading the Principle of Population*, Princeton University Press, 2016

Beinart, William, *Twentieth-Century South Africa*, Oxford University Press, 2001

Berghahn, V. R., *Imperial Germany 1871–1914: Economy, Society, Culture and Politics*, New York, Berghahn, 1994

Bertillon, Jacques, *La Dépopulation de la France: ses conséquences, ses causes et mesures à prendre pour le combattre*, Paris, Libraire Félix Alcan, 1911

Besmeres, John F., *Socialist Population Politics: The Political Implications of Demographic Trends in the USSR and Eastern Europe*, White Plains, NY, M. E. Sharpe, 1980

Bhrolgháin, Marie Ní, and Dyson, Tim, 'On Causation in Demography: Issues and Illustrations', *Population and Development Review*, 33 (1), 2007, pp. 1–36

Bird, Kai, *Crossing Mandelbaum Gate: Coming of Age Between the Arabs and Israelis*, New York, Simon & Schuster, 2010

Bishara, Marwan, *The Invisible Arab*, New York, Nation Books, 2012

Bookman, Milica Zarkovic, *The Demographic Struggle for Power*, London, Frank Cass, 1997

Borrie, W. D., *Population Trends and Policies: A Study in Australian and World Demography*, Sydney, Wellington and London, Australian Publishing Company, 1948

Botev, Nikolai, 'The Ethnic Composition of Families in Russia in 1989: Insights into Soviet "Nationalities Policy"', *Population and Development Review*, 28 (4), 2002, pp. 681–706

Boverat, Fernand, *Patriotisme et paternité*, Paris, Bernard Grosset, 1913

Braudel, Fernand (trans. Richard Mayne), *A History of Civilizations*, New York and London, Penguin, 1993

Bremmer, Ian, *The J Curve: A New Way to Understand Why Nations Rise and Fall*, New York, Simon & Schuster, 2006

Brett, C. E. B., 'The Georgian Town: Belfast Around 1800', in Beckett, J. C., and Glassock, R. E. (eds), *Belfast: The Origin and Growth of an Industrial City*, London, BBC Books, 1967, pp. 67–77

Brezhnev, Leonid, and Tikhonov, Nikolai, 'On Pronatalist Policies in the Soviet Union', *Population and Development Review*, 7 (2), 1981, pp. 372–4

Brimelow, Peter, 'Time to Rethink Immigration?', in Capaldi (ed.), *Immigration*, pp. 33–61

Brouard, Sylvain, and Tiberj, Vincent (trans. Fredette, Jennifer), *As French as Everyone Else? A Survey of French Citizens of Maghrebin, African and Turkish Origin*, Philadelphia, Temple University Press, 2011

Buckley, Mary, 'Glasnost and the Women Question', in Edmonson, Linda (ed.), *Women and Society in Russia and the Soviet Union*, Cambridge University Press, 1992, pp. 202–26

Byron, Margaret, *Post-War Caribbean Migration to Britain: The Unfinished Cycle*, Aldershot, Avebury, 1994

Cairo Demographic Centre, *Fertility Trends and Differentials in Arab Countries*, Cairo, 1971

Caldwell, Christopher, *Reflections on the Revolution in Europe: Immigration, Islam and the West*, London, Allen Lane, 2009

Camisciole, Elisa, *Reproducing the French Race: Integration, Intimacy, and Embodiment in the Early Twentieth Century*, Durham, NC, Duke University Press, 2009

Canadian Encyclopaedia, Edmonton, Hurtig, 1985

Capaldi, Nicholas (ed.), *Immigration: Debating the Issues*, Amherst, NY, Prometheus Books, 1997

Carey, John, *The Intellectuals and the Masses: Pride and Prejudice among the Literary Intelligentsia, 1880–1939*, London, Faber & Faber, 1991

Ceterchi, Ioan, Zlatescu, Victor, Copil, Dan, and Anca, Peter, *Law and Population Growth in Romania*, Bucharest, Legislative Council of the Socialist Republic of Romania, 1974

Chamberlain, B. H., *Things Japanese*, London, Trench, Trübner, 1890

Charlwood, Don, *The Long Farewell*, Ringwood, Australia, Allen Lane, 1981

Cho, Lee-Jay, 'Population Dynamics and Policy in China', in Poston, Dudley L., and Yauckey, David (eds), *The Population of Modern China*, New York and London, Plenum Press, 1992, pp. 59–82

Clements, Barbara Evans, *A History of Women in Russia from the Earliest Times to the Present*, Bloomington, Indiana University Press, 2012

Coale, Ansley J., Anderson, Barbara A., and Härm, Erna, *Human Fertility in Russia since the Nineteenth Century*, Princeton University Press, 2015

Cole, Allan B., 'Japan's Population Problems in War and Peace', *Pacific Affairs*, 16 (4), 1943, pp. 397–417

Coleman, David, 'Projections of the Ethnic Minority Populations in the United Kingdom 2006–2056', *Population and Development Review*, 36 (3), 2010, pp. 441–86

Committee on Population and Demography, *Levels and Recent Trends in Fertility and Mortality in Brazil*, Washington DC, National Academy Press, 1983

Connell, K. H., *The Population of Ireland 1750–1845*, Cambridge University Press, 1950

Cornell, Laurel L., 'Infanticide in Early Modern Japan? Demography, Culture and Population Growth', in Smitka, Michael (ed.), *Japanese Economic History 1600–1960: Historical Demography and Labor Markets in Prewar Japan*, New York and London, Garland, 1998

Corsini, Carlo A., and Viazzo, Pierre Paolo (eds), *The Decline of Infant Mortality in Europe 1800–1950: Four National Case Studies*, Florence, UNICEF, 1993

Cossart, P., 'Public Gatherings in France During the French Revolution: The Club as a Legitimate Venue for Popular Collective Participation in Public Debate 1791–1794', *Annales Historiques de la Révolution Française*, 331, 2003, pp. 57–77

Coulmas, Florian, *Population Decline and Ageing in Japan: The Social Consequences*, Abingdon, Routledge, 2007

Cox, Harold, *The Problem of Population*, London, Jonathan Cape, 1922

Croker, Richard, *The Boomer Century 1946–2046: How America's Most Influential Generation Changed Everything*, New York and Boston, Springboard Press, 2007

Cyrus, Norbert, and Vogel, Dita, 'Germany', in Triandafyllidou, Anna, and Gropas, Ruby (eds), *European Immigration: A Sourcebook*, Aldershot, Ashgate, 2007, pp. 127–40

Davies, Pete, *Catching Cold: 1918's Forgotten Tragedy and the Scientific Hunt for the Virus that Caused It*, London, Michael Joseph, 1999

Dennery, Etienne (trans. Peile, John), *Asia's Teeming Millions and its Problems for the West*, London, Jonathan Cape, 1931

Desai, P. B., *Size and Sex Composition of Population in India 1901–1961*, London, Asia Publishing House, 1969

De Tocqueville, Alexis, *Democracy in America*, New York, George Adlard, 1839

Diamond, Jared, *Guns, Germs and Steel: The Fates of Human Societies*, New York, W. W. Norton, 2005

Diamond, Michael, *Lesser Breeds: Racial Attitudes in Popular British Culture 1890–1940*, London and New York, Anthem Press, 2006

Dikötter, Frank, *Mao's Great Famine: A History of China's Most Devastating Catastrophe 1958–1962*, London, Bloomsbury, 2010

Djerassi, Karl, *This Man's Pill: Reflections on the 50th Birthday of the Pill*, Oxford University Press, 2001

Drixler, Fabian, *Makibi: Infanticide and Population Growth in Eastern Japan 1660–1950*, Berkeley, University of California Press, 2013

Düvell, Frank, 'U.K.', in Triandafyllidou, Anna, and Gropas, Ruby (eds), *European Immigration: A Sourcebook*, Aldershot, Ashgate, 2007

East, Edward M., *Mankind at the Crossroad*, New York and London, Charles Scribner's Sons, 1924

Easterlin, Richard E., *The American Baby Boom in Historical Perspective*, New York, National Bureau of Economic Research, 1962

Eberstadt, Nicholas, *Russia's Demographic Disaster*, Washington DC, American Enterprise Institute, 2009, http://www.aei.org/article/society-and-culture/citizenship/russias-demographic-disaster/

——, 'The Dying Bear: Russia's Demographic Disaster', *Foreign Affairs,* November/December 2011, http://www.foreignaffairs.com/articles/136511/nicholas-eberstadt/the-dying-bear

Edmondson, Linda (ed.), *Women and Society in Russia and the Soviet Union*, Cambridge University Press, 1992

Ehrlich, Paul, *The Population Bomb*, New York, Ballantyne Books, 1968

Ehrman, Richard, *Why Europe Needs to Get Younger*, London, Policy Exchange, 2009

Elliott, Marianne, *The Catholics of Ulster*, London, Allen Lane and Penguin, 2000

Embassy of the Russian Federation to the United Kingdom, 'Population Data', http://www.rusemb.org.uk/russianpopulation/

English, Stephen, *The Field Campaigns of Alexander the Great*, Barnsley, Pen & Sword Military, 2011

Fairbank, John King, and Goldman, Merce, *China: A New History*, Cambridge, MA, Belknap Press, 2006

Fargues, Philippe, 'Protracted National Conflict and Fertility Change: Palestinians and Israelis in the Twentieth Century', *Population and Development Review*, 26 (3), 2000, pp. 441–82

——, 'Demography, Migration and Revolt: The West's Mediterranean Challenge', in Merlini, Cesare, and Roy, Olivier (eds), *Arab Society in Revolt: The West's Mediterranean Challenge*, Washington DC, Brookings Institution Press, 2012, pp. 17–46

Fearon, James D., and Laitin, David D., 'Sons of the Soil, Migrants and Civil War', *World Development*, 39 (2), 2010, pp. 199–211

Fenby, Jonathan, *The History of Modern France from the Revolution to the Present day*, London, Simon & Schuster, 2015

Ferro, Marc (trans. Stone, Nicole), *The Great War 1914–1918*, London, Routledge and Kegan Paul, 1973

Figes, Orlando, *A People's Tragedy: The Russian Revolution 1891–1924*, London, Pimlico, 1997

Financial Times, 'Putin's Hopes for a Rising Birth Rate are Not Shared by Experts', 1 March 2013, https://www.ft.com/content/1dcce460-4ab6-11e2-9650-00144feab49a?mhq5j=e2

Floud, Roderick, and Johnson, Paul (eds), *The Cambridge Economic History of Modern Britain*, vol. 1, *Industrialisation 1700–1860*, Cambridge University Press, 1997

Foner, Nancy, *From Ellis Island to JFK: New York's Two Great Waves of Immigration*, New Haven, CT, Yale University Press, 2000

Freedom House, 'Map of Freedom', 1997, http://www.freedomhouse.org/sites/default/files/MapofFreedom2014.pdf

French, Marilyn, *The Women's Room*, London, André Deutsch, 1978

Gaidar, Yegor (trans. Bouis, Antonia W.), *Russia: A Long View*, Cambridge, MA, MIT Press, 2012

Gaquin, Deidre A., and Dunn, Gwenavere W. (eds), *The Who, What and Where of America: Understanding the American Community Survey*, Lanham, MD, Bernan Press, 2012

Garrett, Edith, Reid, Alice, Schürer, Kevin, and Szreter, Simon, *Changing Family Size in England and Wales: Place, Class and Demography 1891–1911*, Cambridge University Press, 2001

Gatrell, Peter, *Government, Industry and Rearmament in Russia 1900–1914: The Last Arguments of Tsarism*, Cambridge University Press, 1994

——, *Russia's First World War: A Social and Economic History*, Harlow, Pearson Longman, 2005

Geping, Qu, and Jinchang, Li, *Population and the Environment in China*, Boulder, CA, Lynne Rienner, 1994

Gerstle, Gary, *American Crucible: Race and Nation in the Twentieth Century*, Princeton University Press, 2001

Genovese, Eugene D., *The Political Economy of Slavery: Studies in the Political Economy of Slavery*, Middletown, CT, Wesleyan University Press, 1989

Goldberg, P. J. P., *Medieval England: A Social History 1250–1550*, London, Hodder Arnold, 2004

Goldman, Wendy Z., *Women, the State and Revolution: Soviet Family Policy and Social Life 1917–1935*, Cambridge, Cambridge University Press, 1993

Goldschneider, Calvin, 'The Embeddedness of the Arab-Jewish Conflict in the State of Israel: Demographic and Sociological Implications', in Reich, Bernard, and Kieval, Gershon R., *Israeli Politics in the 1990s: Key Domestic and Foreign Policy Factors*, New York, Westport and London, Greenwood Press, 1991, pp. 111–32

Goodhart, David, *The British Dream: Successes and Failures of Post-War Immigration*, London, Atlantic Books, 2013

Gorbachev, Mikhail, *Memoirs*, London and New York, Doubleday, 1996

Grant, Madison, *The Passing of the Great Race or the Racial Basis of Modern European History*, New York, Charles Scribner's Sons, 1919

Gratton, Brian, 'Demography and Immigration Restriction in American History', in Goldstone, Jack A., Kaufmann, Eric P., and Toft, Monica

Duffy (eds), *Political Demography: How Population Changes are Reshaping International Security and National Politics*, Boulder, CO, Paradigm Publishers, 2012, pp. 159–79

Gray, Francis Du Plessix, *Soviet Women: Walking the Tightrope*, New York and London, Doubleday, 1990

Greenhalgh, Susan, *Just One Child: Science and Policy in Deng's China*, Berkeley and London, University of California Press, 2008

Haas, Mark L., 'America's Golden Years? U.S. Security in an Aging World', in Goldstone, Jack A., Kaufmann, Eric P., and Toft, Monica Duffy (eds), *Political Demography: How Population Changes are Reshaping International Security and National Politics*, Boulder, CO, Paradigm Publishers, 2012, pp. 49–62

Hacohen, Dvora (trans. Brand, Gila), *Immigrants in Turmoil: Mass Immigration to Israel and its Repercussions in the 1950s and After*, New York, Syracuse University Press, 2003

Haggard, H. Rider, 'Imperial and Racial Aspects', in Marchant, James (ed.), *The Control of Parenthood*, London and New York, G. P. Putnam's & Sons, 1920

Harvey, Robert, *The War of Wars: The Epic Struggle between Britain and France 1789–1815*, London, Constable & Robinson, 2006

Haynes, Michael, and Husan, Rumy, *A Century of State Murder: Death and Policy in Twentieth-Century Russia*, London, Pluto Press, 2003

Hirschman, Charles, 'Population and Society: Historical Trends and Future Prospects', in Calhoun, Craig, Rojek, Chris, and Turner, Bryan (eds), *The Sage Handbook of Sociology*, London, Sage, 2005, pp. 381–402

Hitchcock, Tim, ' "Unlawfully Begotten on her Body": Illegitimacy and the Parish Poor in St Luke's Chelsea', in Hitchcock, Tim, King, Peter, and Sharpe, Pamela (eds), *Chronicling Poverty: The Voices and Strategies of the English Poor, 1640–1840*, Basingstoke, Macmillan, 1997, pp. 70–86

Hitler, Adolf (trans. Cameron, Norman, and Stevens, W. H.), *Table Talk*, London, Weidenfeld & Nicolson, 1953

Ho, Ping-Ti, *Studies in the Population of China 1368–1953*, Cambridge, MA, Harvard University Press, 1959

Hollerbach, Paula E., and Diaz-Briquets, Sergio, *Fertility Determinants in Cuba*, Washington DC, National Academy Press, 1983

Horowitz, Donald, *Ethnic Groups in Conflict*, Berkeley, University of California Press, 1985

Horsman, Reginald, *Race and Manifest Destiny: The Origins of American Racial Anglo-Saxonism*, Cambridge, MA, Harvard University Press, 1981

Hufton, Olwen H., *The Poor of Eighteenth-Century France 1750–1789*, Oxford, Clarendon Press, 1974

Huntington, Samuel P., *The Third Wave: Democratisation in the Late Twentieth Century*, Norman, University of Oklahoma Press, 1992

——, *The Clash of Civilizations and the Remaking of the World Order*, London, Free Press and Simon & Schuster, 1996, 2002

Iliffe, John, *Africans: The History of a Continent*, Cambridge University Press, 1995

Ishii, Ryoichi, *Population Pressure and Economic Life in Japan*, London, P. S. King & Son, 1937

Iyer, Sriya, 'Religion and the Decision to Use Contraception in India', *Journal for the Scientific Study of Religion*, December 2002, pp. 711–22

Jackson, Richard, and Howe, Neil, *The Graying of the Great Powers*, Washington DC, Center for Strategic and International Studies, 2008

Jackson, Richard, Nakashima, Keisuke, and Howe, Neil, *China's Long March to Retirement Reform: The Graying of the Middle Kingdom Revisited*, Prudential, NJ, Center for Strategic and International Studies, 2009

Jacques, Martin, *When China Rules the World*, London, Allen Lane, 2009

Japan Times, 'Japan's Fertility Rate Logs 16-Year High, Hitting 1.41', 6 June 2013, http://www.japantimes.co.jp/news/2013/06/06/national/japans-fertility-rate-logs-16-year-high-hitting-1-41/#.U6qo4LFnBso

Johnson, Niall, *Britain and the 1918–19 Influenza Pandemic: A Dark Epilogue*, London and New York, Routledge, 2006

Jones, Clive, *Soviet–Jewish Aliyah 1989–1993: Impact and Implications*, London, Frank Cass, 1996

Jones, Ellen, and Grupp, Fred W., *Modernization, Value Change and Fertility in the Soviet Union*, Cambridge University Press, 1987

Jones, Gavin W., and Karim, Mehtab S., *Islam, the State and Population*, London, Hurst, 2005

Judah, Tim, *The Serbs: History, Myth and the Destruction of Yugoslavia*, New Haven, CT, Yale University Press, 1997

Kaa, D. J. van de, *Europe's Second Demographic Transition*, Washington DC, Population Reference Bureau, 1987

Kalbach, Warren E., and McVey, Wayne, *The Demographic Bases of Canadian Society*, Toronto, McGraw Hill Ryerson, 1979

Kanaaneh, Rhoda Ann, *Birthing the Nation: Strategies of Palestinian Women in Israel*, Berkeley, University of California Press, 2002

Karpat, Kemal H., *Ottoman Population 1830–1914: Demography and Social Characteristics*, Madison, University of Wisconsin Press, 1985

Kaufmann, Eric, 'Ethnic or Civic Nation? Theorizing the American Case', *Canadian Review of Studies in Nationalism*, 27 (1/2), 2000, pp. 133–55

——, *The Rise and Fall of Anglo-America*, Cambridge, MA, Harvard University Press, 2004

——, *Shall the Religious Inherit the Earth? Demography and Politics in the Twenty-First Century*, London, Profile Books, 2010

Kaufmann, Eric, and Oded, Haklai, 'Dominant Ethnicity: From Minority to Majority', *Nations and Nationalism*, 14 (4), 2008, pp. 743–67

Kaufmann, Florian K., *Mexican Labor Migrants and U.S. Immigration Policies: From Sojourner to Emigrant?*, El Paso, LFB Scholarly Publishing, 2011

Keegan, John, *The First World War*, London, Hutchinson, 1999

——, *The American Civil War*, London, Vintage, 2010

Kévorkian, Raymond, *The Armenian Genocide: A Complete History*, New York, I. B. Tauris, 2011

King, Leslie, 'Demographic Trends, Pro-natalism and Nationalist Ideologies', *Ethnic and Racial Studies*, 25 (3), 2002, pp. 367–89

Kirk, Dudley, *Europe's Population in the Interwar Years*, Princeton, NJ, League of Nations Office of Population Research, 1946

Klein, Herbert S., *A Population History of the United States*, Cambridge University Press, 2004

Klopp, Brett, *German Multiculturalism: Immigration, Integration and the Transformation of Citizenship*, Westport, CT, Praeger, 2002

Knight, John, and Traphagan, John W., 'The Study of Family in Japan: Integrating Anthropological and Demographic Approaches', in Traphagan, John W., and Knight, John (eds), *Demographic Changes and the Family in Japan's Aging Society*, Albany, University of New York Press, 2003, pp. 3–26

Kraut, Alan M., *The Huddled Masses: The Immigrant in America*, Arlington Heights, IL, Harlan Davidson, 1982

La Ferrara, Eliana, Chong, Alberto, and Duryea, Suzanne, 'Soap Operas and Fertility: Evidence from Brazil', *American Economic Journal: Applied Economics*, 4 (4), 2008, pp. 1–31

Leroy-Beaulieu, Paul, *La question de la population*, Paris, Libraire Félix Alcan, 1928

Lewis, Robert A., Rowland, Richard H., and Clem, Ralph S., *Nationalist and Population Change in Russia and the U.S.S.R.: An Evaluation of Census Data 1897–1976*, New York, Praeger, 1976

Lieven, Dominic, *Towards the Flame: Empire, War and the End of Tsarist Russia*, London, Penguin, 2015

Lipman, V. D., *A History of Jews in Britain since 1858*, Leicester University Press, 1990

Livi-Bacci, Massimo, *The Population of Europe*, Oxford, Blackwell, 2000

——, *A Concise History of World Population*, Chichester, Wiley-Blackwell, 2012, 2017

Luce, Edward, *The Retreat of Western Liberalism*, London, Little, Brown, 2017

Lustick, Ian S., 'What Counts is the Counting: Statistical Manipulation as a Solution to Israel's "Demographic Problem"', *Middle East Journal*, 67 (2), 2013, pp. 185–205

Lutz, Wolfgang, Scherbov, Sergei, and Volkov, Andrei, *Demographic Trends and Patterns in the Soviet Union before 1991*, London and New York, Routledge, 1994

McCleary, G. F., *The Menace of British Depopulation*, London, Allen & Unwin, 1937

——, *Population: Today's Question*, London, Allen & Unwin, 1938

——, *Race Suicide?*, London, Allen & Unwin, 1945

Macfarlane, Alan, *The Savage Wars of Peace: England, Japan and the Malthusian Trap*, Oxford, Blackwell, 1997

MacKellar, Landis, Ermolieva, Tatiana, Hoclacher, David, and Mayhew, Leslie, *The Economic Impact of Population Ageing in Japan*, Cheltenham, Edward Elgar, 2004

McLaren, Angus, *Birth Control in Nineteenth Century England*, London, Croom Helm, 1978

McNeill, William, *Plagues and People*, Oxford, Basil Blackwell, 1976

Macunovich, Diane J., *Birth Quake: The Baby Boom and its Aftershock*, Chicago University Press, 2002

Maddison, Angus, *Phases of Capitalist Development*, Oxford University Press, 1982

Mahdi, Mushin, *Ibn Khaldun's Philosophy of History*, Abingdon, Routledge, 2016

Malthus, Thomas, *The Works of Thomas Robert Malthus*, vol. 1, *An Essay on the Principle of Population*, London, William Pickering, 1986

Maluccio, John, and Duncan, Thomas, *Contraception and Fertility in Zimbabwe: Family Planning Services and Education Make a Difference*, Santa Monica, Rand Corporation, 1997

Marshall, Alex, *The Russian General Staff and Asia 1800–1917*, London and New York, Routledge, 2006

Marshall, Monty G., and Gurr, Ted Robert, *Peace and Conflict: A Global Survey of Armed Conflicts, Self-Determination Movements and Democracy*, Centre for International Development and Conflict Management, University of Maryland, 2005

Martin, George, 'Brazil's Fertility Decline 1965–1995: A Fresh Look at Key Factors', in Martine, George, Das Gupta, Monica, and Chen, Lincoln C.,

Reproductive Change in India and Brazil, Oxford University Press, 1998, pp. 169–207

Meacham, Carl, and Graybeal, Michael, *Diminishing Mexican Immigration into the United States*, Lanham, MD, Rowman & Littlefield, 2013

Merk, Frederick, *Manifest Destiny and Mission in American History*, New York, Alfred A. Knopf, 1963

Ming, Su Wen (ed.), *Population and Other Problems*, Beijing Review Special Features Series, 1981

Mirkin, Barry, *Arab Spring: Demographics in a Region in Transition*, United Nations Development Programme, 2013, https://www.yumpu.com/en/document/view/48347156/arab-spring-demographics-in-a-region-in-transition-arab-human-

Mokyr, Joel, 'Accounting for the Industrial Revolution', in Floud, Roderick, and Johnson, Paul (eds), *The Cambridge Economic History of Modern Britain*, vol. 1, *Industrialisation 1700–1860*, Cambridge University Press, 2004, pp. 1–27

Money, Leo Chiozza, *The Peril of the White*, London, W. Collins & Sons, 1925

Moreton, Matilda, 'The Death of the Russia Village', *ODR*, 3 July 2012, https://www.opendemocracy.net/od-russia/matilda-moreton/death-of-russian-village

Morland, Paul, 'Defusing the Demographic Scare', *Ha'aretz*, 8 May 2009, https://www.haaretz.com/1.5049876

——, 'Israel's Fast Evolving Demography', *Jerusalem Post*, 21 July 2013, https://www.jpost.com/Opinion/Op-Ed-Contributors/Israels-fast-evolving-demography-320574

——, 'Israeli Women Do It By Numbers', *Jewish Chronicle*, 7 April 2014, http://www.thejc.com/comment-and-debate/essays/117247/israeli-women-do-it-numbers

——, *Demographic Engineering: Population Strategies in Ethnic Conflict*, Farnham, Ashgate, 2014, 2016, 2018

Mouton, Michelle, *From Nurturing the Nation to Purifying the Volk: Weimar and Nazi Family Policy 1918–1945*, Cambridge University Press, 2007

Mullen, Richard, and Munson, James, *Victoria, Portrait of a Queen*, London, BBC Books, 1987

Müller, Rita, and Schraut, Sylvia, 'Women's Influence on Fertility and Mortality During the Industrialisation of Stuttgart 1830–1910', in Janssens, Angélique (ed.), *Gendering the Fertility Decline in the Western World*, Bern, Peter Lang, 2007, pp. 237–73

Myrskylä, Mikko, Goldstein, Joshua R., and Cheng, Yen Hsin Alice, 'New Cohort Fertility Forecasts for the Developed World: Rises, Falls and Reversals', *Population and Development Review*, 39 (1), 2013, pp. 31–56

Nakamura, James I., and Miyamoto, Matao, 'Social Structure and Population Change: A Comparative Study of Tokugawa Japan and Ch'ing China', *Economic and Cultural Change*, 30 (2), 1982, pp. 229–69

National Birth-Rate Commission, *The Declining Birth Rate: Its Causes and Effects*, London, Chapman & Hall, 1916

Navarro, Armando, *The Immigration Crisis*, Lanham, MD, Altamira Press, 2009

Neillands, Robin, *The Hundred Years War*, London and New York, Routledge, 1990

Noin, Daniel, and Woods, Robert (eds), *The Changing Population of Europe*, Oxford, Blackwell, 1993

Novikoff-Priboy, A. (trans. Paul, Eden and Cedar), *Tsushima*, London, Allen & Unwin, 1936

Obuchi, Hiroshi, 'Demographic Transition in the Process of Japanese Industrialization', in Smitka, Michael (ed.), *Japanese Economic History 1600–1960: Historical Demography and Labor Markets in Prewar Japan*, New York and London, Garland, 1998, pp. 167–99

Offer, Avner, *The First World War: An Agrarian Interpretation*, Oxford, Clarendon Press, 1989

Office for National Statistics (ONS), 'Ethnicity and National Identity in England and Wales: 2011', 2012, http://www.ons.gov.uk/ons/rel/census/2011-census/key-statistics-for-local-authorities-in-england-and-wales/rpt-ethnicity.html

Ogawa, Naohiro, Mason, Andrew, and Chawla, Amonthep, 'Japan's Unprecedented Aging and Changing Intergeneration Transfer', in Takatoshi, Ito, and Rose, Andrew K. (eds), *The Economic Consequences of Demographic Change in East Asia*, University of Chicago Press, 2009, pp. 131–66

Okie, Howard Pitcher, *America and the German Peril*, London, William Heinemann, 1915

Omran, Abdel-Rahim, *Population in the Arab World*, London, Croom Helm, 1980

Osterhammel, Jürgen, *The Transformation of the World: A Global History of the Nineteenth Century*, Princeton University Press, 2014

Paddock, Troy R. E., *Creating the Russian Peril: Education, the Public Sphere and National Identity in Imperial Germany 1890–1914*, Rochester, NY, Camden House, 2010

Passell, Jeffrey S., and Cohn, D'vera, *US Population Projections: 2005–2010*, Pew Research Center Hispanic Trends Project, 2008, http://www.pewhispanic.org/2008/02/11/us-population-projections-2005-2050/

Passell, Jeffrey S., Cohn, D'Vera, and Gonzalez-Barrera Ana, *Net Migration from Mexico Falls to Zero and Perhaps Less*, Pew Research Center Hispanic Trends Project, 2012, http://www.pewhispanic.org/2012/04/23/net-migration-from-mexico-falls-to-zero-and-perhaps-less/

Pearce, Fred, *Peoplequake: Mass Migration, Ageing Nations and the Coming Population Crash*, London, Eden Project Books, 2010

Pearlman, Moshe, *Ben Gurion Looks Back in Talks with Moshe Pearlman*, London, Weidenfeld & Nicolson, 1965

Pearson, Charles S., *On the Cusp: From Population Boom to Bust*, Oxford University Press, 2015

Pedersen, John, Randall, Sara, and Khawaja, Marwan (eds), *Growing Fast: The Palestinian Population in the West Bank and Gaza Strip*, Oslo, FAFO, 2001

Pelham, Nicolas, *Holy Lands: Reviving Pluralism in the Middle East*, New York, Columbia Global Reports, 2016

Perelli-Harris, Brienna, and Isupova, Olga, 'Crisis and Control: Russia's Dramatic Fertility Decline and Efforts to Increase It', in Buchanan, Ann, and Rotkirch, Anna (eds), *Fertility Rates and Population Decline: No Time for Children?*, Basingstoke, Palgrave Macmillan, 2013, pp. 141–56

Peritz, Eric, and Baras, Mario, *Studies in the Fertility of Israel*, Jerusalem, Hebrew University Press, 1992

Pew Research Center, *Religious Composition by Country 2010–2050*, 2015, http://www.pewforum.org/2015/04/02/religious-projection-table/2050/number/all/

Pinker, Steven, *The Better Angels of Our Nature: The Decline of Violence in History and its Causes*, London, Allen Lane, 2011

Pogson, Ambrose, *Germany and its Trade*, London and New York, Harper & Bros., 1905

Pomeranz, Kenneth, *The Great Divergence: China, Europe and the Making of the Modern World*, Princeton University Press, 2000

Poston, Dudley L., Jr, and Bouvier, Leon F., *Population and Society: An Introduction to Demography*, Cambridge University Press, 2010

Potter, David S. (ed.), *A Companion to the Roman Empire*, Chichester, Wiley-Blackwell, 2010

Putin, Vladimir, 'Vladimir Putin on Raising Russia's Birth Rate', *Population and Development Review*, 32 (2), 2006, pp. 385–9

Qobil, Rustam, 'Moscow's Muslims Find No Room in the Mosque', BBC Uzbek Service, 22 March 2012, http://www.bbc.co.uk/news/world-europe-17436481

Quinlan, Sean M., *The Great Nation in Decline: Sex, Modernity and Health Crises in Revolutionary France c. 1750–1850*, Aldershot, Ashgate, 2007

Ransome, Stafford, *Japan in Transition: The Comparative Study of the Progress, Policy and Methods of the Japanese since their War with China*, London, Harper Bros., 1899

Rashid, Saharani Abdul, Ghani, Puzziawati Ab, Daud, Noorizam, et al., 'Fertility Dynamics in Malaysia: Comparison of Malay, Chinese and Indian Ethics', *Proceedings of INTCESS2016 3rd International Conference on Education and Social Sciences*, 8–10 February 2016, Istanbul, Turkey, https://pdfs.semanticscholar.org/0355/29de3c6a18e9ab357ad33e6764520e8d1e26.pdf

Reggiani, Andreas H., 'Procreating France: The Politics of Demography, 1919–1945', *French Historical Studies*, vol. 19, no. 3, 1996, pp. 725–54

Reich, Emil, *Germany's Swelled Head*, London, Andrew Melrose, 1914

Reinhard, Marcel R., *Histoire de la population mondiale de 1700 à 1948*, Paris, Éditions Domat-Montchrestien, 1949

Riddell, Katrina, *Islam and the Securitisation of Population Policies: Muslim States and Sustainability*, Farnham, Ashgate, 2009

Riezler, Kurt, *Tagebücher, Aufsätze, Dokumente*, Göttingen, Vandenhoeck & Ruprecht, 1972

Roediger, D. R., *The Wages of Whiteness: Race and the Making of the American Working Class*, New York and London, Verso, 1991

Rozanova, Marya S., 'Migration Process, Tolerance and Migration Policy in Contemporary Russia', in Popson, Nancy (ed.), *Demography, Migration and Tolerance: Comparing the Russian, Ukrainian and U.S. Experience*, Washington DC, Woodrow Wilson International Center for Scholars, 2010, pp. 36–64

Saito, Hiroshi, *Japan's Policy and Purposes: Selections from Recent Addresses and Writings*, Boston, Marshall Jones, 1935

Schierbrand, Wolf von, *Russia, Her Strength and Her Weakness: A Study of the Present Conditions of the Russian Empire, with an Analysis of its Resources and a Forecast of its Future*, New York and London, G. P. Putnam's Sons, 1904

Schuck, Peter H., 'Alien Ruminations', in Capaldi (ed.), *Immigration*, pp. 62–113

Seeley, J. R., *The Expansion of England: Two Courses of Lectures*, London, Macmillan, 1883

Segal, Ronald, *Islam's Black Slaves: The History of Africa's Other Black Diaspora*, London, Atlantic Books, 2001

Sen, Ragini, *We the Billion: A Social Psychological Perspective on India's Population*, Thousand Oaks, CA, Sage, 2003

Shaw, Stanford J., 'The Ottoman Census System and Population 1831–1914', *International Journal of Middle East Studies*, 9, 1978, pp. 325–38

Sherwood, Joan, *Poverty in Eighteenth Century Spain: Women and Children of the Inclusa*, University of Toronto Press, 1988

Sigmund, Anna Maria, *Die Frauen der Nazis*, Munich, Wilhelm Heyne, 1998

Slack, Andrew J., and Doyon, Roy R. L., 'Population Dynamics and Susceptibility for Ethnic Conflict: The Case of Bosnia and Herzegovina', *Journal for Peace Research*, 28 (2), 1998, pp. 139–61

Smith, James P., and Edmonston, Barry (eds), *The New Americans: Economic, Demographic and Fiscal Effects of Immigration*, Washington DC, National Academy Press, 2007

Smitka, Michael (ed.), *Japanese Economic History 1600–1960: Historical Demography and Labor Markets in Prewar Japan*, New York and London, Garland, 1998

Snyder, Timothy, *Bloodlands: Europe Between Hitler and Stalin*, London, The Bodley Head, 2010

Soloway, Richard Allen, *Birth Control and the Population Question in England, 1877–1930,* Chapel Hill, University of North Carolina Press, 1982

Sporton, Deborah, 'Fertility: The Lowest Level in the World', in Noin, Daniel, and Woods, Robert (eds), *The Changing Population of Europe*, Oxford, Blackwell, pp. 49–61

Statistics Canada, *Women in Canada: A Gender-Based Statistical Report*, 2011, http://www.statcan.gc.ca/pub/89-503-x/89-503-x2010001-eng.pdf

Statistics New Zealand, *Demographic Trends: 2011*, 2012, http://stats.govt.nz/browse_for_stats/population/estimates_and_projections/demographic-trends-2012.aspx

——, *Major Ethnic Groups in New Zealand*, 2013, http://www.stats.govt.nz/Census/2013-census/profile-and-summary-reports/infographic-culture-identity.aspx

Stockwell, Edward G., *Population and People*, Chicago, Quadrangle Books, 1968

Stoddard, Lothrop, *The Rising Tide of Color Against White World-Supremacy*, New York, Charles Scribner's Sons, 1920

Stolper, Gustav, *The German Economy 1870 to the Present*, London, Weidenfeld & Nicolson, 1967

Stone, Norman, *World War Two: A Short History*, London, Allen Lane, 2013

Sunak, Rishi, and Rajeswaran, Sarath, *A Portrait of Modern Britain*, London, Policy Exchange, 2014

Suny, Ronald Grigor, *They Can Live in the Desert but Nowhere Else: A History of the Armenian Genocide*, Princeton University Press, 2015

'Sydney', 'The White Australia Policy', *Foreign Affairs*, 4 (1), 1925, pp. 97–111

Szayna, Thomas S., *The Ethnic Factor in the Soviet Armed Forces: The Muslim Element*, Santa Monica, CA, Rand Corporation, 1992

Szporluk, Roman, *Russia, Ukraine and the Breakup of the Soviet Union*, Stanford, CA, Hoover Institution Press, 2000

Tabutin, Dominique, 'Les Relations entre pauvreté et fécondité dans les Pays du Sud et en Afrique-Sub-Saharienne – bilan et explications', in Ferry, Benoît, *L'Afrique face à ses défis démographiques: un avenir incertain*, Paris, Agence Française de Développement, 2007, pp. 253–88

Tarver, James D., *The Demography of Africa*, Westport, CT, Praeger, 1996

Tauber, Irene B., *The Population of Japan*, Princeton University Press, 1958

Teitelbaum, Michael, *The British Fertility Decline: Demographic Transition in the Crucible of the Industrial Revolution*, Princeton University Press, 1984

——, 'U.S. Population Growth in International Perspective', in Westoff (ed.), *Towards the End*, pp. 69–95

Tessler, Mark, *A History of the Israeli-Palestinian Conflict*, Bloomington, Indiana University Press, 2009

Thomas, Antony, *Rhodes*, London, BBC Books, 1996

Thompson, Leonard, *A History of South Africa*, New Haven, CT, Yale University Press, 2001

Thompson, Warren S., and Whelpton, P. K., *Population Trends in the United States*, New York, McGraw Hill, 1933

Tien, H. Yuan, *China's Strategic Demographic Initiative*, Westport, CT, Praeger, 1991

Tolischus, Otto D., *Through Japanese Eyes*, New York, Reynal & Hitchcock, 1945

Tooze, Adam, *The Deluge: The Great War and the Making of the Global Order 1916–1931*, London, Penguin, 2014

Townsend, Charles, *Ireland in the Twentieth Century*, London, Edward Arnold, 1999

Trading Economics, https://tradingeconomics.com/japan/government-debt-to-gdp

Tranter, N. L., *Population since the Industrial Revolution: The Case of England and Wales*, London, Croom Helm, 1973

Udjo, Eric O., 'Fertility Levels, Differentials and Trends', in Zuberi, Tukufu, Sibanda, Amson, and Udjo, Eric, *The Demography of South Africa*, Armonk, NY and London, M. E. Sharpe, 2005, pp. 40–64

United Nations Development Programme, *Arab Human Development Report 2002: Creating Opportunities for Future Generations*, 2002, http://www.arab-hdr.org/Reports/2005/2005.aspx

——, *The Arab Human Development Report 2005: Towards the Rise of Women in the Arab World*, 2006, http://www.arab-hdr.org/Reports/2005/2005.aspx

——, *Arab Development Challenges Report: Towards the Developmental State in the Arab Region*, 2011, http://carnegieeurope.eu/2012/05/11/undp-s-arab-development-challenges-report-2011-towards-developmental-state-in-arab-region-event-3664

——, *The Arab Development Report 2016: Youth and the Prospects for Human Development in a Changing Reality*, 2016, http://www.arabstates.undp.org/content/rbas/en/home/library/huma_development/arab-human-development-report-2016--youth-and-the-prospects-for-.html

United Nations Economic and Social Commission for Western Asia, *Population and Development Report – Second Issue: The Demographic Window – An Opportunity for Development in the Arab Countries*, 2005, http://www.arab-hdr.org/Reports/2005/2005.aspx

United Nations Population Division, 2010 and 2012 Revisions, http://esa.un.org/unpd/wpp/Excel-Data/population.htm

United Nations Social Indicators: Literacy, 2012, http://unstats.un.org/unsd/demographic/products/socind/

United Nations World Population Year, *The Population of New Zealand*, n.p., Cicred Series, 1974

Urdal, Henrik, *The Clash of Generations?: Youth Bulges and Political Violence*, New York, United Nations Department of Economic and Social Affairs, Population Division, 2006, http://www.un.org/esa/population/publications/expertpapers/Urdal_Expert%20Paper.pdf

Waters, Mary C., and Ueda, Reed, *The New Americans: A Guide to Immigration Since 1965*, Cambridge, MA, Harvard University Press, 2007

Weber, Cynthia, and Goodman, Ann, 'The Demographic Policy Debate in the USSR', *Population and Development Review*, 7 (2), 1981, pp. 279–95

Westoff, Charles F. (ed.), *Towards the End of Population Growth in America*, Englewood Cliffs, NJ, Prentice Hall, 1972

Westoff, Charles F., and Jones, Elise F., 'The End of "Catholic" Fertility', *Demography*, 16 (2), 1979, pp. 209–17

White, Tyrene, *China's Longest Campaign: Birth Planning in the People's Republic 1949–2005*, Ithaca, NY, Cornell University Press, 2006

Wilcox, Walter F., *Studies in American Demography*, Ithaca, NY, Cornell University Press, 1940

Wilkinson, H. L., *The World's Population Problems and a White Australia*, Westminster, London, P. S. King & Son, 1930

Willetts, David, *The Pinch: How the Babyboomers Stole Their Children's Future – and Why They Should Give it Back*, London, Atlantic, 2010

Wilson, Peter H., *Europe's Tragedy: A New History of the Thirty Years War*, London, Penguin, 2010

Winckler, Onn, 'How Many Qatari Nationals are There?', *Middle East Quarterly*, Spring 2015

Winter, Jay, 'Demography', in Horne, John (ed.), *A Companion to World War One*, Chichester, Wiley-Blackwell, 2012, pp. 248–62

Wood, Clive, and Suitters, Beryl, *The Fight for Acceptance: A History of Contraception*, Aylesbury, Medical and Technical Publishing, 1970

Woods, Robert, 'The Population of Britain in the Nineteenth Century', in Anderson (ed.), *British Population History*, pp. 283–358

Woods, Robert, Williams, Naomi, and Galley, Chris, 'Infant Mortality in England 1550–1950: Problems in the Identification of Long Term Trends and Geographical and Social Variations', in Corsini, Carlo A., and Viazzo, Pierre Paolo (eds), *The Decline of Infant Mortality in Europe 1800–1950: Four National Case Studies*, Florence, UNICEF, 1993, pp. 35–51

Woolf, Leonard, *Sowing: An Autobiography of the Years 1880–1904*, London, Hogarth Press, 1960

Woycke, James, *Birth Control in Germany 1871–1933*, London and New York, Routledge, 1988

Wrigley, E. A., *Poverty, Progress and Population*, Cambridge University Press, 2004

Wrigley, E. A., and Schofield, R. S., *The Population History of England 1541–1871: A Reconstruction*, London, Edward Arnold, 1981

Wrigley, E. A., Davies, R. S., Oeppen, J. E., and Schofield, R. S., *English Population History from Family Reconstitution 1580–1837*, Cambridge University Press, 1997

Zakharov, Sergei, 'Russian Federation: From the First to the Second Demographic Transition', *Demographic Research*, 19 (24), 2008, pp. 907–72

Zubrin, Robert, *Merchants of Despair: Radical Environmentalists, Criminal Pseudo-Scientists and the Fatal Cult of Antihumanism*, London and New York, New Atlantis Books, 2012

Zweig, Stefan (trans. Bell, Anthea), *The World of Yesterday: Memoirs of a European*, London, Pushkin Press, 2014

Index

abortion: in Cuba, 259; laws relaxed, 142; legalised in Soviet Russia, 123, 168; in Romania, 188; Russian rates reduced after Soviet era, 180

Acton, William, 75

Afghanistan: birth and death rates, 30; fertility rate, 21, 262–4; life expectancy, 265–6; median age, 166; migration to Europe, 245; militants, 20; population growth, 166, 171–2; Russian war in, 165–6

Africa: birth and death rates, 30; British imperialism in, 60; demographic trends, 273–4; emigration to Europe, 280; fertility rates, 269–71; losses from slave-trading, 271; median age, 270; population growth, 14–15, 271–2; prospective rise to power, 162; sub-Saharan, 267, 271, 281; urbanisation, 280

age: and behaviour, 16–17, 275–6; and welfare provision, 276–8

ageing, 148–52

Agincourt, Battle of (1415), 19

Aids: in southern Africa, 268–9

Albania, 189

Albanians: in Serbia, 27

Albert, Prince Consort, 76

Albrecht, Hans, 93

Alexander the Great, 19

Alexandra, Queen of Edward VII, 71

Algeria: Europeans in, 31, 227–8; population growth, 230

Alliance National pour l'Accroissement de la Population Française, 121

Allon, Yigal, 252

Americas, the: migration to, 108; see also Latin America; United States of America

Andrew, Prince, Duke of York, 132

Andrillon, Henri: The Expansion of Germany, 69, 117–18

Andropov, Yuri, 164

Anglo-Saxons: as emigrants, 64, 70; population expansion, 279; proportionate decline, 278

Anne, Princess Royal, 132

Anne, Queen of Great Britain, 12–13

anti-Semitism, 112, 115

Arab Spring, 224, 242

Arab world: conflict with Israel, 245–6, 249; economic and social problems, 237–41

Arafat, Yasser, 250

Argentina: as advanced country, 257; European immigrants, 87, 108, 110, 259; life expectancy, 257

Armenians: genocide, 227

Asia: emigrants, 118; individual countries' populations, 222; median age, 274; mortality rates decline, 222

United States of America (*cont.*)
religious attitudes to sex and
procreation, 143–4; rise as
superpower, 127, 129–30; Scotch–
Irish immigrants, 52–4; territorial
expansion, 65; urbanisation, 134
urbanisation: in Britain, 50, 72; effect
on fertility rates, 107, 134, 167; in
Europe and North America, 67; in
Germany, 81; slowness in France,
50; in USA, 134
Uruguay: ethnic Europeans in, 259
Uzbekistan: fertility rates reduced, 180;
infant mortality rate, 171;
population growth, 176

Vauban, Sébastien le Prestre de, 20
Victoria, Queen: on childbirth, 76,
133; children, 15, 71
Victorian age: changing social
conditions, 72; family size, 13;
world population, 12
Vienna: improved conditions, 5
Vietnam: life expectancy, 23
Vietnam War, 138
violence: and average age, 16
Voltaire, François Marie Arouet, 20

Wales: population growth, 59; *see also*
England (and Wales)
Warburg, Sigmund, 111
water consumption and supply, 237–9
Waugh, Evelyn: *Black Mischief*, 133
Webb, Beatrice, 90
Webb, Sydney (Baron Passfield), 90–1
Wellington, Arthur Wellesley, 1st Duke
of, 19
Wells, H. G., 45
West, the: decline, 162
West Bank (Israel): fertility rate,
249–50, 252

West Side Story (musical), 256, 275
Wilhelm II, Kaiser of Germany:
Edward VII's antipathy to, 92; urges
Nicholas II of Russia to wage war
on Japan, 195; on 'Yellow Peril',
203
Wilson, Woodrow, 88, 130, 228
women: attain old age, 149; decision
making, 37; delay marriage, 75;
educational levels, 140–1, 167, 244;
emancipation, 130; falling numbers
of children, 71–2; fertility rates, 6,
10, 13, 23, 31–2; in Japan, 204;
Muslim, 232–3, 238, 244; as political
leaders, 142; in Soviet Russia, 106,
174, 179–80; *see also* feminism
Woolf, Leonard, 4–5, 126
World Economic Forum, 205
world population: changes in rate and
distribution, 11–12, 14–15; increase
to present day, 6–7
World Trade Organisation, 56

'Yellow Peril', the, 118, 203
Yeltsin, Boris, 178, 183
Yemen: average age, 16; child deaths,
48–9, 230; fertility rate, 230, 263;
instability, 242; low water
consumption, 237; population
growth, 103, 224–5; social change,
224–5
youth culture, 137–8
Yugoslavia: conflicts, 189–90

Zaire/Congo: wars, 8
Zimbabwe: rise of indigenous
population, 228
Zionism, 246–50, 252
Zuma, Jacob, 268
Zweig, Stefan, 5